SOCIOLOGY FOR
SOCIAL WORK

SOCIOLOGY FOR
SOCIAL WORK
AN INTRODUCTION

Edited by
Chris Yuill & Alastair Gibson

Los Angeles | London | New Delhi
Singapore | Washington DC

SAGE Publications Ltd
1 Oliver's Yard
55 City Road
London EC1Y 1SP

SAGE Publications Inc.
2455 Teller Road
Thousand Oaks, California 91320

SAGE Publications India Pvt Ltd
B 1/I 1 Mohan Cooperative Industrial Area
Mathura Road
New Delhi 110 044

SAGE Publications Asia-Pacific Pte Ltd
33 Pekin Street #02-01
Far East Square
Singapore 048763

Library of Congress Control Number: 2010924615

British Library Cataloguing in Publication data

A catalogue record for this book is available from the British Library.

ISBN 978-1-84860-650-0
ISBN 978-1-84860-651-7 (pbk)

Typeset by C&M Digitals (P) Ltd, Chennai, India
Printed and bound in Great Britain by TJ International Ltd, Padstow, Cornwall
Printed on paper from sustainable resources

Mixed Sources
Product group from well-managed
forests and other controlled sources
www.fsc.org Cert no. SGS-COC-2482
© 1996 Forest Stewardship Council
FSC

Contents

Contributors

Robert Buckley

Angela Duvollet

Alastair Gibson

Neil Gibson

Tatenda Govera

Steve Hothershall

Colin Keenan

Joan Leece

Rory Lynch

Rob Mackay

Steven MacLennan

Donncha Marron

Frankie McLean

Jeremy Millar

Muzz McKinnon

Keith Muir

Angie Mutch

Tuck-Chee Phung

Val Sheach-Leith

Mike Shepherd

Michael Sutherland

Susan Thoms

Chris Thorpe

Megan Todd

Emmanuelle Tulle

Chris Yuill

Preface

For years we have wanted to create a text that would introduce students to Sociology and what Sociology actually means in everyday life. Our experience of teaching social work students has led us to the creation of a text that provides not only the basic sociological theory, but, just as importantly, how such theory can be of practical use to social workers, and examples of how that sociological theory applies to 'real' life.

The above ambition, to be applied in addition to being theoretical, is evident in the structure of the chapters presented throughout the book. Each chapter shares the format outlined below; a sequence that guides the reader through that journey of theory, practice and experience:

- *A sociology focus*: the main sociological theories and insights relevant to the topic of the chapter introduce each chapter;
- *A social work focus*: consideration is then given to how those sociological insights and theories can inform and assist social work practice in that area;
- *The lived experience*: the voice of either a service user or service provider indicates how the theories, concepts and approaches outlined in both the sociology focus and social work focus can assist in understanding their situation. Doing so, demonstrates the relationships between theory, practice and the 'real world'.

We have also sought to go beyond the conventional 'voices' traditionally present in many academic texts: that solely of the academic. Contributors to this textbook do include academic university lecturers, but also practising professional social workers, and service users (some of whom have chosen to remain anonymous for their own reasons). All of the above authors have extensive knowledge and experience of the topics and issues presented in the chapters to which contributed.

A range of activities (reflective exercises, definitions, and text navigation) are also incorporated within each chapter. Their addition makes the book of use to both full-time students and also for students on distance learning courses. We are also aware of the subtle (and not so subtle!) differences that exist in both practice and legislation throughout the increasingly devolved nation state of the United Kingdom. Where legislation or policy differs between countries in the United Kingdom, we have attempted to provide equivalent references within the text.

More than ever, it is vital that social workers have a sound knowledge base and an ability to apply that knowledge purposefully to practice. We hope you will learn from the contents of this book and that you will also enjoy the experience as you progress through the text.

Chris Yuill and Alastair Gibson

Acknowledgements

The editors gratefully acknowledge the support they have received from all contributors: from the university lecturers who provided the sociology and social work theory, from the professional social workers who provided the practical applications and the lived experience, and from the service users who also provided the lived experience. We also thank Professor Joyce Lishman for her valuable advice and enthusiastic support.

Finally, our thanks go to students past and present for providing the stimulus and our best wishes to all students who are about to embark on a career in social work.

Chris Yuill and Alastair Gibson

1

Sociology for social work – an overview

Chris Yuill, Alastair Gibson
and Chris Thorpe

Key themes

- Social work and sociology have a great deal in common.
- Understanding service users requires an understanding of their social context.
- Our lives are shaped and greatly influenced by social and cultural processes.
- The sociological imagination provides a useful tool for understanding society.
- Much of what we encounter in our daily lives is not 'natural' but 'socially constructed'.
- Sociological theories assist in making sense of a very complex world.
- Different theories provide different insights into the same social phenomenon.

Keywords

sociology, social work, social construction, modernity, the Enlightenment, theory, Marx, Weber, Durkheim, feminism, symbolic interactionism, postmodernism

Introduction

Sociology and social work share many affinities, the most obvious one being that both are concerned with society. Sociology as an academic and as an applied discipline seeks to study society, exploring the deeper and inner mechanisms of certain social phenomena and, more importantly, why they occur. Social work is also concerned with improving society, both for the community as a whole and for individuals who, for whatever reason, have not done so well in life. Both also share an interest in social inequalities: sociology in ascertaining the extent and causes of inequalities, and social work in dealing with the social effects of those inequalities.

This chapter outlines, first, why, sociology is vital for social workers. The simple reason is that sociology can reveal why and how so many of the problems and issues that social workers have to deal with in their daily working lives in regard to their service users occur in the first place. Having such knowledge greatly assists the social worker in working with service users, by identifying the deeper causes of their problems and informing how their needs could be more fully met. Importantly, the focus here is that problems are social and structural, not individual, in origin. Second, this chapter then turns to outlining what sociology is, defining what it seeks to do, and describing how sociology goes about scientifically investigating society. Here, theories and some of the main key concepts of sociology are visited and summarized.

Why is sociology important for social work?

In your social work practice you will spend a great deal of time working one to one with individual service users. As such, they will present you with a host of challenges, issues and problems that you will have to resolve and work through either with them or on their behalf. In professional–service user encounters, the reasons for a service user requiring social work services may appear to lie with that *individual* and the consequences of *their* actions. They perhaps have made certain, possibly questionable, decisions that have led them to act in such a way that has broken the law or caused themselves, or others, harm or problems. Focusing on such an individual interpretation of someone's problems is not surprising since it is just the service user and yourself speaking to each other in a small office, or in their home, for example. What sociology provides you with is the understanding that, for many people, the problems and challenges are not theirs in origin, but rather the causes of these issues are to be found in the *social background in which they live*. The service user may have made certain decisions but these may be in a context not defined or chosen by themselves, where certain options are or are not available to them. Sometimes in these decisions they may have violated certain social norms or laws, but in the context of their lives what they decided to do possessed a certain logic.

Or perhaps you may have a service user who because of ill-health, disability, sexuality or ethnicity experiences difficulties in their day-to-day life. They may find themselves rejected by others, patronised in conversation, left unable to carry out day-to-day tasks, discriminated against in the job market, or verbally or physically abused in the street. Again, it may be individuals who behave 'badly', who utter the hurtful phrases and engage in prejudicial behaviours, but such actions and activity do not mean that discrimination and inequalities are the result of a few bad individuals. What is more important to understand is how such ideas come into existence in the first place and why such prejudicial and negative views continue to endure in our society.

ACTIVITY

Reflect on the central point in the above paragraphs. How much does the social context influence, limit or assist people in the decisions they make?

For the social worker the greatest insight and benefit that sociology offers is an understanding of the wider processes and deeper structures of society that frame and help shape the lives of their service users and that lie at the heart of the inequalities and oppression that social workers seek to overcome. After all, it is not possible to refer to someone, an individual, without reference to some of the structural aspects such as class, gender or ethnicity that are part of that person's identity. These particular social entities are crucially not the creation of individuals. People themselves do not just spontaneously conjure up ideas of class, gender or ethnicity. Rather society presents us with ideas about and ways of doing class, gender and ethnicity that have been developed and enacted long before we were born. These pre-existing ideas frame and form the social world which we inhabit. They provide the coordinates that indicate what we can do and cannot do, and, critically, enable or inhibit what we can do in life.

The following hypothetical case study may serve to illustrate the above points more clearly.

Let us take two individuals born on the same day but into quite different backgrounds and, for the sake of simplicity, say that they are of equal ability in terms of intelligence and furthermore both enjoy the same levels of good health. One, Alex, was brought up in a peripheral social housing estate that, when it was built in the 1960s, promised a bright future for all those who lived there. Brand new buildings, fully fitted with all the mod-cons of the time and inside toilets, were light years ahead of the run-down inner cities that the estate's planners sought to replace. Over the years, however, the estate had gone into deep decline brought about by the steady running down of the local car industry and both a national and local lack of investment in social housing. When Alex was born in the 1980s crime and drug misuse were further hastening the decline of the estate. At school he was highly motivated but had begun to notice that no one from his estate seemed to land the dream jobs they had wished for when they were younger. In fact, no one can find work of any real substance. Sure, there was occasional part-time work but nothing that could help to build the foundations for a comfortable, secure, independent family life of your own. Even though work was hard to come by, he consciously avoided slipping into the dangerous drug use that appealed to many of his contemporaries and did his best by picking up whatever employment he could find. One Christmas, however, short of cash, he agreed to help a mate shift some 'second hand' goods in local pubs. It seemed a good idea at the time, not really hurting anyone, and resulting in a quick profit of fifty quid. A no-victim and financially rewarding outcome would have been the case had Alex's first customer not been a plain-clothes policeman. In the middle of a government-backed drive to crack down on petty-crime Alex found himself with a criminal record and a stint doing community service. Suddenly, his life seems even worse.

Our other individual, Alexander, also grew up outside the city, but in a more affluent suburb. Even though his family was not particularly well off he had a comfortable if uneventful childhood, most of which was spent doing quite well at school in the winter and going on holiday in the summer. Since his primary school grades were good his parents bit the financial bullet and decided that for his next level of education Alexander could attend a fee-paying private secondary school. Again, he did well and when he left to attend university he had not just a good raft of qualifications but also some good friends. University passed in what seemed like an instant, and Alexander gained a good First Class degree. It was his friends from school who proved highly useful on graduating. One of them knew of a finance company with which his brother worked that was seeking to recruit good graduates. Alexander applied, dazzled his prospective employers at the interview and secured the job. Suddenly, his life seemed even better.

The above vignette may appear clichéd in certain respects, but unfortunately it contains many truths about the times in which we live. The research of MacDonald et al. (2005), for example, has found that while people living in highly deprived neighbourhoods develop all sorts of interesting and ingenious methods of dealing with poverty (what they term doing 'poor work'), ultimately the combined effects of class and place serve to limit people's horizons as to what is possible and achievable in life. The highly influential work of French sociologist Pierre Bourdieu (1984), on the other hand, revealed the power of connections and networking for the social elite in both advancing and maintaining their privileged position in society.

The effects of social structure can operate in some instances quite obliquely. In the case study, as in real life, where one lives, the quality and type of housing one grows up in, are pretty much determined by class. Social structures can also at times operate in a more subtle and less direct manner. In the case study the various choices and options that were available to Alex and Alexander would have seemed quite normal to them and would go unnoticed, most of the time.

DEFINITION

In sociology **structure** or **social structure** refers to enduring patterns of inter-action that exist in society. These structures, such as gender, ethnicity and class, in turn shape and mould people's behaviours and interactions with others. The ability of people to make up their own minds and decide on their own course of action is to be found in the concept of **agency**. There is much debate in sociology as to how much power social structures can exert over people and how much power individuals have to control their own lives as they wish.

It should not be read, however, that people are prisoners of some predeter-mined social 'fate'. Where we begin our lives is undoubtedly shaped by history and the circumstances into which we are born, but people can exert agency that can re-shape and transform their own lives, or even that of the wider society. There are numerous examples where that outcome is evident. What should be appreciated is that, yes, people can exercise free will and make their own decisions but *crucially* the context in which they attempt to do so can either inhibit (as in Alex's case) or enable (as in Alexander's case) the successful enactment of their wishes and desires. So, in theory then, one may be free to do what one wants or desires, but hav-ing the opportunities and resources to enable that to happen is quite a different story. Those resources, such as adequate housing, suitable educa-tion and being able to pursue a healthy existence, are unevenly distributed across society.

We examined class above, but gender and ethnicity can also play equally decisive roles in outlining the contours and possibilities of people's lives. One point with which to conclude our discussion of structure and its influences on people's lives is that, the research reveals that for the vast majority of people, one's class position, gender and ethnic heritage substan-tially condition what kind of life they can lead. So, for example:

- Researchers from the Brookings Institution identified that in the United States and United Kingdom it would take six generations given the current trends for family economic advantage bestowed by family background to be levelled out. Basically, if you come from a rich background chances are you will end up rich, with the reverse being true for those born into poorer backgrounds – if you are born poor chances are you will stay poor.
- The Fawcett Foundation has noted that women in the UK still earn on average 17% less per hour than men. Within employment women face both a 'sticky floor' and a 'glass ceiling': they are stuck in low-paid, insecure employment, while finding it difficult to obtain the promotions they can see their male colleagues achieving.
- People from ethnic minorities in the UK tend to do worse than the white population in both of the above studies. Overall, people from ethnic minorities will be found in the poorest sections of society, with women from ethnic minorities experiencing an even worse hourly pay gap.

ACTIVITY

Once again, reflect on the points raised above. This time reflect on your own life and circumstances. How much of your life has been shaped by society and social processes? Remember that these influences can be very subtle at times.

In addition to providing the social worker with insights into the inner workings of society, sociology can develop what are termed 'transferable skills'. The workplace of today is highly complex and fluid, requiring a quite different skill-set from previous times. A lack of fixity and surety entails that pre-set procedures for dealing with situations do not always work or are even appropriate. Each situation has to be addressed on its own individual merits. To do so requires skills such as analysis, reasoning and reflection. Student social workers are required to 'critically reflect on and take responsibility for their actions' (SiSWE, 2005, p. 19) and, although written some time ago, Donald Schön's (1983) work on 'Reflection in Action' and 'Reflection on Action' continues to provide social workers with an important practice model. The awareness of sociological concepts combined with the worker's awareness of his or her own experience is an inherent part of the process of reflection.

Thinking Sociologically

In his key (1959) work *The Sociological Imagination*, Charles Wright-Mills, the highly influential American sociologist, expressed what we have been discussing succinctly as 'private troubles and public issues': the way in which what we may experience as individual malady and unease (a private trouble) is inextricably bound up in society and the problems that society is facing as a whole (public issues). Even though published more than fifty years ago, his work stands the test of time, providing a succinct commentary on modern life with its 'earthquakes of change' and constant personal difficulty and challenge. His work also provides us with a useful approach to the 'doing' of sociology and how to begin thinking sociologically. Of prime importance here is to develop what he calls 'the sociological imagination'. Such a mindset allows us to perceive and understand society in a novel, objective and more productive manner. It requires us perhaps to put aside our own subjective viewpoint of the world and shift between different foci and perspectives, in an attempt to grasp objectively what is going on and to see beyond the private and individual surface world and look at the deeper levels of social structure. As Wright-Mills ably summarized the same point:

> The sociological imagination enables its possessor to understand the larger historical scene in terms of its meaning for the inner life and the external career of a variety of individuals. It enables him to take into account how individuals, in the welter of their daily experience, often become falsely conscious of their social positions. Within that welter, the framework of modern society is sought, and within that framework the psychologies of a variety of men and women are formulated. By such means the personal uneasiness of individuals is focused upon explicit troubles and the indifference of publics is transformed into involvement with public issues. (1959, p. 5)

ACTIVITY

Why is it necessary to be objective and put aside one's own experiences in studying society?

The sociological imagination in a variety of applications is encountered throughout this book. You will discover how sociology makes interesting and challenging claims as to how and why certain social phenomena, such as poverty, sexism and racism for example, come into being. The following key concepts are of use in easing that process. These are important ideas within sociology that can help to clarify and make sense of what can otherwise be quite baffling to comprehend.

Modernity

Being aware of history is vitally important. As highlighted before, social phenomena do not simply occur of their own accord; there is no 'well, that's how it is', or 'people are just like that'. Everything can be traced to a cause or a series of events that brought it into being. A historical perspective allows us to understand how ways of being and thinking came about, granting us an even deeper level of understanding of why the issues and challenges occurred in the first place. Modernity is our historical epoch, the name attached to the period in which we live. It refers to the society in which we live, the values we hold, the experiences we have, the ideas in our heads and, indeed, to all parts of our lives. As a historical epoch modernity was ushered in by the massive social, intellectual and technological transformations brought about by the Industrial Revolution, the French Revolution and the Enlightenment, all occurring during the 1700s.

Living in modernity is characterized by the following trends and impulses:

- *Secular* – religion and sacral belief play very minor roles in modernity. Organized religion is in decline in many Western countries with religion no longer being the main way that people will take to explain or understand social and natural phenomena.
- *Rational* – following on from the above, rational logical science and scientific methods are the dominant mode of explanation of both society and the natural world in modernity. Also, life is highly regulated and organized.
- *Industrial* – technology and mass production create the goods that people use in the workplace and in the home.
- *Urban* – the majority of people around the globe live in urban and not rural environments. May 23rd, 2007 (Wimberley et al., 2007) was apparently the day the global urban–rural balance shifted in favour of urban dwelling.
- *The nation-state and citizenship* – people are not subjects of a king or clan chief living in a relatively small principality or fiefdom, for example, but are citizens of substantial nation-states.
- *Fast-changing* – modernity moves at a fast pace. Constant change is a feature of modernity, where traditions and settled ways of living are swept aside by the creation of new forms of interpersonal relationships and technologies.

As a point in history, modernity is unique and very different from previous historical times. Even though it is always inadvisable to indicate an exact date when a historical period begins, modernity can be said to have its roots somewhere in the mid-eighteenth century. That date may appear to be a long time ago, but in historical time it is very recent and really marks the beginning of contemporary history and a society that we would recognize. The early phases of modernity witnessed a dramatic shift away from the previous historical period of feudalism, a historical period that would be quite unfamiliar to us now. The king or feudal lord dominated society, and the world was understood through religious narratives and doctrines. In fact, religion pervaded all aspects of life, infusing even the most ordinary of acts with religious meaning and ritual. A useful example can be found in the tradition of Plough Monday, held on the first day of work after the Christmas holidays. Work could not begin until the local priest blessed the peasants' ploughs and farming tools. Religion also functioned as the main mode of understanding both people and nature: everything was the result of God's will; divine will was the cause of planets moving, seasons turning and disasters taking place.

As an individual you would also notice other substantial differences in feudal times. For a start you would be a subject not a citizen. Such a status would severely limit the capacity you would have to exercise your free will and act in the way that you wanted. The idea of individuals possessing what we would now term human rights is very much part of modernity and a consequence of the Enlightenment. The French and American revolutions in the late 1700s exemplify the transition from people as subjects without rights to citizens with rights that were inalienable and to be supported by the state. The promise of a better, freer society in which individuals would be able to exercise greater control over their lives and enjoy greater equality was a prime reason why these revolutions enjoyed so much popular support. The French Revolution captured such a desire for a better world with its rallying call of 'liberty, equality and brotherhood'.

Much of social work is concerned with ensuring, if not advancing, the rights of various oppressed, discriminated against and marginalized groups in society. The fact that social workers have to advance an agenda of social justice indicates one further feature of modernity. Even though modernity is built upon highly egalitarian impulses, current society is far from being equal. The idea and notions of equality are there, often enshrined in laws, human rights charters and in the constitutions of nation-states, but unfortunately full equality is far from being fully realized. Various inequalities and examples of oppression are highlighted throughout this text in relation to gender, class, ethnicity, sexuality and disability. In fact, one could claim that the majority of people in society experience some form of disadvantage

The reason for the endurance of inequality lies within the social structures and social processes that shape modernity. Throughout this text we shall explore and discuss how social structures and social processes such as class, gender and ethnicity create and maintain inequalities. The power of society and social structures, as we shall see, is an important point for social workers to grasp; that the problems and issues they encounter in their everyday work are *social* and not individual in origin.

ACTIVITY

The comments on modernity stress the importance of possessing a historical perspective on what happens in society – what have you understood from the above and what is its relevance for social work?

Social Construction

The concept of social construction arises frequently throughout this book and, in itself, constitutes an important sociological insight into what we experience and encounter in society. At its simplest, social construction refers to an element of life that may seem perfectly 'natural' and as always having been that way, but actually turns out to be something that has emerged out of social, cultural and historical processes and events. Sociology understands that there is very little in society and in the way that people act and interact that can be attributed to processes and influences outside of society. Actions, perceptions, thoughts and even feelings are all in their own ways framed and shaped by the society in which we live.

An example may be useful to clarify the point being developed here. Childhood, on first inspection, may seem a fairly straightforward and easy-to-explain element of our lives. It is, after all, a special time imbued with images of innocence and naivety. When one takes a long-term historical view of childhood, what has actually constituted childhood has varied considerably over time and where one was in the world. In the early phases of the Industrial Revolution in Britain, for instance, childhood, especially a working-class childhood, was non-existent, or quite different from what we would recognize as childhood today. Children were regarded as economic resources, who were deemed capable of working twelve-hour days, often in quite dangerous and unhealthy circumstances. Their small fingers were useful, for example, for picking loose threads out of early cotton spinning machines while the machinery was working at high speeds. Working with these dangerous machines could, and quite often did, result in lost fingers and limbs. Modern ideas of protecting children from risk did not pertain at all. Indeed, if we turn our attention away from history and examine contemporary global childhoods, we can notice that for many children childhood is a period of work and economic activity. What we in the West regard as 'childhood' must, therefore, be recognized as being specific to a particular time and place.

ACTIVITY

Besides childhood, can you identify and discuss other examples of everyday taken-for-granted phenomena that are socially constructed?

Inherent in the above discussion is the importance of social context and how what we accept as being 'natural' or 'normal' is related to the society in which we live. The next concept we explore illuminates the process by which people come to accept the norms and values of their particular society.

Socialization

Sociology rejects the view that people are born with a pre-set range of beliefs, behaviours or attitudes that explain all social action. What is striking about humanity is just how much variety there is both across and within different cultures and societies, in addition to notable differences between people across historical time. What would be considered as being perfectly reasonable behaviour in one context may seem utterly alien in another. So, for example, ideas about marriage, sexual behaviour and drinking alcohol will vary by country and culture. Drinking is a useful example. In the United Kingdom the drinking culture emphasizes what can be quite heavy consumption, often in loud bars and clubs, while in Mediterranean cultures drinking is often associated with family meals and moderate consumption, with the emphasis being on the social interaction rather than on drinking as much as possible.

The main point here is that there is nothing automatic about people's behaviour; there are no genes that will make humans act in a predetermined manner. If such processes were at work then we would expect to see much more consistency and similarity between humans across time and across all societies. A very positive message is contained here. By drawing attention to the fluidity or changeability of human behaviour this means that types of behaviour that are oppressive, harmful or negative are not fixed and can be transformed, hopefully for the better. People are, for example, not naturally racist or homophobic, nor are women naturally better at doing the house-work than the men in their households.

Socialization is the concept that sociologists use to explain how a person learns to exist as someone within their given society. By indirect and direct means, as we grow we are exposed to or instructed in what is expected of us and how we should behave by learning and absorbing the various norms and values of our society. So, for example, people will become aware of the norms regarding gender by perhaps observing what activities in the household their parents undertake, or by being directly told that playing with dolls is for girls and skateboarding is for boys.

It is not just in childhood that people are socialized. It is a process that continues throughout life. Think of the position you are occupying at the moment. As a social work student you are not simply being instructed in what it is to be a social worker, you are also being socialized into *being* a social worker. Almost subconsciously you will adopt values and ways of acting that may or may not be quite different from how you are now, changing both yourself and how you view others.

Theory

Theory is an important element within the sociological imagination. Trying to understand and make sense of what can be highly complex social situations can be extremely challenging. The vast array of information, data and research concerning what sociologists study is partly responsible for the complexity. For example, Figure 1.1 outlines the rise in poverty since 1979. On examination, the graph provides some very useful information. A clear rise in poverty from 1979 onwards is evident, as is the current number of people who are deemed to be in poverty using a certain measure. These statistics are in themselves highly fascinating, providing illuminating information about a contemporary social malaise. They do not, however, inform us about why that has occurred. Nor do they tell us why poverty exists in the first place. On the one hand statistics are ideal for informing us about something of the surface of the social world, about the various patterns and trends that exist, but on the other they are limited in explaining why these patterns and trends exist in the first place. This is where social theory comes in useful. Theory explains *why* certain events and trends occur and assist us in achieving a deeper level of understanding of those events and trends.

One point has to be made concerning sociology and theory. There is no single over-arching 'master theory' to which all sociologists will subscribe and refer to in their work. Sociology is a broad church, welcoming in a variety of voices and perspectives, most of which do not agree with each other. Reading through any sociology journal, such as *Sociology* or *The British Journal of Sociology*, reveals many divergent perspectives. The vigorous debates and disagreement generated in the aforementioned journals actually assist in

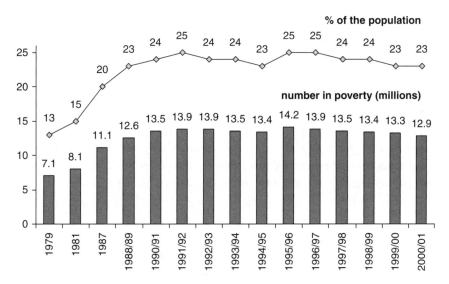

Figure 1.1 *The number of households below 60 per cent median income (after housing costs and including self-employed); 1979–2000/01; UK*

Source: Scottish Poverty Information Unit, 2002

stimulating further research and allow us to sharpen and to hone the conclusions and analyses that sociologists advance about contemporary society.

The main theories that sociologists rely on and that have been prominent within sociology are outlined next. The classic founding figures of sociology, Marx, Weber and Durkheim, are treated first before moving onto the more contemporary theories of symbolic interactionism, feminism and postmodernism.

ACTIVITY

Read the following theoretical perspectives and as you do so try to identify how they may assist you as a social worker.

Marx and Marxism

Strictly speaking, Karl Marx (1818–1883) was not a sociologist, and definitely not an academic sociologist with a chair and tenure in a university like Durkheim and Weber, who will be discussed next. He was a political activist and philosopher who dedicated his life both to attempting to understand

and to change what he regarded as the unjust and exploitative capitalist society he witnessed emerging in nineteenth-century Europe. In attempting to do so, his works contained many sociological insights into capitalist society. In particular, Marx devoted much of his time and energy to exploring how exploitation and inequalities were built into the structures of capitalist society and the emotional consequences of such inequalities for people in their everyday lives. Marx viewed capitalism overall as being deeply flawed, in that it can create so much unhappiness and misery in the world while simultaneously possessing the resources to end all social problems and to create a society that is free of want and deprivation.

Constant and enduring inequalities are core and defining features of capitalist societies. A particular form of class structure is responsible for generating and perpetuating inequality. It rests on the existence of two opposing classes. The ruling class (or bourgeoisie) are a small elite core in society who possess the capacity to exercise a great deal of power over the rest of society. The type of people Marx would be is referring to here are not the land-owning heirs to the feudal lords nor members of the gentry, but rather people who own or run substantial companies, or organizations.

DEFINITIONS

The **ruling or executive class (bourgeoisie)** are the people who own or run large companies or organizations. Their class position allows them to exercise considerable power that possesses the ability to alter and change the lives both of people in their companies or organizations, and in the wider society. The **working class (proletariat)** are those who work for employers in order to have some form of socially relative standard of living. They have little individual power but much greater collective power.

The key criterion to be included in the ruling class is ownership of what Marx termed 'the means of production'. i.e., possessing the ability to control what happens in their company and organization, issuing instructions and making policy. This power can be considerable. An example here would be Sir Fred Goodwin, the former Chief Executive Officer of the Royal Bank of Scotland. He had the power to decide high-risk deals that ultimately affected the lives of millions of people during what has become known as the 'credit crunch'.

The working class (or proletariat) is basically everyone else. As a class the working class includes a wide range of people and does not merely refer to manual or unskilled labourers. These are people who work in the companies and organizations mentioned above and who comply and follow the commands (albeit reluctantly) of the bourgeoisie. The reasons for this are to be found in another feature of capitalist society. Considerable compulsion exists to work for a wage as there are very few, if any, opportunities anywhere to have a reasonable standard of living by any other means. By taking up working for a wage or salary one effectively surrenders control over a considerable part of one's life.

ACTIVITY

How much control do people have in their workplace? Are there differences by occupation?

The inequalities that Marx concentrated on flow from the basic logic that, for the ruling class to continue to maintain their social position and the profitability of their companies or organizations, those who work for them must be paid at a much lower level, with as much labour as possible demanded of them during the working day. As Green (2001) has identified, for example, the working day for most people has steadily intensified since the 1970s.

Marx was also concerned with the emotional and psychological consequences of living in an unjust and unequal society. His theory of alienation talks to the pain and suffering that arises out of having little control over the day-to-day running of one's life, whether in the workplace or in the wider society. Instead of working, for example, being an activity that leads to self-fulfilment and self-realization, it results in tedium, depression, ill-health and frustration. These emotions in turn can lead individuals into engaging in acts that are harmful to themselves and others.

ACTIVITY

In what ways could Marx's theory of alienation assist us in understanding the circumstances of social work service users and service users?

Overall, Marx and Marxism identified that our society is one riven by power imbalances and inequalities. The cause of those disparities in wealth and power emerges from the existence of a class system that privileges one small elite core over a larger mass of people.

Durkheim and Functionalism

Emile Durkheim (1858–1917) was the first university-based sociologist. His life's work was devoted to establishing sociology as an independent discipline in its own right, and to raising it above being regarded as a mere derivative of the more established disciplines of social philosophy, economics and psychology. Durkheim's vision of the purpose of sociology was one that was deeply shaped by the tumultuous times (chiefly, the considerable political upheaval following the defeat of his native France in the 1870 Franco-Prussian war) in which he lived. As such, he was underpinned by one over-riding and highly practical aim: namely, to develop a specific set of scientific tools whose function and application were to maintain and regulate the healthy state of the 'social body' during the potentially traumatic period of transition from traditional life to modernity.

In his studies of society he observed that certain patterns of behaviour and ways of acting were replicated again-and-again and by different people. These patterns of behaviour also endured over time. Society for Durkheim was also therefore not just the sum total of the random actions of people, but was something rather more structured and organized. Society seemed to be comprised of phenomena that made society function and each phenomenon required the existence of other systemic parts for itself to exist.

As such, much of Durkheim's focus was on how society functioned. Indeed, his sociology and that of his followers was referred to as 'functionalism'. Society for Durkheim was akin to a human body where each organ would perform a particular role (more of which later) in keeping the overall organism alive. The heart, for example, pumps the blood, while the lungs supply oxygen and so on. In society each institution and each person also performs a role that enables society to function much in the same way that the heart, lungs and other organs keep the body alive. Key to the functionalist perspective is the concept of 'role'. A role requires either a person or institution to act in certain ways. So, for example, the 'student role' requires that a person attends lectures, diligently takes notes and studies late into the night, while the 'lecturer role' requires someone else to provide knowledge, in addition to guidance and support, to assist people with learning. With both people acting out their roles the social institution of education takes place.

ACTIVITY

From a functionalist perspective, outline what a social worker role would be and what a service user role would be.

The identification of such patterns allows for a study of society. So, if a heart may be a 'biological fact', which can be studied and examined by biologists, then being a student is a 'social fact', which is open to investigation by sociologists. Durkheim referred to these phenomena as 'social facts'. Social facts are those aspects of our own individual 'mental existence' that affect and shape us, but that at the same time are independent of our individual lives and thus cannot be said to 'belong to us'. The institution of the family, language, religious beliefs and professional careers (such as being a social worker) all stand as examples of social facts.

Overall, Durkheim stressed that society is, and should be, essentially stable and functional. Each of us fulfils a variety of social roles that can assist in the smooth running of society. The existence of these roles can be studied as if they are 'social facts', making the study of society, and hence sociology, possible.

Weber and Social Action Theory

Max Weber's (1864–1920) thought was grounded in the view that the study of social life must take as its starting point real individual social actors *first and foremost* and not 'objective' social structures, a notion he referred to as 'methodological individualism'. Such a view represents a very clear and influential departure from the types of impersonal and abstract 'structural' thinking which Durkheim and Marx favoured. In fact, Weber disliked the theories of Marx and Durkheim as for him, they overestimated or exaggerated the extent to which social structures are something that has an independent existence and reality outside of the people who create them. For Weber, focusing so greatly on social structure was a very mistaken understanding of society. Instead, he sought to understand the motives behind people's behaviour. To do so, different forms of action in which people engage were identified by Weber and he used them as ways of trying to work out why people act as they do. The main forms of action are summarized below:

1. *Instrumental rational action* – the actions and motives of an individual are based on cold, clear, hard-headed logic concerning the realization of precise goals or outcomes by the most effective and efficient means possible.
2. *Value-rational action* – as a form of action, value-relational action relates more to expressing social and cultural values than it does to the strict, cold, rational logic expressed in the first form of action. Hence, the rationality can only be understood as being rational by reference to a system of religious belief, for example. Most religious activity is not in itself inherently rational but can be seen to be rational in the context of the norms and culture of that religion. So, for example, one may

want a war to be avoided. Logically, it may make sense to write to an MP or to join an anti-war movement, but for a religiously motivated person it may make more sense to pray.

3. *Traditional action* – action is prompted here by the demands and impulses of tradition. Little thought or reflection is given to why one engages in a particular course of action beyond acknowledging that is how a particular action has always been done and so that is how it shall remain.

4. *Affectual action* – action is prompted by emotions with no recourse to any of the forms of action mentioned here. Cold logic, values or tradition are replaced by the immediate feelings (anger, sadness, love and so forth) that someone may be experiencing.

ACTIVITY

How may the above forms of action as put forward by Weber can help you as a social worker understand the motives and actions of a service user or service users?

Weber's criticisms about the tendency to prioritize the existence of society and social structures above the individual did not stop here. In what was arguably his most important contribution to sociology, the notion of *verstehen* (or 'understanding' when translated from the German), Weber argued that the proper study of social life comprised the interpretation of individual social actions and the beliefs and ideas that would motivate people to act in the ways they do. Indeed, it is essentially Weber's approach to studying social life that underpins what is referred to as 'action theory', which seeks to explore and understand the 'actions' of people in society.

ACTIVITY

Why is it important to have an understanding of what motivates people to act in certain ways and how they interpret the world around them?

Weber was also concerned with how the increasing emphasis in modernity on cold, hard logic and rational action created not a happy world but instead one of increasing rigidity and conformity. In effect, life in modernity becomes 'disenchanted', losing its vibrancy and spontaneity. The central metaphor Weber advanced to capture what he thought of modernity was that it was akin to an 'iron cage', all very structured and orderly, but at the same time restrictive and constraining. Large and powerful bureaucracies exemplify the over-rational impulses of modernity that help to create the cold and unrewarding life to which Weber alludes. Many aspects of our contemporary lives are shaped by and dependent on such bureaucracies, whether they are found in the public or private sector. As a social worker you will be involved in the substantial bureaucracy of the welfare state, the various structures of which will at times be able to provide substantial resources that will drastically improve the lives of the people with whom you work. At other times its quite labyrinthine structures will frustrate and impede your attempts to do as you think best and will potentially alienate service users who may be overwhelmed by what can appear as a cold, uncaring and impersonal system.

Overall, Weber draws attention to the importance of understanding the actions, motives and interpretations of people in order to understand society. The various forms of action he identified provide a useful way of doing so. One form of action though, for Weber, could produce quite negative outcomes. The prominence of rational action in society can make all life just too ordered and too controlled, leading to it becoming disenchanted and restricted.

Feminism

There is one immediately noticeable feature concerning the theorists that we have reviewed so far: they are all men (in addition to all being white and all now dead!). During the 1960s and 1970s, and influenced by events taking place in the wider society, it became clear that sociology did not pay sufficient attention to gender issues. In response to the shortcomings of 'malestream' (that is male-biased mainstream) sociology, feminism, which was at that time more of a political movement as opposed to an academic concern, became part of the discipline, bringing with it a specific focus on the private sphere of everyday life, particularly the family, and, of course, the unequal power relations between men and women. The feminist perspective has therefore acted as an important challenge and corrective to malestream sociology. Feminists argued that male sociologists were often gender-blind in their approach and had a vested interest as men in not exploring gender inequalities since they were the beneficiaries of women being oppressed in the home and workplace.

The theory of patriarchy was one of the many significant contributions that feminism brought to sociology. The theory of patriarchy makes claims that all parts of society are organized and constructed for the benefit of men, who have greater resources of power and control in all fields over women. British sociologist Sylvia Walby, in her earlier (1990) work, mapped out how patriarchy operated and endured in society. She noted that while the situation between men and women was in no way fixed, with no inevitability that women will always occupy a subordinate position compared to men in society, the various gains won by the women's movement in the 1960s and 1970s had by no means fully realized gender equality. The reason for the incomplete realization of feminist goals was that patriarchy influenced many aspects and spheres of men and women's lives. Sources of male domination were also multiple and responsive to change, making it harder for a thorough transformation in gender relations to occur.

ACTIVITY

Feminism as both a movement and an academic pursuit has its roots in the 1960s and 1970s. Discuss whether or not you believe that women and men are now equal in both the public and private spheres of social life.

DEFINITION

The feminist concept of **patriarchy** refers to the male domination of society where all spheres and areas of social life are constructed for the benefit of men rather than women.

Walby identifies how patriarchy functions in the following spheres of life:

1. *Paid employment* – as indicated earlier in this chapter, women experience a much poorer working environment than men. On average, women are paid less than men and are clustered in low-paid service employment, and are more likely than men to find their chances of mobility impaired by being caught between the 'glass ceilings' and 'sticky floors' of the contemporary workplace.
2. *Household production* – men and the State benefit from many forms of unpaid labour that women perform in the household by running the family home, looking after children and being the prime carer for older, disabled and ill family members. The domestic division of labour remains in men's favour.
3. *Culture* – despite shifts in traditional cultural stereotypes concerning gender roles, women are culturally presented, particularly in relation to pornography and wider media representations, in a way that accords with dominant male desires and interests.

4. *Sexuality* – a double-standard exists where sexual activity and conduct that is acceptable for men is regarded as being unacceptable for women. This discriminatory contradiction is further reinforced by the presence of hegemonic sexuality that claims primacy over other forms (i.e. lesbian) of sexuality.
5. *Violence* – even though laws exist that seek to punish and limit male violence they are neither extensive nor effective enough to consistently challenge the enduring patterns of male violence that exist in society.
6. *State* – the State is not gender-neutral but perpetuates male dominance in society. While some redress to gender inequalities has been advanced by the State these measures do not go far enough, and, while opening up new opportunities for women in the public sphere, they do not adequately address the barriers and discrimination that women encounter.

Greater detail on gender issues can be found in Chapter 3.

Overall, feminism draws much-needed attention to the importance of gender relations and the power imbalances between men and women. From the work of Walby and others, patriarchy (male dominance) is seen to operate, sometimes quite subtly, on different levels throughout society, therefore making it hard to tackle and to bring about equality between the sexes.

Symbolic Interactionism

The above theories, especially those of Durkheim and Marx, all deal with large-scale observations of society and understandings of the deeper levels of society. Focusing on large-scale issues in sociology is termed 'macro-sociology' and is quite different from the 'micro-sociology' that focuses on the small-scale interactions between people and how people rehearse and present their identity to others. In effect, the micro-sociological approach is the reverse of the large-scale theories, by understanding society as emerging from the small, day-to-day interactions of individual people as opposed to emerging from large, impersonal social structures.

The 'symbolic' in symbolic interactionism refers to a wide variety of objects, actions and sounds, or symbols, which convey some form of meaning. Anything can count as a symbol so long as it refers to something else and conveys some form of meaning. Gestures, clothes, titles, actions, words and images are all examples. When people wear a certain item of clothing, to extend one of the above examples, they do so with the intention of communicating something about their identity and sense of who they are. Using clothes in a symbolic manner applies to everyone; the disaffected youth who pulls on a hoodie is symbolically using clothing just as much as the mainstream businessman who presents himself in a smart designer suit. In many respects the use of costume and other props is not dissimilar to an actor portraying a character on a stage, and that is why symbolic interactionism is sometimes referred to as being 'dramaturgical', in that the social world is akin to a stage on which people act out who they are. This theatrical analogy provides a useful route into understanding symbolic interactionism. Essentially people in their everyday lives (or social actors to use the preferred symbolic interactionist term to denote people) perform who they are, or rather, perform who they would like to be.

ACTIVITY

Provide examples of symbols that you use to convey your sense of self. Remember that symbols can be any item, gesture or act that is meaningful both to yourself and to others.

A certain fragility and fluidity can be found in the daily presentation of self. For one leading proponent of the symbolic interactionist approach, Erving Goffman (1968), social actors have to be careful about the information and symbols they use to communicate their sense of self and identity. In some instances, for certain people an event or aspect of self in their past or present may result in them being excluded from full social acceptance. They may possess what Goffman terms a 'stigma' and therefore run the risk of becoming stigmatized. A stigma may be anything from a bodily difference to a criminal record, drug use, or any number of other ways of being that can be regarded as being socially problematic. Consequently people may have to devise what are sometimes quite elaborate techniques that will either obscure or hide what may potentially be causing them problems.

ACTIVITY

How could possessing a stigma affect a service user or service users? What steps could you take to support them?

More detail on stigma and social work is outlined in Chapter 9.

Overall, the symbolic interactionist approach assists in understanding the small-scale, everyday interactions of people and how people construct and present who they are to others. It also provides insights into how aspects of the self can be viewed negatively by society and the routines that someone may have to develop in order to be socially accepted.

Postmodernism

In the past twenty years or so the terms 'postmodern' and 'postmodernity' have established themselves as important, if not contested, concepts in trying to understand modern life. As has often been remarked, perhaps the best way to think about and define what is meant by the term 'postmodernity' is to think about it in direct relation to its predecessor, 'modernity'. Modernity, as we outlined earlier in this chapter, is the term used to denote the period in the West from the time of the Industrial Revolution onwards whereby society is characterized by increased 'rationality' – faith in scientific reason – 'social structural differentiation' – the division of society into complex and smaller parts – and social 'order' and 'certainty' – the highly predictable nature of Western societies, and the ordered 'roles' and 'identities' of the individuals therein. Postmodernity, then, is intended to denote a completely different type of society from that of its modern predecessor.

On this view, postmodern society is one that has moved beyond the boundaries of modern society, such that in place of the modern emphasis on 'stasis' postmodernists emphasize 'movement' and 'flux', in place of 'design' there is now 'chance', where there was 'determinacy' there is 'indeterminacy', and lastly, where there was certainty 'uncertainty' now prevails.

Several implications follow on from the postmodernist rejection of certainty. First, it means that the idea of a fixed, one-size-fits-all solution to social problems is to be rejected. The evidence is multiple of the failures of big-scale attempts to create a better society. The Holocaust and the brutalities of Soviet-era communism can be cited as examples. Instead, for postmodernists many viewpoints should be welcomed and respected, with no one perspective being privileged over another. All is equal. Second, by claiming that no ultimate truth exists, for postmodernists it is better to see ideas, in particular so-called expert ideas, concerning a social phenomenon as being a particular 'discourse', or a way of talking about something. Some discourses can be more dominant than others, however, and will maintain that dominance by excluding and dismissing other discourses. This is not because those discourses inherently contain 'the truth' but rather because they are advanced by powerful groups within society in order to protect their own position.

ACTIVITY

Postmodernists urge us to accept all viewpoints as being of equal merit. Can you identify instances where according the same validity to all perspectives could be highly positive and other times when it could be problematic?

One leading figure associated with postmodernism is Michel Foucault (1926–1984). Though he himself never liked being described as a post-modernist, many of his ideas and writings influenced other writers and academics who subscribed to postmodernism. One of his key ideas was in relation to power. Unlike Marxists, who see power as being exclusively held by the ruling class, and certain feminists, who identify power as being in the hands of men, Foucault claimed that power was diffused and spread out through society and that power was an entity that one could exercise and not just merely possess. So, for example, as a social worker you may not have as much power as other people in society but you will be able to exercise considerable power over service users. Your gate-keeping role to services and resources is one example of this power, where your decisions can have a substantial effect on the lives of your service users.

Overall, postmodernism makes us think about what is true and sceptical about taking the words of experts as being intrinsically true or correct, and reminds us of the validity of different viewpoints. How power is diffused throughout society is another lesson that postmodernists provide; power is not always held just by large bodies or organizations but rather can spread out throughout society, with people being able to exercise power in different contexts.

How to use this book

The power of society to shape, mould and influence our lives has been a central theme throughout this chapter. It is to the social and to society that we must look if we are to understand and comprehend fully the wider processes that frame and contextualize the problems of service users and minority groups. The discipline of sociology is the tool, the technique and the method that make the many complexities of society intelligible and open to investigation. The main processes and structures of society are dealt with next.

You will find each chapter is written by a number of authors. Every one represents a different and equally valid but complementary viewpoint and input into a particular issue. The objective is to present you with the *theory*, *application* and *experience* of an issue. So, each chapter begins with the *theory*, where a sociologist outlines and explains important sociological observations, theories and research. That opening in turn provides the basis for a social worker, who will discuss the practice aspects and relate how the *application* of sociology will inform that practice. All of which leads up to either a service user or a frontline practitioner discussing their *experiences*. All in all, you will be provided with a resource that will take you through not just the sociological theory but also how this makes a difference in a social work situation and to the lives of real people.

2

Social Inequality and Social Class

Donncha Marron, Robert Buckley and
Joan Leece

Key themes

- Class, however defined, is a constant feature of British life.
- Social inequality between social classes continues to exist in Britain.
- Class is more than just an economic relationship – it shapes the cultures and experiences of everyday life.
- Childhood poverty is a serious, but often poorly addressed issue.
- Poorer disadvantaged families are disproportionately represented in the child welfare and child protection systems.

Keywords

Class, Weber, Marx, functionalism, social inequality, capital, culture

---

Introduction

Inequality remains a persistent feature of both British and global society. Considerable disparities exist between people in terms of the power and resources they have available to pursue their ambitions, live the lives they desire, or even maintain a reasonable level of health and well-being. These differences are structured around the social processes of class, gender and ethnicity. In the following chapters, gender and ethnic inequalities are explored, but class, as a source and form of inequality, is under consideration here. As becomes clear, an understanding of class is important for social workers. Class is one of the main influences as to why certain people become users of social work services, and being able to appreciate how class shapes, conditions and influences all our lives provides insights into one of the most powerful social structures that exists in contemporary society.

The main sociological theories of class are outlined first in the sociology focus. Here, we consider the ideas and insights provided by the classical sociologists before considering contemporary debates on the salience and relevance of class in contemporary society. The social work focus develops these discussions and perspectives further, highlighting how class impacts on the lives of service users. In the closing lived experience a social worker reflects on how class has shaped both her working experiences as a social worker and the experiences and lives of service users.

Sociology Focus

There are many ways to understand and conceptualize economic and material inequality – by gender, ethnicity, geographical location, and so on. Traditionally, however, sociologists have favoured concentrating on the category of social class. There are many ways to define class sociologically, and there are complex arguments over which is to be preferred. In general, sociologists understand an individual's class by his or her relationship to economic activity; in other words, by what they do for a living. Class, though, has much wider consequences for one's life beyond work. It shapes where one lives, where one goes to school, one's view of the world, politics, accent and interests among other things. Class, therefore, has been, and continues to be, important in terms of how individuals relate to the wider social world around them and how that social world impacts upon them. What is less clear today, however, is whether class is an important form of identity in terms of how the individual understands *him or herself* (Savage, 2000).

Class is a widely understood, though much debated, topic. Most people tend to accept, almost intuitively, that society is divided into an 'upper class' of wealthy businessmen, aristocrats and celebrities, a 'middle class' of salaried professionals and managers, and a 'working class' of wage-earning manual workers. Sociologists, more or less, accept such a tripartite structure as a general description of class today. Sociologists do attempt, though, to go beyond description in an attempt to explain how classes are created. Let us examine some of the different sociological perspectives that have been developed to explain how social classes and inequality develop.

Sociological Theories of Social Inequality

Functionalism: The Necessity of Inequality

The functionalist approach to class has been most widely associated with the work of Kingsley Davis and Wilbert Moore, two American sociologists who worked in the middle decades of the twentieth century. They argued that stratification–that is, the layering of individuals into an economic hierarchy–has a crucial relationship for the maintenance of social order (Davis, 1942; Davis and Moore, 1945). Their point of departure was to see society as a mechanism, a system like a machine, which must put people to work within specific roles if the whole is to function. If our social class is determined by our economic activity, a key question is how people are motivated to come to fill certain positions over time. And, once they are in that position, how they are encouraged to keep on performing the duties attached to that role.

Now, if the array of work roles in society were all equally pleasant, all equally important and all equal in terms of requiring the same kinds of talents and qualifications, then it would not matter who went where. If this was true, then the problem for society of sorting people into social positions would not be an issue. But, Davis and Moore argue, it does make a difference. Some jobs are simply more agreeable than others, some require special talents and training, and some are simply more important than others. The question, then, is how does society, as a system, locate people to do certain jobs that are essential to the maintenance of society, be it as stockbrokers or window-cleaners?

Society must have some kind of rewards at its disposal to induce people to take certain jobs. It must also, then, be able to distribute those rewards appropriately. According to Davis and Moore, the three main rewards are: 'sustenance and comfort' (salary received and effort required to do the job), 'humour and diversion' (how interesting the job is), and 'self-respect and ego-expansion' (how prestigious the job is). A stratified society is thus one where the income and other benefits of different positions are unequal. Davis and Moore conclude then that 'social inequality is an *unconsciously* evolved device by which societies insure that the most important positions are conscientiously filled by the most qualified persons' (1945, p. 243). So, society always treats individuals differently in terms of the financial benefits and prestige they enjoy for the jobs they do. And, most importantly from the functionalist perspective, social inequality must always exist.

Most sociologists today strongly disagree with this functionalist approach. First, it is not really a theory of class, as it examines only how individual inequality arises within society. It does not examine how individuals come to form particular class groups. It also fails to convince that the high rewards enjoyed by the likes of sports stars and famous musicians are really necessary to get people to do those jobs, or that these rewards are purely a reflection of intrinsic talents and abilities (Tumin, 1953). Furthermore, functionalists also ignore the question of power, opportunity and intergenerational inequality. Whether one attends university, for example, is heavily dependent upon the social class of one's parents. University is an expensive undertaking, and parents who are better resourced are more able to facilitate their children's education. One's occupation is, in turn, heavily determined by university attendance and so plays a major role in forming one's class position. The class position of one's parents ultimately has, therefore, a strong effect on one's own class position. Class cannot then be simply a matter of individual 'effort' or 'talent'.

The functionalist position is, perhaps, still relevant in terms of understanding how the Labour government in Britain after 1997 attempted to create what it called an 'Opportunity Society' based on the principle of meritocracy (cf. Saunders, 1996). What this means is that in attempting to give everyone equal opportunities in education and training, regardless of class background, everyone's class position in society should be determined solely by their individual talents and effort. The persistent and deeply ingrained ability of advantaged social classes to preserve opportunities for their children and so exclude other individuals suggests, on the contrary, that the functionalist interpretation of class inequality, and the 'Opportunity Society', are not quite so straightforward as they are presented.

ACTIVITY

Consider well-rewarded occupational groups like accountants, solicitors or doctors. Are these individuals drawn from across society or do they come from a particular type of social background?

Marx: Class and Class Conflict

One of the most influential perspectives on class has been that developed by the nineteenth-century thinker Karl Marx (1818–1883). He attempted to show that within capitalist societies – societies characterized by industrial production, wage labour, free markets and the pursuit of profit – there were two great classes forming in opposition to each other (Marx, 1975;

Marx and Engels, 2005). On the one side there is the bourgeoisie, the capitalist class. These are the exclusive owners of productive property – 'capital' – who constantly try to drive down the wages they pay to workers and accumulate more and more capital through producing goods and selling them for a profit. On the other side there is the proletariat, the working class. This class possesses no productive wealth or property. The workers attempt instead to get by on selling their labour to the bourgeoisie and earning wages. Here, Marx firmly defined these evolving classes on the basis of property ownership and argued that the bourgeoisie exploit the proletariat ever more intensively by not paying them the full valuc of the labour they purchase. This 'surplus value', he argued, formed the basis of profit, which was always kept by the bourgeoisie to reinvest in production.

The big shift that Marx anticipated under capitalism was the working class developing a 'class consciousness' and becoming aware of the real reasons for its unequal condition. As workers became more and more exploited, Marx anticipated, they would also become more united, organized into trade unions and politically aware of their position within capitalism. Within Marxist thought, then, it is not only the economic determination of class that is important but also how the working class identifies itself as belonging to an exploited class. Marx ultimately envisaged that the working class would rebel against their exploited condition. The proletariat would overthrow the bourgeoisie and institute a new kind of social and economic system characterized by common ownership of productive property.

Such revolutionary uprisings never occurred within advanced Western countries. On the contrary, the twentieth century witnessed shifts in the organization of capital ownership, a growing middle class, rising incomes and the development of mass consumption (Saunders, 1989). Since the 1960s and 1970s, as manufacturing employment has gone into decline, the nature of work itself has been transformed. In consequence, as Savage et al. (2001) have argued, members of the working class today do not posses a strong sense of belonging to a class, even if they recognize the importance of class inequality. Marx's ideas nevertheless still continue to be relevant for sociologists in attempting to understand persistently high levels of inequality and how certain groups continue to be exploited by capitalism. Erik Olin Wright (2000), for example, has argued that the growth of the middle class can be explained in terms of the rise of a number of 'contradictory class locations' based on the level of control individuals exercise in the workplace and the skills they possess. Leslie Sklair (2000) has also put forward the idea that exploitation now occurs on a global basis, exerted by a transnational capitalist class, rather than simply existing within specific societies.

ACTIVITY

In relation to Marx's ideas about class exploitation and conflict, what do you think has changed since his time? What has stayed the same?

Weber: Class, Status and Party

Another very influential sociological perspective on class has been that developed by Max Weber (1864–1920). Weber initially is pretty close to Marx in terms of defining the major division of class: the possession or lack of possession of productive property (Allen, 2004). He thought that this basic category of class profoundly affected what an individual could do and what financial rewards they could draw. However, Weber, unlike Marx, drew a distinction between ownership and control of capital and saw this as according different power to different groups. Many powerful business-men and women today are board members of companies as opposed to owners. They are salaried employees whose job it is to produce a profit for shareholders and who are well rewarded for doing so.

For Weber, class operated in relation to a market (Weber, 1946, 1992). On the one hand, property is unequally distributed. Some people possess it and others do not. This then shapes what the individual can do in rela-tion to the market and what kinds of rewards they benefit from. Owning productive property allows one to produce profit. On the other hand, people selling labour power might lack property but they bring to the market for labour a lot of different skills and qualifications that are recog-nized and rewarded differently. Weber called this the 'market situation'. For example, while neither doctors nor nurses own productive property, doc-tors receive much higher salaries for their qualifications than nurses do. Weber, in contrast to Marx, thought it unlikely that a single unifying 'working class' identity would develop among workers who did not possess property. Multiple classes would develop, on the contrary, on the basis of different skills, qualifications and future career opportunities.

Weber also took a multidimensional view of stratification. Class is only one way groups are divided – for him 'status' is also important as expressed through people's styles of life. Symbols and dispositions like housing, dress, speech, background and occupation can serve to mark out individuals with a certain status identity in the eyes of the wider community. Although it sometimes overlays class, it may also vary independent of class or cut across class divisions. A good example of this might be a drug dealer. He or she might possess considerable wealth and enjoy a strong market position in the buying and selling of illegal narcotics. Yet their social status in the eyes of the wider society is low. The third key potential social division that Weber identified was what he called 'party'. He regarded this as the ability of individuals to group together into particular forms of political organization for the achievement of certain goals.

Weber's work has been extremely influential within sociology and Weber's ideas about class tend to form the bedrock of much contemporary sociological research (e.g. Goldthorpe, 1987). Indeed, the current ONS–SEC class model used in government research derives, in part, from a Weberian understanding of class (Crompton, 2008).

However, one of the weaknesses of a Weberian understanding of class is that, if class operates in relation to a market for skills, it does not explain how markets themselves are constructed so as to demand and reward skills in particular ways. To give a simple example, why are professional footballers paid more than sprinters, or golfers more than table-tennis players? More broadly, then, how and why do individuals become rewarded in different ways? An important distinction between Marxist and Weberian perspectives is that the Weberian does not give precedence to class as a social division and refuses to claim that class necessarily matters more than any other kind of social division (Savage, 2000). Another important difference is that the Weberian perspective does not stress an inherent relationship between the *objective* position of belonging to a class by virtue of one's market situation and the *subjective* understanding of oneself as belonging to a class. Put more simply, just because you belong to a class does not mean you *think* you do.

The Death of Class?

Over the past several years, sociologists have been debating at length the relative usefulness of the concept of class. Class has historically, thanks to the theoretical legacy of Marxism, been the crucial social division that has preoccupied sociologists. Yet, in recent times, all this attention class has received has been challenged. Sociologists have questioned whether class is actually a useful concept at all for understanding the individual's relationship with society (Beck, 1992; Pahl, 1989) or whether it is slowly losing its salience in terms of structuring inequality, identity and experience within contemporary Western societies (Clark and Lipset, 1991; Pakulski and Waters, 1995, 1996). Others have sought to develop a more multidimensional view of inequality that combines the concepts of class with gender and race/ethnicity (Bottero, 2005; Bradley, 1996).

The most extreme questioning of class as a concept is contained in Jan Pakulski and Malcolm Waters's (1995) book *The Death of Class*. The title says it all really! These sociologists put forward the position that class has now completely lost the significance it had in the past. They argue that globalization, the decline of industrial manual employment and the erosion of traditional working-class communities, are making class increasingly irrelevant. People no longer understand themselves in terms of a common class identity or acting in the interests of a class. On the contrary, they are more likely to understand themselves and their conditions of life as individuals.

On the one hand, Pakulski and Waters argue that economic inequalities are simply not what they used to be. They suggest that wealth is not so concentrated any more and cite a number of changes, including the growth of public companies, wider ownership of property and the maintenance of savings and pensions by a large bulk of the population. They also point to the fact that wages are higher so that absolute poverty is less pervasive. They see, of course, that inequalities do persist but argue that these may result from individual differences in lifestyle, status and consumption patterns rather than an individual's relationship to work. Alternatively, they may result from a whole host of social divisions beyond class, including ethnicity, gender, age, nationality and so on.

They argue, therefore, that we have moved to a 'status-conventional society'. Differences are based not on economic factors between groups but on cultural differences such as identity, taste and consumption practices between individuals. With greater wealth and higher incomes across the board, individual consumption becomes extremely important in terms of how status and inequality are expressed and experienced. For them, it is not the collective experience of class exploitation where inequality shows itself but through individuals' relative inability to consume. So, lifestyle, fashions, interior decor and type of job are deemed to be more important than economic value, income, wealth or occupation.

ACTIVITY

Do you agree with Pakulski and Waters? Have we seen the death of class? Does class matter in your life?

Against this belief in the death of class, the influential French sociologist Pierre Bourdieu has sought to trace a very definite ongoing relationship between class and status. Rather than status or consumption divisions replacing class inequality, he argues (1984) that tastes for a whole range of cultural objects and practices – for example, pastimes, music, art, food – can be clearly seen to be structured by social class. The general thrust of Bourdieu's argument is that social class groups consciously and unconsciously attempt to distinguish themselves from lower social class groups through the appropriation and consumption of distinctive forms of culture.

Just as different people possess different levels of income and wealth – what he calls economic capital – they also possess different levels of cultural capital. The latter is acquired over the course of an individual's lifetime through formal education and informal learning and it manifests itself as the ability to appreciate particular kinds of cultural objects and practices. Think, for example, of the cultural capital required to order wine in a restaurant, itself a generally esteemed or 'legitimate' form of consumption. In order to appreciate wine fully, one must have an acquired knowledge of wine-producing countries, regions, grapes and estates. One must also have a knowledge of different vintages and an awareness of the suitability of different types of wines for accompanying different kinds of food. Liking the taste of wine is not enough. What gets valued as culture, however, is always being challenged and contested. For Bourdieu, class positions tend to be reproduced through the family as parents pass on their levels of economic capital and cultural capital to their children. In consequence, at any point in time, particular class groupings can be identified through the combinations of economic and cultural capital possessed by individuals.

Within this section, we have looked at the concept of class and how sociologists have thought class to be important in terms of structuring inequality within society. We examined three distinctive sociological perspectives on class inequality: the functionalist perspective, which emphasizes the social necessity of inequality, the Marxist perspective, which emphasizes ownership of property and the gradual polarization of two classes, and the Weberian perspective, which emphasizes the role of the 'market situation' and how this leads to a multiplicity of different classes.

We then addressed the question of whether class is still an important concept with which to understand inequality today. While some sociologists have questioned the usefulness of class as a concept, others–like Pakulski and Waters–believe that class is disappearing and being replaced by other kinds of status inequality. Where economic wealth used to be important in shaping class as the most important form of inequality, now inequality is based upon individuals' relationship to culture and their consumption practices. Yet other sociologists, like Bourdieu, have argued that class and culture are not separate. On the contrary, they are two sides of the same coin: class is important in shaping consumption while consumption gives expression to, and reinforces, class differences.

Social Work Focus

Class pervades so much of social work practice. That is why it is important for social workers to have an understanding of the debates, theories and issues that have been visited in the sociology focus. Throughout this book you will repeatedly encounter the powerful effect that social class exerts on a variety of issues that substantially affect peoples' lives. It is by no accident that crime rates are higher, long-term illness and poor health more persistent, and poverty more keenly experienced by certain sections of the population. Class plays a fundamental role in influencing and determining people's life chances, the conditions in which they live and the choices they can make concerning what they do. Often for people at the 'bottom' of society, their class position blunts opportunities that in turn create an environment whereby they can possibly come into conflict with the norms and laws of wider society.

Sayer (2008) makes the point that some political scientists and sociologists have argued that class is an outmoded concept, and that we are all middle class now. Jones (1998), however, argues that historically social work is an overwhelmingly 'class-specific' activity, and that social work's preoccupation with those at the bottom of the social hierarchy is an important feature in its evolution. However, he also makes the point that, by the late 1990s, social work was uneasy with this long-standing class specificity, and this is reflected in the language used in social work writing and texts, the limited emphasis on class in social work courses and the organizational context of service delivery.

Whatever the dominant perspective on the 'death of class' debate, the reality is that the majority of social work services users come from the poorest people in our society (Davis, 2007; Walker and Walker, 2002). It is therefore imperative that social workers have a sound understanding of different theoretical perspectives that comment on the societal impact of social exclusion, disadvantage and poverty (Davis, 2007). Three controversial, but nonetheless influential, sociological explanations of poverty are outlined below, and these reflect the value-laden attitudes that often prevail towards the poorest people in society.

In the 1960s the US sociologist Oscar Lewis (1961) stated that a 'Culture of Poverty' existed within the poorest people in society, whereby people adopted negative attitudes and helplessness about their circumstances that led to inter-generational poverty within certain families and communities. A similar position was taken in the 1970s by Conservative MP Sir Keith Joseph (cited in Welshman, 2006), who coined the term 'Cycle of Deprivation' in reference to what he termed the chaotic lifestyle of the poorest people in the UK, which was then perpetuated by the next generation. Both perspectives have been criticized for not explaining why people find themselves in poverty and for their emphasis on people living in poverty as a result of their own shortcomings. Neither takes cognizance of structural disadvantage or social exclusion.

> See Chapter 5 for greater detail and discussion of poverty.

Finally, one of the most controversial theoretical concepts to emerge from sociology has been 'underclass theory' (Giddens, 2006; Llewellyn et al., 2008). This perspective, promoted by Murray (1990), adopted an individualist explanation of poverty and argued that the underclass group within society were largely drawn from ethnic minorities or from white people from areas of social disadvantage and social disintegration (Giddens, 2006). Murray (1990) highlighted unemployment, crime and increasing illegitimacy as evidence of the existence of an underclass of almost dispossessed people in society and claimed that the welfare state contributed to a dependency culture that failed to promote individual responsibility and, by default, encouraged a reliance on the state (Llewellyn et al., 2008). Giddens (2006) has pointed out that many sociologists have been strongly critical of Murray's (1990) theory of an underclass in the way that Murray describes and Giddens suggests that the concept of social exclusion is a much more meaningful and informed way of highlighting the living situations which incorporate deprivation and inequality.

It is important to recognize the fact that, whilst these perspectives have been extensively criticized within sociological circles, they have also not been without influence. For example, underclass theory had an influence on the social welfare policies of the Conservative government in the 1990s (Bochel et al., 2009; Cunningham and Cunningham, 2008). Similarly, Bochel et al. (2009) highlight the influence of the Cycle of Deprivation on New Labour's social exclusion strategies in the late 1990s/early 2000s. As recently as 2004, the Social Exclusion Unit suggested that the Cycle of

Deprivation was especially unfair to children, who were disadvantaged and missed out on life chances and the opportunity for enhancement because of their family or geographical background. Although we may criticize the oppressive and highly negative tone within all three theories towards the poorest in society, these did arguably highlight the often understated issue of intergenerational poverty and deprivation. Webb (2006) argues that the management of an Urban Underclass–that is, people who live in the worst social economic conditions–by a range of agencies and experts on social exclusion is tied in with the idea of a safety net for society, which is a neo-liberal approach to welfare provision. Social workers need to understand these issues and debates and make connections with the wider discourse on the nature of state intervention in family life (Adams, 1996; Fox Harding, 1997; Webb 2006). They need to be able to view the problems that service users experience, not only in terms of individual feelings and personal circumstances, but also in the wider context of social class, inequality, structural disadvantage and the wider society (Davis, 2007). Social work is not just about striving for change in individuals and families; there is an expectation and responsibility within social work that seeks change in the wider values, attitudes and perspectives of society through emancipatory practice. A discussion of which follows next.

ACTIVITY

Reflect on the above discussion. There are two different paths for social workers suggested above. One is to act as a form of 'police', where the disenfranchised elements of society are kept in order so as not to cause problems for mainstream society. The other is for social work to effect some form of social change and to alter society so as to alter the circumstances that cause problems in the first place. Which path would you take and why?

Empowerment, participation, and service user and carer involvement

In recent years there has developed a growing body of evidence of positive developments in emancipatory practice through the evolution of empowerment as a conceptual framework. There is also a greater degree of consumerism as a result of genuine improvements in partnership working and a greater recognition of the rights of service users and carers. Sayer (2008) stresses the importance of critical thinking and critical analysis in social work and highlights the need to look at the underlying influences that may emerge in the form of individual practice dilemmas, or the wider living context in which a particular service user operates, or perhaps the organizational structure of service delivery. He stresses the point that social workers need to be able to take account of wider societal perspectives and illustrates how, for example, within a structural analysis of disability, 'the disability movement would argue that it is the barriers within society rather than individual impairment that exclude people with disabilities' (Sayer, 2008, p. 4.) This change has to be viewed within the context of how social work has evolved through the years and how it has struggled at times with its combined and often conflicting role as an agent of social change and an agent of social control.

Historically social work has been set within a number of professional dichotomies, such as care and control, support and supervision, and voluntary and compulsory intervention. The development of a plethora of complex legislation to underpin social work, and the role of state intervention in the lives of families, for instance, has resulted in a much more adversarial and legalistic approach to many aspects of social work practice. Nowhere is this more apparent than in social work with children and families. Within this sector in local authorities and voluntary organizations, there has been more of an emphasis on viewing social problems from an individualist perspective, or what Sayer (2008) has referred to as *individual blaming* rather than viewing these issues from a wider structuralist point of view, which would acknowledge that people's problems are not an outcome of poor character but a condition of their class location in society. There is a clear power dynamic at work within the welfare system, given that Smale et al. (2000) stress that people who choose to, or are compelled to, engage with social work services are invariably from poor, disadvantaged and working-class family circumstances.

In the 1970s the ideology of social work as a radical force for social change gained considerable credence. Bailey and Brake heralded radical social work as 'understanding the position of the oppressed in the context of the social and economic structure they live in' (1975, p. 9). Part of accepting such a perspective on social work entailed understanding the influence social class as a social structure has on people's lives. The demise of radical social work according to Sayer (2008) was due largely to the years when Margaret Thatcher was the influential prime minister of a Conservative government. There was an unwillingness for the state to pay employees to be critical of the services they were providing and a shift away from more collective (and by implication class-based) approaches to intervention, as had been envisaged by the Barclay Report

(1982), to a more statutory orientated and procedurally defined delivery of services. The spirit of 'radical social work' did not die, however. Radical social work re-emerged in the form of emancipatory practice encompassing anti-oppressive practice, empowerment and, more recently, wider service user and carer participation. One effect of coming from a lower social class background is that you have less control over your life and circumstances than people from other social classes. By empowering people and offering them the opportunity to participate in how their support is structured, you are assisting people in gaining back some of that control. The following discussion of social work with working-class children and families illustrates how emancipatory social work may be realized in practice.

The role of social work with children and families is highly complex. Fox Harding (1997) created a model that attempted to outline a range of theoretical value positions that would influence how the child welfare system evolved in terms of role, policy, legislation and practice. In short, the *laissez-faire* position is that family life is a private matter and that state intervention should be kept to a minimum. The *kinship defender* position argues that the role of the state is to support vulnerable children and families in society. A third perspective, the *state paternalist view,* argues that ultimately the state has responsibility for the protection of children in society and that, in some situations, this may have to be achieved by a permanent removal from the birth parents. The final position is that of the *children's rights perspective*, which argues that not only is the child welfare system insufficiently child-centred, it is also on occasion actually quite oppressive in how it deals with children's rights. Fox Harding (1997) highlighted the fact that there are differences on a range of issues, such as the causes and remedies for deficient parenting, which will influence how individuals, agencies and policy-makers view the operational success of the system. Of particular interest to this discussion is her identification and acknowledgement of a 'class transaction' that can create problems for children who invariably come from poorer families in society and who are then placed with carers who have very different lifestyles to those of their natural parents.

We need to acknowledge that social work with children and families is often a very controversial, emotive and polarized aspect of practice. There is also a wide spectrum of roles, responsibilities, service provision and diverse activity that is carried out under this heading. These factors may partially explain why this area of social work has arguably been slower than other sectors of practice to include and develop service user and carer perspectives. Another explanation, however, may rest within the array of feminist perspectives where there is consensus that the family has been an important vehicle in the perpetuation of the subordination of women in society (Cunningham and Cunningham, 2008). They also argue that given the fact that much of social work intervention is aimed at women within families, where good enough parenting has in reality meant good enough mothering, the social work professional has contributed to the disempowerment of women within the child welfare system, where there are already imbalances of power between the state-run service provision and a diverse range of service users, often with conflicting and competing needs and rights.

There are, however, positive indicators that social work with children and families is embracing service user and carer perspectives, and thereby tackling some of the class disadvantage experienced by working-class children. A growing body of research exists on this dimension of practice, including the particular challenge of engaging with children and young people on their views of service provision. Historically this has been a somewhat tentative area of research, where writers such as Lindsay (1999) have very effectively highlighted the specific and complex ethical dilemmas researchers have had to take into account in undertaking research with children.

In recent years the prevalence of legislation, statutory duties and performance indicators has changed the nature of social work, whereby the needs and rights of service users are often compromised by agency policies, the lottery of limited resources and a preoccupation with risk management and defensive practice. The net result is that despite the growth of consumerism in social work in the 1990s, the service user agenda has always been set and controlled largely by local authority social services departments. The development of empowerment and emancipatory practice in social work has been a complex and difficult process. Davis (2007) argues that social work has been caught between two contrasting theoretical perspectives in developing a structural approach to practice. One is the maintenance approach, where social workers recognize the significance of social divisions in society and work within the restrictions imposed by the social order. The second advocates a more radical approach, whereby social workers go beyond a recognition and understanding of structural issues in society and actively engage with service users to challenge the current social order and change their world for the better (Davis, 2007).

Chapter Summary

This chapter set out to examine the relationship between sociology, social work and social class. It presented the key theoretical sociological theories of class followed by a discussion on how sociology should be a central component within social work education and practice. Finally, the discussion centred on class, social exclusion and the child welfare system.

Perhaps in a professional climate preoccupied by procedures, outcomes, quality assurance indicators and the management of individual risk, social work inadvertently embraced the now rejected and often scorned Thatcherite mantra that 'there is no such thing as society', from an interview given to *Woman's Own* magazine in 1987, and as a result lost its focus on wider societal perspectives and issues. It is arguable that middle-class social workers are striving to impose social control on socially excluded families through service provision and statutory frameworks, but that there is also a significant 'social transaction' at work in terms of the personal values and different perspectives of social workers and service users on the role of statutory social work intervention.

Lived Experience

The lived experience in this chapter has been provided by Joan Leece, a Social Work Services Manager with a large urban local authority. Joan has worked in a variety of practice settings and for the past fifteen years she has been employed as a social work practitioner, team leader and manager in a hospital/community care setting.

As you read Joan's reflections on her experiences of social work and its relationship with social class it would be useful to consider the issues that have been discussed in both the sociology and the social work focus. Doing so should help you relate what can seem quite abstract theories and concepts to individual people.

The following prompts should prove helpful:

- Reflect on one of the debates highlighted in the sociology focus on the existence of class in contemporary society and on how class has influenced both Joan's personal and professional biography.
- Consider how class structures and other social hierarchies are also mirrored in health and social care. Think about how this could shape the care and support a service user may receive.

- Compare Joan's feelings and her thoughts on how her perception of her own class position altered on becoming a social worker, with your own position as a student and how you perceive and understand your own class position.
- Assess which of the sociological perspectives on class best understands the situations that Joan describes.

I come from what people would call a traditional working-class background. I grew up on a council estate in a large town in the North West of England. Reflecting on my motivation to become a social worker, I am very conscious of the role that my working-class roots played in this process. Having grown up as a child of the welfare state, I developed a strong commitment to the principles of positive state intervention in the lives of citizens. I grew up with a passion to believe that state welfare services should go beyond providing a 'safety net' for the disadvantaged in society and be concerned with the creation and development of learning opportunities that empower people to make positive changes in their life. Although I am very proud of my working-class roots, I am also conscious that I have experienced the benefits of social mobility in that I work in a middle-class profession. I own my own home and I enjoy very different leisure activities and lifestyle from my parents. I have no doubt that my upbringing shaped my personal values, which in turn led to a career in social work. As a social worker I gained knowledge, skills and a professional value base that is rooted in respect for people and anti-oppressive practice. From a professional perspective, I am only too aware of how important it is for legislation and social policy to support and enable the most vulnerable in society.

My knowledge and experience in social work have led me to understand that there are a number of significant social problems that transcend class, such as ageing, disability, ill-health and bereavement. At the same time, it also reinforces the significance of social class given that, almost fifty years after the creation of the welfare state, the most vulnerable and disadvantaged people in society are from working-class backgrounds. Only too well do I recall, when working as a main grade worker with cancer patients, the relief I would feel if the patient was employed in the oil industry, as they were generally well paid and had good health benefits, such as full pay for six months. However, if the patient was employed in the fishing industry for example, my heart would sink as I knew they would initially only be in receipt of Statutory Sick Pay, and their financial worries would begin, on top of having to deal with a life-threatening illness.

Historically the Health Service has been a class-ridden organization, although in recent years this has lessened somewhat. The social class barriers between the diverse professions are beginning to break down, but have not yet been eliminated. At the top of the hierarchy are the consultants, senior medical staff who still wield considerable power which is gradually being eroded by management systems that aim to meet government targets. Below the consultants are the numerous grades of doctors who, if they originate from the UK, predominantly come from a middle-class background. Then there are the allied medical professionals such as physiotherapists and occupational therapists, again generally from middle-class backgrounds. The largest professional group is the nurses who, in my experience, are mainly working class, but there is also a shift here, with a greater emphasis on nurses being trained to degree level!

So where does social work fit into this hierarchy? I always felt it related more closely to the allied medical professionals; however, on one occasion the hospital management attempted to map out the different professional groupings within the hospital and social work was aligned with the ancillary staff, namely the domestics, porters and kitchen staff!

The main task for a new social worker in a hospital setting is to gain credibility, and this is not easy when one considers the competing demands and to whom they are answerable. Hospital social workers are not employed by the NHS but by the local authority and therefore their work agenda and priorities may be different from those of their medical colleagues. As mentioned earlier, consultants still wield considerable power and their priority is to treat the patients and empty beds as quickly as possible. The majority of consultants will not be at all concerned about the patient's social situation. Hospital social workers can be stuck between 'a rock and a hard place': they need to act as the advocate for the patient, to work to the LA priorities, but at the same time endeavour to ensure there is a steady throughput of patients and to not cause unnecessary delays. This is where the worker's credibility is vital if they are to achieve their primary aim and act as the patient's advocate.

How is this achieved? First and foremost it is by providing a prompt professional service; however, in my view there are also other subtle influences at work. As a team leader in a hospital setting I was aware that workers who obviously came from a working-class background and had a strong dialect had greater difficulty becoming accepted and gaining credibility than their middle-class counterparts. Mode of dress is another factor. It may be regarded as acceptable for a child care worker to wear jeans, but it is not acceptable in a hospital setting, where a smart mode of dress is required in line with the other professions.

Despite what some sociologists claim, we are not a classless society and a significant number of services users and carers are very class conscious. I recall one situation when a member of my staff was involved in an assessment for a care package for a man of eighty-nine, who could be described as middle or upper-middle class. He was no longer able to live at home, and part of the social work assessment process meant seeking the views of his only close relatives, his two elderly sisters who were his main carers. The sisters were quite distressed that they had to meet a social worker, because to them, a social worker worked with the lower-status people. To me this was a clear example of how social work can be perceived, and that the recipients of its services are often those from dysfunctional or working-class backgrounds. This can be an initial barrier when endeavouring to work with families who certainly do not consider themselves in either category.

This problem can be further exacerbated by the social background of the individual worker, and the issue of language and class can be a very important consideration. Higher Education Institutions are rightly seeking to address issues of structural disadvantage and recruit students into professional training courses from 'non-traditional backgrounds'. On the one hand, this approach has to be applauded, but on the other it brings with it a tension and a challenge. The social work code of practice says that we should value diversity, and this would obviously include people from areas with very strong local dialects and accents. Indeed, I am still proud that I have retained much of my Lancashire accent after living in Scotland for over thirty years. In professional social work, however, clear concise verbal communication is essential. We need to speak clearly and avoid colloquial terms.

Further Reading

The following two texts provide excellent commentaries on sociological approaches to class:

Bottero, W. (2005) *Stratification: Social Division and Inequality*. London: Routledge.

Crompton, R. (2008) *Class and Stratification: An Introduction to Current Debates*, 3rd edn. Cambridge: Polity Press.

The following book provides information on radical social work:

Bailey, R. and Brake, M. (1975) *Radical Social Work*. London: Edward Arnold.

3

Gender

Val Sheach-Leith, Michael Sutherland and Neil Gibson

Key themes

- Gender is an example of social construction. What it means to be male or female varies across cultures and throughout history. There is no 'set way' to be a man or a woman.
- A particular society's norms about what is gender are learned and performed throughout life.
- A great deal of gender inequality still exists in contemporary society.
- The gender of service users impacts on and is affected by social work in all arenas of practice.
- The gender of social workers impacts on service users.

Keywords

gender, sex, social construction, performativity, hegemonic masculinity, inequalities, patriarchy

---

Introduction

Issues of gender exert a great influence on social work, whether in shaping what social workers do, or in how social workers present themselves in their daily working surroundings. In this chapter we begin by outlining and discussing the sociological material and concepts relating to gender. The one key message to emerge here is the social construction of gender, and that how men and women are in society is not explainable by a reference to biology or an innate sense of what it is to be a man or woman. Rather, it is down to how a particular society defines the roles, cultures and activities of women and men. Attention then turns to how the social processes of gender outlined in the sociology focus influence the practice of social work in a variety of social and care settings. The key point here is how the obvious and also the subtle performances and expectations have to be understood and negotiated to ensure effective practice. Finally, in the lived experience, two social workers discuss how issues of gender affect their working lives.

Sociology Focus

The top ten toys for Christmas 2008 included a crying baby doll with a musical potty and a *Star Wars* helmet. On Christmas morning it is highly likely that it was a girl who sat quietly nursing the crying baby doll on its potty, whilst her brother ran round the room wearing the *Star Wars* helmet, busily 'saving the world' for humankind. Whilst the variations in physical and emotional behaviour between girls and boys, women and men appear, on the surface, to be derived from biological differences, these variations are actually *socially constructed*. This means that they are not only innate (natural), but are also based on strongly held beliefs circulating in society which inform and shape (construct) appropriate feminine or masculine behaviour.

These beliefs and accompanying social processes shape the experiences of females and males, old and young, in the family, in school, in the workplace, in the private and public sphere. In the same way as social class (see Chapter 2) impacts on the way people live and experience their lives, similarly there is no area of life that is untouched by the social construction of *gender*. As Holmes (2009, p. 3) notes, 'We live within a *patriarchy,* a society largely controlled by men and in which men usually have a greater share of the rewards (both in terms of wealth and status) available' (emphasis in the original). Although some theorists believe that patriarchy is too simple a concept with which to explain the situation of men and women in contemporary society, it does allow us to consider how our life choices and life chances are shaped by gender.

DEFINITION

Patriarchy as a concept refers to the male domination of society. This domination is maintained through cultural, linguistic, and political and legal means and is evident in many aspects of everyday life, such as the media and representations of gender and gender roles.

Social work as a career and as a practice is a gendered sphere. It is still predominantly women who become social workers and this affects how social work as a profession is perceived and rewarded in terms of status and pay. Women are believed to be 'naturally' caring, therefore the emotional labour that is an integral part of social work goes unrecognized and unrewarded. Social and welfare policies are also influenced by gender norms in society (Marchbank and Letherby, 2007), shaping decisions on who cares for young children or elderly relatives for example. The impact of gender on social work practice is explored further below.

Sex and Gender

DEFINITION

Sex refers to the physical and biological differences between men and women. **Gender** refers to the cultural, social and psychological differences between men and women. Gender is therefore not a fixed concept or set of behaviours but instead changes over time and between and within societies.

In order to understand why women and men experience the world differently, and often unequally, we need to distinguish between two important terms, namely *sex* and *gender*. In the early 1970s, feminist sociologist Anne Oakley highlighted how a focus on the biological differences between women and men failed to explain women's subordinate position in Western society. Focusing on *sex*, the biological attributes of female and male bodies could not explain, for example, why at that time it was predominantly men who worked outside the home (in the public sphere), whilst women stayed at home to look after young children (in the private sphere). There is no biological reason why this should be the case. Therefore, we need to look at socially constructed ideas in society, for example as noted above, that women are 'naturally' more caring than men, to explain these differences.

Oakley (1972) argues that it is only through exploring the ways in which society expects and encourages women and men to behave, through focusing on the social rather than the biological, that we can begin to understand why this division of labour existed (and to some extent still does). *Gender* therefore refers to the social, psychological and cultural differences between women and men (Giddens, 2006), and relates to what it means to be *feminine* or *masculine* in particular societies. Gender is *not* fixed but differs across time and space. Let's look at two examples to illustrate this point.

In respect of masculinity, in the Western world, it is now increasingly acceptable for men to express their emotions, particularly in the sporting arena, something that would have been frowned upon by previous generations. Therefore, beliefs about what it means to be 'masculine' have changed over time. Similarly, ideas about femininity vary across cultures. As Holmes (2009, p. 26) notes, whilst women in the West have often been viewed as physically weak, in many other cultures (e.g. in Africa and Asia) women carry heavy loads in the course of their everyday lives. Because gender is not fixed and does not derive automatically from sex, sociologists argue that 'masculinity' and 'femininity' are either learnt, through the processes of *socialization*, or, as some theorists maintain, are something that we '*do*' on a day-to-day basis. We look at both perspectives below, beginning with gender socialization.

ACTIVITY

Identify and discuss what types of activities and ways of behaving would be considered as being feminine or masculine in contemporary society? Are these contemporary femininities and masculinities different from previous generations' ideas of being feminine and masculine?

Gender Socialization

Although gender is not fixed, Western society nevertheless has very clear ideas about what it means to be feminine or masculine; from the clothes women and men wear, the careers they enter into, to who should do the washing up. Traditionally sociologists have used the concept of *socialization* to explain the processes by which the family, schools, the state and the media help children learn gender. To simplify greatly, baby girls are dressed in pink dresses, baby boys in blue dungarees; they are given gender specific toys (dolls or train sets) and encouraged to participate in different sports (gymnastics or football). Children are taught to use their bodies (Young, 1980) and express their emotions differently; girls to take care of their appearance, boys to engage in physical rough and tumble, girls to cry, boys to keep their tears at bay. As a result of these socialization processes, girls and boys mature to fulfil particular roles in society (Connell, 2002).

More recently, sociologists have questioned just how useful the concept of socialization is for understanding gender. Connell (2002) argues that there is not just *one* masculinity or femininity which society transmits to passive individuals, but a plurality of masculinities and femininities. All women and all men are not the same: therefore masculinity and femininity can be done differently. In addition, although gender socialization is predominant in the formative years of life, it continues throughout life. This means that although we always have to take into account the social structures (such as class) that shape gender, becoming gendered (learning and 'doing' masculinity and femininity) is more open to resistance and change than a passive socialization model suggests.

DEFINITION

Gender socialization refers to the process by which people learn what it is to be a woman or a man in their society. This involves being directed in often quite subtle ways towards particular activities and modes of behaviour that are deemed to be gender appropriate in that society.

ACTIVITY

Discuss how children and adults are socialized into male and female gender roles in your country. Is socialization necessarily a passive process or can people challenge and transform prevailing social conventions concerning gender?

'Doing' Gender

Socialization theories tend to have the effect of making gender seem like a natural attribute of individuals. However, some theorists suggest that gender is not so much a property of individuals but something that we '*do*' in our day-to-day social relationships and interactions. Interactionist sociologists explore the ways in which individuals and groups interact and suggest that we can view society as a stage on which a drama is set. On this stage gender is very significant, as it shapes the ways we play our 'parts' or roles in different contexts–in the home or at work, for example. From this interactionist perspective, 'we are all actors trying to give a good performance of femininity or masculinity' (Holmes, 2007, p. 51). We act out femininity or masculinity in our interactions with others. This approach moves us away from thinking about gender as an attribute of individuals to focus instead on gender as a part of social situations.

A key interactionist theorist, Erving Goffman, argues that in our day-to-day lives we manage our behaviour to create a favourable impression to others. Part of this impression management includes displaying gender. For Goffman, the social scripts available to us are so familiar that displaying gender (being masculine or feminine in social situations) is relatively straightforward and not something we give a lot of thought to. In contrast to Goffman, West and Zimmerman (1987) argue that whilst this display of gender may appear 'routine' it nevertheless requires physical and emotional effort. Displaying femininity may require considerable body work (dieting, waxing and tanning, for example) and also emotion work (working to adopt a caring attitude). Similarly, displaying masculinity requires that men work to embody certain physical attributes (muscular strength, for example) and to display certain emotions (such as toughness). West and Zimmerman (1987), therefore, see working at gender as central to all social interaction.

We now move on to explore a radically different and influential perspective, which moves away from gender as something that we perform (from a pre-existing gendered script) towards something that we bring into being through our performances.

Gender as 'performative'

DEFINITION

As developed by Butler the concept of **performativity** refers to how social actors create their identities through acting them out and performing them on a daily basis as opposed to having them pre-configured or made up beforehand.

Separating sex from gender and emphasizing the social aspects of gender has been very fruitful for sociologists of gender. It has, however, tended to reinforce the idea of the biological body as a fixed, (pre-) sexed entity onto which gender is then placed, like putting clothes (gender) onto a hanger (sex). There remains the assumption that *femininity* will be attached to a *female* body, *masculinity* to a *male* body. Although sex and gender would appear to be linked, it is important to recognize that having a female/male body need not necessarily lead to the display of feminine/masculine characteristics or behaviours. The work of the feminist philosopher Judith Butler is important here because it allows us to consider that our understanding of both sex *and* gender result from the effects of social practices in society. From Butler's perspective, individuals are not pre-sexed or pre-gendered, but rather in 'doing' gender individuals effectively *produce* sex and gender. It is through the 'doing' of gender (what Butler [1999] terms the 'stylized repetition of acts') that we create ourselves as gendered beings. Gender, therefore, is *performative*. This framework allows us to break away from unproblematically attaching femininity and masculinity to female and male bodies. Although, as noted above, society has clear ideas about what it means to be feminine or masculine, people can, and do, do femininity and masculinity differently. Butler (1999) calls this 'gender trouble'.

Moving on from this section on how we come to learn, do, or bring gender into being, we turn now to exploring the concept of masculinity in contemporary society.

ACTIVITY

Identify ways in which masculinity and femininity are performed in everyday life.

Masculinities

DEFINITION

Connell has developed the concept of **hegemonic masculinity** in order to describe the dominance of masculinity in society. This form of masculinity exerts its influence by being accepted by society as the 'best way' to be a man. As such, control and aggression, heterosexuality, being successful and displaying 'macho' behaviours are elements of this form of masculinity.

Initially, influenced by the feminist movement, much of the sociological work on gender focused largely on women and ideas about femininity. Since the late 1980s, however, more attention has been paid to men and the social construction of masculinity (Giddens, 2006). Connell (1995) explores the relationship between masculinity and femininity and how gender is structured in society. He argues that we can only understand what masculinity is by relating it to femininity. Masculinity and femininity do not exist in isolation but in relation to each other. Connell (1995), therefore, is interested in *gender relations*, the ways in which gender is created in interaction between women and men, between women, and between men. Thinking about interaction between men, Connell, as we noted previously, argues that a plurality of masculinities exist in contemporary society. These different masculinities emerge as a result of the way society is structured, for example, by class and ethnicity. Our structural location influences how we are socialized into and do gender (this is the case for femininity as well as masculinity). Put simply, a black middle-class man will experience and do gender differently from a white working-class man. Significantly, upper- and middle-class ways of doing gender are more valued in society (Holmes, 2009).

Connell (1995) describes the dominant form of masculinity in Western society as hegemonic masculinity. The term 'hegemonic' relates to the concept of hegemony – the social dominance of a particular group that is maintained not by force, but by their beliefs and values being accepted as the norm in society. Hegemonic masculinity, therefore, is the form of masculinity that underpins patriarchal society and legitimates the subordination of women. Hegemonic masculinity is associated with physical strength, control and aggression and, most importantly, heterosexuality. Men who might be said to embody hegemonic masculinity include the Hollywood actors Arnold Schwarzenegger and Bruce Willis, and successful businessmen such as Gordon Ramsay and Donald Trump. Whilst most individual men do not embody all the features of 'hegemonic masculinity', this form of masculinity has cultural dominance in society as whole and as a group they benefit from it. Within the dominant framework of hegemonic masculinity there are specific *gender relations* between different groups of men, in which some are marginalized. In this gender hierarchy, Connell (1995) argues that homosexual men stand in a relationship of subordination to heterosexual men as they do not embody the masculine 'ideal'. Other men, such as those from different ethnic groups, may also be marginalized in this gender hierarchy that privileges hegemonic masculinity. What Connell's work highlights is the need to take into account the structures in society that shape gender and furthermore that gender is created through social relationships; it is not a static fixed category. Having looked at various aspects of the social construction of gender, let us now look at some of the ways in which gender shapes the life experience differently.

ACTIVITY

Identify other examples of men who conform to Connell's concept of hegemonic masculinity. In what other ways does this type of masculinity pervade contemporary society and affect the ideas and behaviours of both men and women?

Gender Differences

While some gender differences may be viewed as benign, for example the clothes we wear, others are less so. The values and norms inherent in the social construction of gender mean that women and men experience life differently and sometimes unequally. Two areas that will prove fruitful to explore are health and employment.

For more on gender and health, see Chapter 7.

Gender has a direct effect on health. Traditional masculine occupations (heavy industry and mining) exacted a heavy toll on male bodies. Although employment in these areas has declined greatly, it is still men who undertake the largest proportion of physical and dangerous work, for example, in the offshore oil and gas industry. In proving their masculinity, men are also more likely to engage in risky behaviour and are therefore 'more likely than women to be murdered or to die in a car crash or dangerous sporting activities' (Doyal, 2001). Women, in contrast, carry the major burden of caring for the home, the family, elderly relatives, whilst at the same time, increasingly being employed in part- or full-time work. Women's structural location in society (as subordinate to men) also affects their health, as they are more likely to experience the negative impact of poverty.

Dominant notions of masculinity also affect help-seeking behaviour. Men are much less likely to seek medical help than are women for a range of physical and emotional problems (O'Brien et al. 2005). The men who took part in O'Brien et al.'s study, which explored their help-seeking behaviour, found that many men believed it was 'weak' to consult their doctor with what might be considered a trivial complaint. Being strong and enduring pain was part of 'being a man'. This conception of masculinity can have a direct effect on men's health as an early diagnosis of disease, or treatment of injury, is delayed. These beliefs also made it difficult for men to seek help when they were experiencing mental health problems. As one participant said, 'If I was a woman, I'd probably go to the doctor and get some ... antidepressants ... But as a man you just pull your socks up' (O'Brien et al., 2005, p. 511).

Ideas about gender also shape the world of work. We often perceive particular occupations to be more suited to women (e.g. nurse) or men (e.g. fighter pilot). These perceptions shape not only the type of work women and men engage in, but also pay and conditions. In 2008, women working full time still earned 12.2% less than men, while for all forms of employment the gender pay gap was 22% (ONS, 2009a). The reasons behind the gender pay gap are complex. One line of thought is that women are often employed in the public sphere of health and education, where the 'caring' work they do is seen as a 'natural' part of being a woman and therefore not rewarded in terms of status and pay. Women working part time in order to continue to meet family responsibilities often find themselves in low paid, insecure jobs contributing to the number of women and children living in poverty.

Whilst men are still more likely to work than women, the type of work they do has changed. The loss of heavy industries has meant that more men are now employed in customer services and the caring sector. Although it is now more acceptable for men to show a 'caring side' than it was in the past, the dominance of hegemonic masculinity in society means that men who adopt careers (such as social work or nursing) may have their masculinity (closely tied to heterosexuality) called into question (Cross and Bagilhole, 2002).

One area where assumptions about gender are significant is in work that involves caring for the bodies of others, as in nursing and social care. Bodywork can involve dealing with human wastes and its perception as 'dirty work' can lead to it being given low status and poor rewards (Twigg, 2006). Requiring intimate contact with the body and emotion work, bodywork in the field of social care is predominantly carried out by women. The work they do in caring for bodies in the workplace is similar to that which they are expected to do in the home (e.g. the management and care of the bodies of young children), and both forms of bodywork are perceived as part of being feminine, and therefore as 'natural'. This can lead to women failing to receive proper reward for the work they do (both in the home and in the workplace). The intimacy of bodywork also brings assumptions about male sexuality to bear. Men are viewed as sexually predatory and this can affect the willingness of agencies to employ them in this area of work (Twigg, 2006).

The social construction of gender therefore has real effects on the life experience and life chances of women and men. The two areas explored above, health and employment, provide only a brief insight into these effects; other areas in life are similarly impacted upon.

Having looked in this section at the social construction of gender, we now turn to the significance of this to social work practice.

Social Work Focus

Thompson (2007, p. 88) notes that 'discrimination and oppression are so often central to the situation social workers encounter ... the majority of social work clients are women, yet the significance of gender in a male dominated society is a factor that many practitioners fail to take into consideration ... they adopt what is known as a "gender-blind" approach'. It has been noted earlier on in this chapter that social work as a profession and practice is a gendered sphere. All social work environments can never be gender-neutral. Gender plays a part in social worker and service user relationships, in those between service users and those between colleagues. It is useful then to consider some of these social work environments and how gender impacts upon the practice of the social worker both personally and institutionally.

Social work services are delivered in a variety of settings, and, in all of them, many service users coming into contact with the social work system may be seeking 'normality' (Thompson, 1993, 2006), that is, a return to, or shift to, a sense of balance or relative comfort. This sense of 'normality' may be drawn from learned experiences, observations from daily interaction within an individual's environment, and stereotypes drawn from the mass media, which can place an unnecessary pressure to conform on an individual. One of the aims of social work is to empower service users to assist them to challenge any oppression which prevents the successful achievement of a sense of normality, and not merely to adjust to the situation. Gender plays a significant part in this process, both for the social worker and for the service user, and an awareness of potential issues in various work settings will help to prevent workers adopting a 'gender-blind' approach.

We shall now consider the implications for specific areas of practice.

The Criminal Justice Environment

Statistics in the United Kingdom show that male offenders outnumber female offenders by approximately four to one (Scottish Government, 2006; Ministry of Justice SOL HMSO, 2009). This can make the field of criminal justice social work a male-orientated environment. Doyal (2001) noted that males are more likely to engage in risk-taking behaviour and, typically, criminal activity can be linked to machismo where a purvading attitude of alpha-maleness exists. If we also consider Connell's (1995) *hegemonic masculinity* and O'Brien et al.'s (2005) statement that dominant notions of masculinity affect help-seeking behaviour, these barriers pose a potential stumbling block to social workers in this particular field.

The majority of service users within the criminal justice system do not 'choose' to be there and may not be willing to engage with or seek to be empowered to make changes in their behaviour, lifestyle or environment.

The work of Connell (1995) comes into play in terms of considering how society and social relationships help shape gender, and consequently, how gender is used to conduct social relationships. The relationship between social worker and service user will be influenced by each other's knowledge of gender and how this can be utilized to make gains.

Consider a female social worker working with a male service user. The male service user may have been brought up in an environment where he was encouraged to use his masculinity to assert power and to regard females as the caregivers and providers of his needs. He will use this in his relationship with the social worker, and she will have to empower herself to assert her professional identity over her gender, whilst at the same time he will need to adjust to the notion that his needs will only be met if he is willing to empower himself to embrace positive change, which may need to begin with a change in his view of gender roles. Similarly, a female service user may have to overcome gender issues when working with a male social worker, but gender issues may also occur in same-sex relationships. Cross and Bagihole (2002) highlight the fact that male social workers may be challenged about their sexuality by male service users. Certainly this may stem from the fact that they are being asked to consider uncomfortable changes and may be retaliating against the worker.

Consideration may also need to be given to the type of crime committed and the nature of the worker/service user relationship. A female offender who funds drug use through prostitution may have issues working with a male social worker, which could impact on the responsiveness and impact of any programme-based work on the offender. She may feel resistant to a male worker due to the nature of her experience with males and her feelings of oppression within her environment. Similarly, if a service user has grown up with a poor role model, this will also impact on the working relationship. A male service user may be unresponsive to a male worker if there has been a lack of positive male role models in his upbringing.

Issues with gender should not negate social workers working with particular service users, but merely inform social workers that any potential barriers in the working relationship *may* stem from each other's understanding of their gender and how to use this.

Substance Misuse

There are many theories to suggest why an individual may use substances to such an extent that it becomes problematic. It may be a factor of social isolation, the environment, mental health difficulties and self-medication, learned behaviour, or simply a desire to recreate a pleasurable experience over and over again. Gender does play a role in substance misuse, both in why a person may use substances, and how a social worker can approach interventions with a service user.

Consider an individual's route into substance use. The most common first experiences of substance use are related to school, peer group pressure, conformity and curiosity. It is plausible that gender influences the types of substances experimented with. Alcohol is a common drug of choice for experimenting at an early age and can be consumed in a group environment where peer group pressure is rife. Desires to experiment with alcohol may be borne out of social norms, witnessing parental use of alcohol, watching television where the majority of soap operas are set around a pub, and digesting other forms of media that perpetuate the idea that alcohol use is 'normal' and 'cool'. Holmes (2007) believes we act out masculinity and femininity as we grow, and this can be incorporated into our actions and experiences, particularly in relation to how society dictates that males and females should act. Indeed, Oakley (1972) also states that gender is defined by how males and females are expected and encouraged to behave, and recognition should be given to reported statistics over the increase of alcohol use by females and how our learning experiences as we grow influence this behaviour.

Throughout an individual's career of experimenting with substances, various experiences, gains, losses and consequences will be accumulated. Problematic substance use may well stem from these learned experiences when an individual recognizes that a certain substance has a certain masking effect, or produces a certain coping strategy. For some the connection might be that a certain substance—for example, alcohol—produces confidence in social situations, making it easier to perform to members of the opposite sex. The more this substance is used and relied upon, the more difficult it becomes to perform without it. For others it may be that a substance helps numb the pain of uncomfortable experiences. All of these issues may be related, in some way, to gender. It is also important to recognize that criminal activity is often linked to substance use and can place an individual within the criminal justice system.

For the social worker working in the field of substance misuse, one of the biggest challenges is working with the service user to identify the reasons behind their use. Assessments generally cover a wide area of topics but do focus on upbringing, schooling and significant events in a person's social history. Gender issues should come into play for the social worker, who should consider the potential relevance of alienating experiences, role models, peers and sexuality.

Interventions can often include group work programmes, but issues of gender do need to be considered when thinking about this approach. First, does a worker opt for a single-sex group or a mixed-sex group? Single-sex groups can focus on gender-specific issues and eliminate any risk of sexual distractions, but mixed sex groups reflect society and may be more beneficial in enhancing social skills across genders. Another question to consider is who should facilitate the group? If you are working with a female group, there may be a risk that a patriarchal society, as described by Holmes (2009), has played a role in their oppression and subsequent route into substance use. Therefore a male facilitator might alienate group members and further feelings of oppression. However, the other line of argument would be that to employ male facilitators in this environment could demonstrate a positive male role model.

Care Management

Since the introduction of the National Health Service and Community Care Act (1990) care management has become a significant role within the social work field. Perhaps it is within the field of care management where 'traditional' gender stereotypes are perpetuated – the role of female being seen as providing a naturally caring role, as noted by Marchbank and Letherby (2007). Certainly this image of a 'naturally' caring social worker who takes on the emotional labour of a situation may assist in the relationship formation between social worker and service user, but it is professional identity that needs to override gender identity.

Female social workers within care management need to be aware that older service users may have an engrained idea about the role of women in society and therefore will have a greater expectation as to what should be provided for them. For example, a housebound service user who struggles with domestic chores may feel it is appropriate to ask his/her social worker to take some of their laundry home and wash it for them. In a few exceptional circumstances this might be appropriate on a one-off basis, but a long-term arrangement like this does nothing to empower the service user and in fact does more to disempower the social worker and the professional relationship. Role boundaries and professional identity need to dominate work in this field.

Male social workers in this field also face challenges. Older service users may challenge younger men working in the caregiving industry, sexuality might be challenged, and gender stereotypes over 'traditional' male occupations might be raised. Similarly, it is important to assert the professional nature of social work in this setting if being faced with issues such as these.

It also becomes important for the social worker to recognize gender issues they themselves may have. These issues could be based on their role and gender within society; for example, a young male social worker may only be able to base experiences with older people on his relationship with his grandparents. This relationship will carry with it expectations on gender roles which the young male social worker will need to be aware of when forming new, professional, relationships with service users.

The Residential Child Care Environment

Residential child care environments, particularly where there are groups of teens, can be particularly macho or challenging (Berridge and Brodie, 1996). If external and internal managers are predominantly male, there may be a greater emphasis on, and imbalance between, control over care, and recreational activities may be geared more towards traditional, boys' interests. There tends to be a greater number of boys in particular residential settings—for example, residential schools and secure accommodation (a point of interest in itself)—than there are girls. These factors can contribute to the creation of such a 'macho' atmosphere.

Girls who may be resident in such a male-dominated environment may enjoy the traditional male activities and this particular masculine atmosphere, but others may feel that their interests are not being catered for and their identities are being subsumed into such a 'malestream' environment.

Similarly how will any number of boys feel if they are uncomfortable relating to men who express themselves in a very traditional way or if they would prefer to take part in activities that some may see as 'girly'? In a residential, looked after, setting, staff have to find a balance between recognition of an individual's developmental needs and the importance of peer group membership as a part of those needs.

Similarly staff, depending on their own value base and belief systems, may place different expectations on boys and girls when it comes to appearance and behaviour. Some staff will have particular views on how adolescent boys and girls should look based on notions of acceptable masculinity and femininity. Boys can be allowed to bare a degree of flesh but girls doing the same may meet with disapproval. Likewise in behaviour, staff may accept particular behaviours in boys—'rough and tumble' play or overtly sexual (male and heterosexual) posturing—that they would not accept in girls.

ACTIVITY

Think about your own experience as a child. Try to remember playing with other children, and how comfortable or uncomfortable you felt. How easy was it to join in or opt out, and did you find playing with same sex or other sex children more preferable?

A further gender issue that often comes to light in residential child care is that of who assumes the tasks of care and control. When confronted with challenging behaviours it may be assumed by male and female staff that a physically larger male, apparently more authoritative and likely to be in a more senior position, will undertake a physical restraint. Likewise assumptions can be made about who is in a better position to comfort an upset youngster, to give that youngster a hug, if this is permitted (Johnson et al., 2000). It is assumed and expected that a female member of staff will undertake this task for two reasons: women are the 'natural' caregivers and men are treated with suspicion and will feel discomfort when attempting to touch children (Finkelhor, 1994).

Work with Families: Fieldwork

Social workers working with families will need to consider how family dynamics are shaped and influenced by particular expected gender roles. They will need also to recognize that families come in all shapes and sizes and in varying forms, for example, the two- or the single-parent family, kinship caring families, same sex parent families, reconstituted families and other familial combinations. This said, gender and the expectations placed on a parent based on his/her sex will play a significant part in how a family functions.

Consider the situation of a traditional family of mother, father and two children, all being of a traditional religious faith. What if father loses his long-standing job and therefore his identity as breadwinner, and mother, as the significant caregiver, feels compelled to go out to work for the first time? The homeostasis of this family—that is, the emotional balance—will be affected. If one parent has difficulty in relinquishing the societal, and perhaps more importantly for this family, the religiously, expected gender and family role, but the other enjoys this change, this could create real tensions, and eventually dysfunction, within this family. Resultant behaviours of any of the family members may bring the family to the attention of a social work agency. So how then does the social worker engage with this family? Is it his or her job to promote a return to the status quo as quickly as possible or to enable the family members to adjust to their new roles? How gendered is the social worker's assessment and intervention likely to be? The family's and the worker's values in relation to faith, gender and family are undoubtedly going to impact on the work to be undertaken here.

ACTIVITY

Think about your own family. Who provides nurture, or discipline, or food, or who decides what activities will be done or where to go for holidays? To what extent are the answers to these questions about role performance gender-based? Think also about how your experience fits with Connell's (2002) concept of gender socialization.

Fostering and Adoption Services

The majority of individuals who apply to adopt and foster are female. This is not surprising given that women are expected to be or become mothers. It reflects the notion, as noted earlier, that women are society's reproducers and carers. Increasingly, however, single men are coming forward to apply to adopt or foster, or if as part of a couple, to be the legal adopter or lead foster carer, which is not without its difficulties for some of the male applicants.

Some men can find that they are entering into a very feminized environment because the social workers who will carry out the assessments are likely to be female; the literature, materials and resources available focus on women being the foster or adoptive carers (Kelly and Gilligan, 2000); membership of panels is dominated by women; and the support available afterwards is likely to be given by a female social worker. The whole process can be a very daunting one for some men (Freeark et al., 2005). Those who are in hetero-sexual couples may find themselves marginalized or may collude with the process of marginalization. One male carer explained to this social worker that he did not usually read the paperwork as it was addressed to his wife.

Also, the additional suspicion that some men sense from professionals when applying to foster or adopt may make these men wonder if it is worth proceeding. Some workers can be overly concerned about sexual abuse (which is mainly perpetrated by men) and they might be insufficiently convinced of the importance of men in children's lives. What messages then are these workers sending out to prospective male carers?

Newstone (1999) identifies some of the challenges faced by male foster carers:

- managing teenage girls' affectionate behaviour;
- being expected to restrain aggressive behaviour;
- dealing with children's negative preconceptions of men;
- carrying the label 'all men are potential abusers';
- being sidelined by professionals (in visits, meetings, correspondence);
- feeling marginalized in a female environment.

But it is not just men who will come up against institutional barriers. Hicks (2000) identifies the challenges that can exist for same-sex couples wishing to foster or adopt, especially for lesbian women. Some professionals will have notions of types of lesbian, usually 'the good lesbian' (automati-cally safe, able to care) or the 'bad lesbian' (threatening, militant), and the former will be more readily approved as a carer than the latter.

Social workers involved in this field need to consider how the processes of assessment, intervention, decision-making and post-placement support with foster and adoptive families are gendered and they also need to reflect on their potential to be sexist and heterosexist. Additionally, agencies need to develop policies that recognize the diversity of experiences and attributes that men and women, whether gay, straight, bisexual, can bring to caring for a child.

A further, but related point, is that of the particular developmental and gender considerations in the needs of looked after and adopted children. It may be that a child's needs would suggest their placement with a carer of a par-ticular gender, or sexuality for that matter, in order to enable him/her to grow and develop healthily. There is some evidence (Flouri, 2005; Ramchandani et al., 2005; Wineburgh, 2000) to suggest that it is important for both boys and girls who are looked after to be provided with healthy role models of both genders, however there is such a low presence of men in the child care and educational systems.

ACTIVITY

If you are a woman, how comfortable would you feel with a male midwife? If you are a man, how comfortable would you feel discussing sexual matters with a female doctor?

The Adult Group Care Environment

Group care environments, be they day care or residential, are mainly staffed by women. Where there is a higher degree of dependency and need, and therefore of care, there can be found a higher number of female, frontline, 'hands on' staff (Coulshed and Orme, 2006). In any group care environment there can be the need for workers to attend to the personal care of service users: washing, bathing, toileting, dressing, etc. When men work in this environment there can be a great deal of ambivalence over their involvement in personal care, especially for children (Christie, 1998; 2006).

Some agencies have policies that state that male staff should not undertake the personal care of female service users, although both male and female staff will be required to do so for male service users (Johnson et al., 2000). Such policies fail to give service users a choice. It is not inconceivable that a male service user may not wish for his personal care to be carried out by a woman, and is it completely inconceivable, though highly unlikely, for a female service user to prefer a male caregiver to attend to her personal care?

Understandably, though unacceptably, such policies come from fears and anxieties around the sexual exploitation of service users by staff (Johnson et al., 2000). Social workers need to be aware of the risks of such power-based exploitation in any staff–service user relationship and not be quick to assume that male workers are likely to sexually exploit male or female service users but female workers are unlikely to sexually exploit at all.

It is, however, not just within the area of personal care in the group care environment that social workers need to be conscious of gender roles and expectations. It is also in the particular relationships that develop between staff and service users. It may be that a 72-year-old male resident gets on particularly well with his 52-year-old female keyworker because she reminds him very much of his departed wife, but his habit of calling her 'My darling' will need to be challenged by the worker as it may be sexist in overtone and certainly crosses a professional boundary.

Likewise staff will need to challenge the routines and practices that may exist in some group care environments that collude with and perpetuate stereotypical gender role expectations–for example, male staff assuming the role of drivers and female staff mending clothing.

It can be worthwhile for any day care or residential establishment to undertake a gender audit in relation to who does what and with whom and to identify thereafter the practices that are sexist and that require challenging and changing.

Sense of a Gendered Self

A fundamental tool social workers are required to make use of in their day-to-day work in any setting is that of the 'use of self'. A social worker's physicality, body language, and mannerisms will transmit particular messages–sometimes conscious to the worker, at other times not–to service users. Social workers need to become increasingly aware of which messages they are 'giving off' to service users in this way. Inevitably, then, how workers 'do' gender and how their genders are perceived by others, service users and colleagues alike, will have an effect on professional relationships.

Social workers need to be aware of how their gender might impact on relationships. Their biological sex, male or female, might make particular areas of work difficult to engage in. Some services may, and legally can, appoint a person from a specific gender to work in settings where either only a man or a woman could undertake the role, for example, a female worker to work with Asian women.

It is not only the social worker's biological sex that may have to be considered, it is also his/her appearance and presentation of masculinity or femininity. Some relationships between social workers and service users may not 'work' because of the degrees of masculinity or femininity presented by, or perceived by, the service user or social worker. This may not mean that the worker needs to alter how she/he behaves as a man or a woman but it does mean that she/he needs to be sufficiently aware of self to enable an understanding of the effects of her/his gender on service users.

On other occasions the worker may need to consider whether or not her/his gender limits her/his abilities in the workplace: the male worker who cannot hug an upset child despite a permissive culture; or the female worker who cannot assert herself with a group of deliberately sexually provocative boys.

Chapter Summary

It can be seen then that gender plays a significant part in the personal, cultural and structural (Thompson, 1993, 2006) provision of social work services. Social workers need to be aware of their gendered selves and their potential for sexism. They also need to consider the organizational cultures in which they work and be prepared to challenge any policies and practices that treat men and women, girls and boys unequally in an unfair and oppressive way. They need to act as agents of social change in pointing to, and endeavouring to, eradicate institutional sexism in the social services.

This is not only an ethical consideration but also a legal requirement. United Kingdom legislation requires service providers to administer their services equally without any discrimination shown towards men or women. This will not mean treating everyone the same, but is likely to mean that existing imbalances and inequalities in service provision need to be readressed.

Social workers need to be feminists, unpopular though this may be in the present day (Dominelli, 2009). Orme (2009) argues for a particular feminist perspective, that is not exclusively women-centred, of 'feminist praxis', which 'recognizes the diverse experiences of all users of social work services and seeks to challenge and transform policy, practice and the organization of the service delivery which constrains people in gender-specific roles or oppresses them by inappropriate exercise of power'.

Lived Experience

For the lived experience Alastair Gibson (AG) interviewed two practising social workers, Alastair Logan (Al) and Adelle Aitken (AA), on their personal reflections and observations concerning how the social process of gender influences the working environment of social workers.

As you read the interview it would be useful to consider the issues that have been discussed in both the sociology and the social work focus. Doing so should help you relate what can seem quite abstract theories and concepts to individual people.

The following prompts should prove helpful:

- Reflect on how the themes discussed by the participants relate to the sociological theories discussed earlier in this chapter.
- Identify how gender is performed by social workers and service users, in particular the expectations that are discussed of how gender should or should not be performed.
- Consider the gendering of social work and other care environments. Which of these would you expect to be 'gendered' in a particular way, where one gender is more powerful or dominant?

AG: How do you think working within social work is influenced by the fact that you are male or female and what are your experiences of the gender issues in social work?

AL: Bearing in mind that I work predominantly with men, in criminal justice the majority of clients are male, and working with sex offenders, the thing that I'm aware of, because I'm male as well is that there's an element or potential for grooming to go on between the client and myself, in that the client will try to side with me or get me on their side and say 'you know what it's like for a man here'. In the case when I worked in Probation there were issues such as domestic argument or domestic violence you would often get a rhetorical question–'come on, Alastair, you know what it's like being a man'–and I think I found that to be an issue about how I work. I guess I can use that to my advantage as well: in that because I often work with female colleagues there can be a gender balance and while there can be a misconception with male clients that women are 'just like this' and 'all men agree with me', you can act as a counter-balance and say 'that's not the case'. So it's something you often have to be aware of, I think. Something I have to keep reminding myself of.

AA: I think that can work for females as well. Sex offenders will manipulate a lot and because we're female they feel, and this is general offenders too, that they can charm you. You can see that people go on the charm offensive to get around you or get you onside. It's quite interesting. I suppose, having worked in the youth justice area briefly, often, when I worked with one of my colleagues who's male and we'd go on the same home visits, if the family wasn't happy they would turn it around. I was 22 at the time, and it would be 'Are you a mother?' And if you're not a mother, 'how dare you come into here and suggest our parenting isn't good enough or there needs to be some intervention', whereas my colleague he never once had that, despite the fact that he wasn't a parent either. He never had that used as ammunition against him ... They make the assumption that because you're younger, because you're a social worker, you wouldn't possibly have children that age, and they did use that, and it could be used in Children's Hearings as well. It was used to possibly undermine our opinions.

AG: Have you ever found in your practice that the organization is more likely to expect you to do certain things based on your gender? If you're male you may be more likely to be expected to do this, if you're female this?

AA: I don't think so in this specific workplace. Although there have been issues where certain clients' needs, or the issues they present, when it's been deemed appropriate to have a male worker.

AG: What's that based on? What's the thinking behind that?

AL: I think sometimes for balance. But sometimes, some women's group that they run, they don't let men facilitate those for some good theoretical reasons if you know what I mean, but that's almost like a closed area for men to go into. I remember being given one specific female client, and I was given the client because I was male, and it was felt she needed the experience of having a positive male role model in her life because all other previous ones had been particularly negative or abusive so it was a case of let's see how she reacts or whether it would help to have a male.

AA: I had that experience at Youth Justice. It was actually a children and families case, and it was a young female. She was only 14 and because I was a younger age group amongst the work staff I was given her case. The senior had explained it as 'there's horses for courses' and I got on very well with her, whereas it was felt if she had an older member of staff or a male she wouldn't have taken to them quite as well. But it doesn't always work like that.

AG: Alastair's example of a man perhaps not being permitted to work with an all - female group … would the same thing happen if there was an all-male group we might prevent a female worker from working with them?

AA: We do have that situation with this job, and there are female facilitators with the sex offenders group, which is all male.

AL: What's interesting though is that in either a group setting, with JSOP [Joint Sex Offenders Programme] or 2-to-1 work assuming, there's a general assumption that the client we're going to work with is male, although we do have some females, and that you would not be allowed to have two men co-work together with another male as regards to JSOP work and I think even, I could be wrong here, but also if it was a female client, it probably wouldn't be allowed to have two men working with her. So again, much as it is useful to have a gender balance, I think in some ways it's seen as OK to have two women work with a man, but it's not OK to have two men. Again, I think there's good reasons behind that, but it does seem a little bit odd sometimes, because I think there's no issue with having two women work with either another woman client or a male client.

AG: That's really interesting. I hadn't thought of some of these issues, I must say, and I guess I was thinking more in terms of the traditional ways of looking at men and women, you know, if you want something done that needs toughness you go to the man, if you want the nurturing done, you go to the woman. That doesn't sound like it's your experience.

AA: I think here we have a large number of very assertive women who would be described as 'just as tough', and to be honest I think the males here are often a softer touch, than the women are I would say, in terms of enforcing compliance. I would say the men are sometimes softer than women.

Further Reading

Two very clear and accessible sociology texts to assist in exploring the sociology of gender in more depth are:

Connell, R.W. (2002) *Gender*. Cambridge: Polity Press.
Holmes, M. (2009) *Gender and Everyday Life*. London: Routledge.

If you wish to access a more challenging text, then try:

Butler, J. (1999) *Gender Trouble: Feminism and the Subversion of Identity*. London: Routledge.

4

Race and ethnicity

Chris Yuill, Angela Duvollet, Tuck-Chee Phung and Tatenda Govera

---

Key themes

- Issues of race and ethnicity are constantly changing in contemporary society.
- Diversity, multiculturalism and new forms of culture combined from different cultures are a feature of modern global life.
- Ethnicity refers to the culture, traditions and language of a group. We are all part of an ethnic group.
- Racism has its origins in the early colonial slave trade.
- Racism changes over time with cultural differences.
- Institutional racism is a distinct issue in British society.
- Social work has a duty to challenge racism.
- The Personal, Cultural and Structural (PCS) model of social work assists the social worker in working with service users from ethnic groups.

Keywords

ethnicity, race, slave trade, racism, institutional racism, discrimination, prejudice, PCS model, critical race theory

---

Introduction

One central insight runs throughout this chapter. It concerns the presence and origins of racism in society. We establish that racism is far from being simply the negative actions and unpleasant attitudes of a few misguided or bad people. Racism should be more accurately regarded as a social phenomenon that emerges out of distinct social, cultural and historical structures and processes. What we mean by this reference to structures and processes is that people do not spontaneously originate racist ideas, or that somehow people just randomly think that other people with a different colour of skin or from another country are inferior, dangerous and should be treated differently from how one would treat people one would regard as being similar to oneself.

Those ideas have to come from somewhere. Where they do come from is the society and culture in which one lives. Racism is, in effect, 'built in' to many social institutions, cultural practices and everyday understandings and interpretations of society. It is from these sources that people can develop racist ideas and structure their individual understandings of society and people. Possessing such an understanding of racism, as we shall explore, greatly enhances social work practice in relation to issues of race and ethnicity.

To provide a deeper understanding of the points raised above, the sociology focus examines a number of core concepts and key issues relating to race and ethnicity. This overview consists of profiling the ethnic composition of the United Kingdom, followed by a critical discussion of the concepts of race and ethnicity, before outlining the various forms that racism takes in contemporary society. Emphasized throughout in the sociology focus is the relationship of social structure with racism, and how social structures both create and maintain racism. The emphasis of the chapter then moves to the social work focus where we apply the sociological insights to social work theories and practice. Thompson's PCS model and the Critical Race Theory (CRT), which assist the social worker in understanding the relationship between social structure and individual action, are explored by building on the material outlined in the sociology focus. In the lived experience focus a young woman who has encountered many different aspects relates her experiences of what it is to be from an ethnic minority in today's increasingly globalized society.

Sociology Focus

Changing Demography – the new ethnic landscape

As the introduction indicated, British society is becoming increasingly diverse, with many different groups from a wide variety of national and ethnic backgrounds becoming resident in the UK. The purpose of this section is to map out that diversity, statistically, before moving on to outline some of the drivers for why modern Britain exhibits this particular profile.

TABLE 4.1   *UK population by ethnic group, April 2001*

	Numbers	Total population %	Non-white population %
White	54,153,898	92.1	–
Mixed	677,117	1.2	14.6
Indian	1,053,411	1.8	22.7
Pakistani	747,285	1.3	16.1
Bangladeshi	283,063	0.5	6.1
Other Asian	247,664	0.4	5.3
All Asian or Asian British	2,331,423	4.0	50.3
Black Caribbean	565,876	1.0	12.2
Black African	485,277	0.8	10.5
Black Other	97,585	0.2	2.1
All Black or Black British	1,148,738	2.0	24.8
Chinese	247,403	0.4	5.3
Other ethnic groups	230,615	0.4	5.0
All minority ethnic population	4,635,296	7.9	100.0
All population	58,789,194	100.0	

Source: Office for National Statistics, 2005
Reproduced under the terms of the Click-Use Licence.

What is immediately noticeable is that even though greater diversity is evident ethnic minorities as a whole still constitute a relatively small part of the overall population, some 7.9% (see Table 4.1). This demography is forecast to increase to somewhere around 10% after the year 2010.

One further interesting observation apparent in the statistics is the increasing number of people from mixed backgrounds in the UK, currently about 14.6% of the non-white population and 1.2% of the UK population as a whole (see Figure 4.1 and Table 4.1). The interesting implications for self-identity of the increasing number of people from a mixed-heritage background will be discussed when we explore ethnicity later in this chapter.

There is one troubling aspect apparent in the official statistics that is useful to highlight. As Nazroo (1998) notes, official categories of ethnicity are often not attuned to the sensitivities and subtleties of how people identify their ethnicity and culture. Consequently, many official government categories are too wide-ranging and loose to provide an accurate outline of the norms and cultures of particular groups of people. A useful example can be found with the classificatory term of 'South Asian' used in some UK health surveys, for example. The problems with this term as an accurate collective name for referring to a distinct group of people become apparent

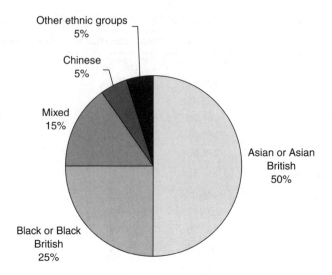

Figure 4.1 *Black, South Asian and East Asian population: by ethnic group, April 2001 (Office for National Statistics, 2005)*
Reproduced under the terms of the Click-Use Licence.

when one considers that it applies to millions of people. Furthermore, these millions of people are located in the different countries of India, Sri Lanka, Bangladesh and Pakistan; are speaking different languages of Punjabi, Bengali, Urdu and English; and are practising different religions such as Islam, Sikhism, Buddhism and Christianity. How useful or accurate the term South Asian is for adequately grasping the cultural and ethnic diversity of such a vast group of people is therefore debatable.

There are many reasons for the increasingly diverse landscape portrayed in the statistics. Before outlining those reasons it is worth pointing out that Britain has always been to some extent a multicultural country. There is good historical and archaeological evidence of a variety of people from outside Britain having a presence as far back as Roman times. For example, a unit of North African Moors served in a Roman Legion that was stationed in what is now Burgh-by-Sands in the north of England. There is even a tantalizing suggestion that the legionnaires settled there (King et al., 2007).

More recently, the main reasons for immigration into the UK can be broadly summarized as follows:

- *The British Empire* – at one point Britain was *the* major global economic and military superpower. It was said that the sun never set on the British Empire; such was its extent that it was always daytime in one of the territories that the British ruled. One consequence of empire was that people from countries ranging from Asia to the Caribbean were either British citizens or regarded Britain as the Mother Country. During the main phases of mass immigration in the 1960s and 1970s many people considered that migrating to Britain was moving to a place where they already possessed an existing symbolic, legal or emotional connection. The lived experience focus discusses the influence that the British Empire continues to exert on self-identity and the choices people make as to where they decide to live.

- *Economic success* – following on from the above, one reason for migration is economic opportunity. People move to where the jobs are. Though it may be more accurate in the British case to say that people were encouraged to move. In the 1960s in particular the British government (but notably not the late anti-immigration Conservative MP Enoch Powell) actively encouraged people from the former British colonies and territories to migrate to Britain to make up for the labour shortages in the British economy, especially in areas such as health and transport.
- *Globalization* – the increasing interconnectedness of the world witnesses the parallel ease of movement or flows of people through various scapes, such as via discount airlines. It is now much easier to be mobile; in fact sociologists such as John Urry (2007) have claimed that mobility defines the current age, as people are increasingly less bound to a particular place.

Race: social construction or biological fact?

The concept of race is commonly used in society. To people in modern society it may seem 'natural' to regard people as belonging to a distinct race. On many official forms, for example, we are often asked to indicate to which racial group we think we belong. What sociology reveals, however, is that the concept of race is highly problematic. There are many issues and controversies arising from both the use and the origins of the concept. Sociologists regard race as being a highly unhelpful, if not wholly redundant and outmoded, concept that does little to help us reach an understanding of the interactions of different peoples and societies. This inadequacy is primarily due to the concept of race emerging from a particularly low point in human history (encompassing plantation slavery and colonial expansion) coupled with a lack of any scientific validity for categorizing people into different 'races': claiming that different 'races' of people exist is akin to making claims that different species of people exist – this is an unsustainable proposition.

DEFINITIONS

Race refers to the mistaken notion that people can be accurately biologically differentiated into separate and discrete groups. **Ethnicity** refers to the social, cultural and historical characteristics of a group of people. Such characteristics are highly fluid and can change over time and be adopted by other groups of people.

The social construction of race

A useful way of understanding why the term race is so controversial is to consider how the history of the concept and how racial differences between people have been socially constructed over time. Doing so also illustrates the assertion made in the introduction to this chapter that racism is located not in individuals but in social structures. The importance of this is explored further in the social work focus when considering the PCS model. The discussion below is based on various writers–Callinicos (1995), Blackburn (1998) and Carter and Virdee (2009)–who are influenced to varying degrees by the Marxist tradition. The relationship between changes in the economic base, the various norms and values of a society, and the ideas that people hold, and the actions they perform, are central to that perspective.

Previous epochs of human history saw very little distinctions being made on what we today would recognize as race. For the ancient Greeks, Romans and Egyptians the defining attribute of someone was not their skin colour, it was whether or not the person was either civilized or a barbarian. To be civilized one had to be a citizen of one of the countries (or city-states, to be more accurate) just mentioned. Citizenship was importantly irrespective of skin colour. During the classical period there were many instances of people who were black becoming prominent figures in those societies. The Roman emperor Septimus Severus, for example, was of black African descent. In the Middle Ages it was religion that marked out the differences between people. The three religions of Islam, Judaism and Christianity dominated how people understood society and the differences between people during that historical period. Critically, people could shift voluntarily (or by force!) from one religion to another. Skin colour or supposed racial group was irrelevant to which religion you belonged to. The historical legacy of these times is still evident today, with populations of white Muslims in Eastern Europe and Arabic Christians in the Lebanon, for example.

The concept of race and the idea of classifying people on the basis of physiological differences critically begin with the need to justify the barbarism associated with the enslavement of Black Africans in order to provide labour for the newly founded European colonies, mainly in the Americas. The British state played a full part in this process, whether in founding the colonies, setting up the companies that were directly or indirectly involved with slavery, or by providing the banking and credit arrangements for those companies. As Callinicos (1995) maintains, slavery and the mass exploitation of captured people played a pivotal role in the development of British capitalism. Many British cities boomed due to the profits of the slave trade or the money made from plantations. Glasgow, Bristol and Liverpool are all examples of British ports whose expansion in the 1800s was funded directly and indirectly by the slave and plantation system.

The enslaving of black Africans began in the mid-seventeenth century and did not fully disappear until the mid-eighteenth century. During that time up to 14 million people were forcibly transported from Africa to the Americas and the Caribbean. The chattel slavery of this period was highly brutal. Many people died in transit. It was common for slave ships to 'tight-pack' (to use an expression of the time) several hundred people in the cargo hold of a ship for the duration of the long voyage across the Atlantic. Conditions on board were harsh, with people chained to their wooden berths for weeks on end. Conditions on arrival were little better. Caribbean field slaves working on plantations were often expected to live for only a year at most.

It was the need to justify the barbarity described above that led to the development of the ideologies of race, racial superiority, and thereafter racism. Many people, both black *and* white, were appalled by the slave trade and in Britain organizations such as The Charterists actively campaigned for its abolition. They often appealed to notions of a common humanity, drawing attention to the rights of Africans, as fellow human beings, to be allowed to access the same freedoms and rights as white Europeans. To counteract opposition to slavery notions of white superiority and black inferiority were developed. Black people were, in effect, assigned a 'non-human' status, and were seen as exhibiting less intelligence, for example, than white people, thus 'legitimating' their oppression and exploitation. Much of the rationale for categorizing people into different groups was based upon highly dubious science (more of which later). It is also important to highlight the self-organization and resistance of black people in this period too. In Haiti in 1791, former domestic slave Toussaint L'Ouverture led a slave rebellion against the Spanish, French and British colonial powers, liberating the island and ending slavery in 1804.

It is from this point in history that what we would understand today as being racism emerges: the notion that people who are 'not white' are different and inferior. These ideas of white racial superiority were also taken up by the British in the founding of the British Empire. One rationale used by the British to conquer and subjugate other peoples was that white British people and British culture were superior and inferior 'non-white' races would benefit from being ruled by Britain and being exposed to British values. Racism therefore emerges as a means to justify the exploitation of one group in order to realize profit and to maintain the functioning of the capitalist system as a whole.

Even though the British empire no longer exists, those ideas still exert an influence in contemporary British society. The importance of slavery and colonial attitudes is revisited in the social work focus and in the lived experience, as they provide an explanation for where racist ideas and racist cultural practices originate from.

ACTIVITY

Why is it important to understand the history of ideas relating to race and classifying people?

The scientific validity of race?

In terms of the scientific validity for classifying people into different races there is very little evidence – if any – for doing so. One notable and vital aspect about humans is that they are a remarkably homogeneous species and those genetic similarities that do exist do not always follow the social conventions for the race someone belongs to. In the nineteenth century pseudo-scientists such as De Gobineau claimed the opposite, and attempted to construct firm differences between groups of people, in terms of abilities and characteristics. Such views are no longer taken seriously by main-stream scientists. Biologist Steven Rose eloquently summarizes the lack of a scientific basis of race as follows:

> The definition of race is essentially a social one, as in reference to Blacks or Jews. While there are differences in gene frequencies (that is, differences in the propor-tions in which particular genetic variants occur) between population groups, these do not map onto the social criteria to define race. For instance, Polish Jews resemble their fellow Polish nationals, non-Jews, more closely than they do Jews from Spain. Gene frequencies in Black Americans differ from those in Black South Africans. And that for that matter, gene frequencies differ between North and South Wales, yet no one would think of classifying those two populations as two different races. This typological thinking has not disappeared: it characterizes, of course, the poisonous propaganda of racist political groups, and has not entirely vanished from popular scientific writing. (Rose, 2005, p. 37)

ACTIVITY

What does the extract from Steven Rose tell you about trying to scientifically classify humans into different 'races'?

Ethnicity: fixed or fluid?

Conceptually, 'ethnicity' has many advantages over race. The false scientific and historical racism baggage associated with race is dropped in favour of what, on the surface, appears to be a more satisfactory social and cultural mechanism for identifying groups of people, and crucially, for how people identify themselves. The emphasis this time is on culture and norms, such as styles of dress, food, language, and so on. Again, though, caution must be exercised as unwittingly (or otherwise) the concept can be misused and misapplied. We have already discussed how official classification can be problematic, by being too blunt and insensitive in how people are assigned to particular categories. Other misuses are discussed below.

Technically and correctly, everyone, regardless of their skin colour, belongs, in some way, to an ethnic group. So, the distinctive speech patterns, diet and dress of a white person from the East End of London are as much an ethnicity as are the speech patterns, diet and dress of a black person with a Caribbean family heritage who lives in Glasgow, the interesting point being that the person in the first example is less likely to be regarded and defined as being from an ethnic group as the person from the second example. What happens, as Davidson (1999), Maynard (1994), and Carter and Fenton (2010) argue, is that ethnicity becomes a coded way of referring to black and ethnic minority groups as opposed to a concept or term that can be applied to any group of people. It can therefore be just another way (or homologue) of referring to race, and, as we have reviewed, all the problems that entails.

Ethnicity too can also often be misused in a way that suggests a cultural fixity, and that the traits of language, dress and diet are akin to a static, unchanging, stereotyped shopping list: for example, that all Asian people have poor English and eat spicy food and Asian women dress only in saris.

In reality, cultures are incredibly dynamic social entities, constantly changing and developing over time, fusing with other cultures and creating new ways of being. In short, all cultures and therefore ethnicities are fluid and *not* fixed. This focus on fluidity chimes with wider treatments of identity in sociology (Giddens, 1991; Jenkins, 2008). What is evident is that people in contemporary societies have access to a more eclectic (or a 'pick-and-mix') approach to how they construct their own identity and, in turn, present their sense of self to the outside world. A lack of determinacy and malleability of self also sits well with postmodernist understandings of society, where people are freed up from restrictive modernist conventions. Referring to the previous Asian example, if we observe contemporary Britain we can note many examples of this cultural fluidity and change. Television programmes such as *Goodness Gracious Me* play with images and ideas of Asian and British culture, producing a fusion of the two.

ACTIVITY

List other instances where different cultures have combined to create new or hybrid cultures.

Following on from the ideas of fluidity and fixity expressed above, the issue of how people define themselves subjectively introduces important nuances. Ethnic identity can be one of a whole array of other identities to which one subscribes. Other parts of people's lives—such as their gender, sexuality, class, religion, membership of a political party, and sporting allegiances—will also influence how people assemble and perform their identities. Coming from a distinct ethnic group, therefore, may influence those other facets of self-identity, but it by no means is the one over-arching, all-encompassing master identity that subsumes other aspects of self. Scots-Asian comedian Hardeep Singh Kohli (2008) neatly sums up some of the nuances and subtleties of fluid and multiple ethnic identities and the tension between subjective self-identities and objective identity:

> My outward appearance may be Indian but my mind, my heart and my stomach are very much from Glasgow. English is my first language, by quite some way. Yet, as a turbaned Sikh, Indians expect me to be a fluent Hindi and/or Punjabi speaker. It seems that wherever I go in the world the expectation of who I might be is never in sync with who I actually am. (Singh Kohli, 2008)

ACTIVITY

What does the above quote from Hardeep Singh Kohli indicate about the complexities of how one perceives oneself and how others do?

Racism

DEFINITIONS

Prejudice refers to the negative or racist attitudes held by people about a particular minority group, while **discrimination** occurs when people and institutions enact that prejudice. **Institutional racism** is the (often) unintended outcome of a public or private body failing to provide a suitable service for people from an ethnic minority and **new racism** refers to how racism today is less about skin colour and more about supposed cultural differences.

'Racism is like a Cadillac: they bring out a new model every year'

The lack of scientific validity of race was highlighted earlier in this chapter. Just because we can identify the immense genetic similarities between people, correctly discuss the falsity of race as coherent concept, and cogently critique the various issues associated with the misuse and use of ethnicity, this does not make the very real social issues of racism, prejudice and discrimination disappear. As the quotation above from Malcom X indicates, racism changes over time. The outright biological racism associated with earlier epochs has given way to a racism based on cultural differences. However, regardless of how racism changes it still persists, and there are many disadvantages encountered by people from black and ethnic minorities.

Institutional Racism

The case of murdered student Stephen Lawrence in 1993 drew attention to 'institutional racism'. The investigation into his death carried out by the London Metropolitan Police was deemed to have been hampered and was far from satisfactory due to an inherent culture in the police that was prejudiced against and dismissive of minority groups.

The ensuing inquiry into the shortcomings of the initial police investigation produced this useful definition of institutional racism:

> The collective failure of an organisation to provide an appropriate and professional service to people because of their colour, culture or ethnic origin. It can be seen in processes, attitudes and behaviour which amount to discrimination through unwitting prejudice, ignorance, thoughtlessness and racist stereotyping which disadvantage minority ethnic people. (MacPherson, 1999)

New Racism

Gilroy (1982) has identified a 'new racism' in contemporary society. This new racism differs from previous expressions of racism. After the horrors of the Holocaust appeals of difference and superiority are no longer made on the basis of race and biology. Rather, the new racism focuses on culture and reveals that it is quite possible to drop the reference to biological 'races' and have, instead, as Balibar (1991, p. 21) notes, 'a racism without races'. New racism expresses difference and superiority by appealing to cultural norms and traditions. Claims are made that ethnic minority cultures are either lacking in sophistication or are deviant and dangerous. Islamophobia provides a useful example of this cultural racism, where all Muslims can be perceived as being supportive of terrorism and opposed to Western social norms.

Social Work Focus

Within the schools of social work we seek to prepare students to practise in a multiethnic, multiracial and multiclass society, to become culturally or multiculturally competent (Dean, 2001). There is no easy solution when trying to achieve cultural competency, defined as 'A set of congruent behaviours, attitudes and policies come together in a system or agency or amongst professionals and enables that system, agency or those professionals to work effectively in cross-cultural situations' (Coello et al., 2004, p. 1). As a process, cultural competency evolves over time as a result of increased cultural knowledge, values and beliefs. Dean (2001) suggests that it is *maintaining* an awareness of a lack of competence rather than the *establishment* of competence that would be the realistic goal and not so much *knowledge* but rather *understanding* is the key to professional competence. Either way, the health care industry and researchers need to become culturally competent, requiring the development of the skills needed to be respectfully aware of the whole person regardless of their culture, religion or race in order to continue to address issues of equity, ethnicity and race to ensure quality of practice.

The Central Council for the Education and Training of Social Work's Paper 30 for the Diploma in Social Work (1989), for example, was ahead of its time in addressing issues of racism and discrimination. The CCETSW paper addressed anti-racist practice in social work education, some ten years before the MacPherson Report into the murder of Stephen Lawrence concluded that there was 'institutional racism' in the police investigation. As the UK is a multicultural society made up of a variety of ethnic groups, all of which have their own characteristics that contribute to making up their cultural identity, race and ethnicity became an important issue not only in how social workers were trained but also in how social work provided services to people from minority ethnic groups. Penketh (2000, p. 52), for example, highlighted that 'many black students and social workers struggled for years to challenge the failure of social work courses to address anti-racism effectively, and this had been among the main catalysts of change'. Paper 30 offered this opportunity for ethnicity and racism to be openly addressed.

There is an expectation that students in training and later as qualified practitioners will have a clear understanding of how to challenge these issues in the wider structural context. To assist this, the standards of professional conduct and practice by which social workers are governed, are identified in the British Association of Social Workers (BASW) Code of Ethics and the Scottish Social Service Council's Codes of Practice. These address racism in general terms; however, the National Association of Social Workers (NASW) Code of Ethics is more specific under section 1.05 (c):

> Social workers should obtain education about and seek to understand the nature of social diversity and oppression with respect to race, ethnicity, national origin, color, sex, sexual orientation, gender identity or expression, age, marital status, political belief, religion, immigration status, and mental or physical disability. (NASW, 2008)

As social workers, acknowledging the direct link to our own cultural experiences (or 'cultural baggage') will allow us not only to reflect on how this may have an impact on our practice and professional development, but will also provide us with the means to challenge the institution, the state, policy and procedures and how services are provided at community level. To manage the potential tensions between the intra-psychic, the social, the systemic and the political, it is paramount that a reflection and evaluation of practice is developed and maintained to ensure that social work remains anti-racist and socially inclusive in practice. It would therefore be useful to draw on conceptual frameworks to support practice.

The Theory Base

As highlighted in the first part of this chapter, within society ethnic minority groups are often viewed as different and inferior, which can result in the inseparable relationship between discrimination, oppression and racism. As a practitioner, consider that racism 'is a multi-dimensional and complex system of power and powerlessness' (Burke et al., 2000, p. 283) operating at micro and macro levels with the more powerful groups in society dominating and able to influence policy and procedure in institutions and social systems.

Neil Thompson's PCS analysis, first introduced in his book *Anti-Discriminatory Practice* in 1993, provides a framework to assist the practitioner,

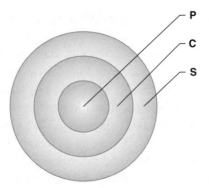

Figure 4.2   *PCS analysis*

to analyse inequality, oppression and discrimination operating at three interrelated levels: Personal, Cultural and Structural. One fundamental insight that Thompson provides with his PCS model chimes with one of the basic tenets of this book: that ideas and actions are not solely the creation of individuals, nor are they the result of 'natural' dispositions. If we are to adequately explain why certain social phenomena (such as racism) occur then this must be made in reference to the social structures in which people live their lives. Ideas, after all, have to come from somewhere. These are ideas and attitudes that are created by society, emerging out of various processes and cultural developments, and adopted, often unwittingly, by individuals. The PCS model assists us in understanding and analysing how society influences the thoughts and actions of both individuals and organizations.

Incorporating the PCS model into your practice will also assist us with *developing* our cultural awareness and practice strategies in order to promote anti-racist and anti-oppressive practice. The PCS model also assists in developing an understanding and analysis of the multifaceted phenomena of oppression, discrimination and racism, and the interlocking nature of oppression. Incorporating the sociological issues raised in the first section of this chapter will also crucially provide us with additional information and insights into all three levels of the PCS model (Figures 4.2).

Beginning in the centre of the diagram in Figure 4.2, the P (**personal** or **psychological**) level constitutes the most intimate and immediate element of oppression and discrimination. It is at this level that we encounter the individual's level of thoughts, feelings, attitudes and actions, and it is here that an individual's discriminatory behaviours and language are practised and rehearsed. The P also refers to the practitioner's interaction with service users' **practice** and **prejudice**; the holding of pre-formed opinions by the practitioner, based on a lack of knowledge and an inflexibility of mind.

Possessing such a mindset often stands in the way of non-judgemental practice for the social worker. For example, we may unintentionally and unconsciously contribute to racism and social exclusion of others through our own experiences, customs and habits.

The P level is embedded in the C (**cultural**) level. Culture plays an important role in legitimating what is normal and acceptable in a given society. As we discussed earlier in relation to ethnicity, who and what we are, our beliefs and social values, are strongly shaped and influenced by prevailing cultural norms. These cultural norms permit and encourage, in turn, the types of behaviour evident in the P level. Thus, if one lives in a culture that positively sanctions notions of white superiority, then racist jokes become permissible and acceptable at the P level.

Lastly, Thompson identifies that the C level is embedded in the wider S (**structural**) level. This level is the most powerful level in the model. The structural level ultimately influences and conditions the other two levels and is formed by the deepest levels of society. Here, the various power relationships, social divisions (class, gender and race, for example) and historical forces all interweave and give shape to the overall form of a society. For Thompson (2001, p. 23), the structural level is the 'interlocking matrix of social divisions and the power relations that maintain them'. Due to a society developing and being organized in a particular way, certain attitudes and forms of oppression therefore become 'built in' or 'sewn in' to that society. In the sociology section we encountered how racism and exploitation were part of the development of Western capitalist society, the legacy of which is that, both in terms of power relations and in popular culture, black and ethnic minority people are accorded a secondary or subaltern status.

The case concerning Victoria Climbié provides a useful example to link, in the wider context, the PCS model to practice. Victoria, a seven-year-old black-African child from the Ivory Coast, was killed in 2000 while living in the administrative area of Haringey Council in North London by her two black 'carers', her great-aunt, Marie-Therese Kouao, and Kouao's boyfriend, Carl Manning. There was an over-simplification and generalization of cultural issues (C) in the assessment of Victoria. There was, for example, a stereotyping of African culture by professionals (C), including her social worker's (P) assumption that Victoria's 'standing to attention' in front of her carers was a sign of 'respect and obedience', and the assumption by medical staff that the marks on her body resulted from her being raised in Africa. The pathologist on examining Victoria's body after her death found '128 separate injuries, many of them cigarette burns' (*BBC News*, 22 January 2009).

As Lord Laming's report indicated, there are dangers with generalizations: 'cultural norms and models of behaviour can vary considerably between communities and even families' (2003, 16.4). In addition, the report highlighted how 'fear of being accused of racism' (S) (P) undermined professional assessment and intervention. Ultimately, it was the failure to consider the safety of the child first which contributed to Victoria's death. The welfare of the child is paramount and the Children Act 2004 was a response to the concerns that arose from the Victoria Climbié case. It should be noted that Victoria's social worker was black, an African-Caribbean. This highlights the importance of anti-racist training for all social workers irrespective of their ethnic background. The ethnic identity of a worker does not guarantee cultural competency. Hence in the training of social workers, critical race theory is an important aspect of the curriculum (see below).

ACTIVITY

Can you think of examples of how the safety and culture of the child may be in conflict?

Critical Race Theory

A highly radical approach to both the understanding of racism and the course of action one adopts to counter racism is evident in the next theory under consideration. Critical race theory (CRT) began life as a movement in the American legal profession and system. It developed as a result of a compilation of work based on extensive research by a group of progressive law professors in America: Derrick Bell (an African-American), Alan Freeman (a Caucasian), Richard Delgado (a white-Hispanic), and various others, covering two decades starting from the mid-1970s.

The goals of CRT are to critically explore race relations in a broader context, 'transforming the relationship among race, racism and power' (Delgado and Stefancic, 2001, p. 2). Whilst maintaining the importance of the structural causes of racism, it is the subtler forms of racism and the insidious and corrosive effect that racism has on the experiences of black and other minority groups that occupy a central place in this theory. Racism from the CRT standpoint is much more than name calling in the street or preventing black people securing a promotion at work. Racism structures, pervades and conditions the very textures and rhythms of social life, the psychological dispositions of white and black people, privileging a 'white' perspective and interpretation in every social phenomenon. In effect, all social values, customs and norms perpetuate the superiority of being white while simultaneously denigrating and denying black people their status and humanity. Delgado and Stefancic (2001) offer a threefold typology of racism from a CRT perspective:

- A 'normal science' – the everyday experiences of black and ethnic minority people (or 'people of colour' in American usage) in society are saturated knowingly or unknowingly by racism and racist discourse.
- An 'interest convergence' – racism advantages all white people regardless of social class (hence their otherwise differences converge). A white person whether situated in the social elite or in the working class makes some form of gain from the existence of racism. For the elites their advantage is material, while the white working classes are psychologically advantaged, by believing that, despite their own relative material inferiority, they are somehow culturally or biologically superior to black people.
- 'Social construction' – where race and races are not so much biological but categories, invented by society, which can be manipulated or removed when convenient (Delgado and Stefancic, 2007). We investigated the social construction of race and ethnicity in the sociology focus.

As a consequence of the all-pervasiveness of white perspectives and superiority, CRT embraces a different race-consciousness, challenging the ways in which race is constructed and represented. This challenge occurs in both in the legal system and our society, covering a myriad of issues, and refers to a 'broad constellation of historical and contemporary theories that have actively engaged the prevailing racial theories of particular times and/ or social contexts' (Collins, 2007, p. 1).

Critical race theorists are concerned 'with disrupting, exposing, challenging, and changing racist policies that work to subordinate and disenfranchise certain groups of people and that attempt to maintain the status quo' (Milner, 2008, p. 2). Possessing such a perspective can lead to critiquing seemingly liberal perspectives on race and ethnicity. Take, for example, the practice of not allowing people's ethnicity to inform a decision, opinion or judgement; that is acting in a manner commonly termed as 'colour blind'. Such an approach may appear to be fair and progressive, but CRT suggests that colour blindness will only encourage us to consider and redress blatant forms of racism, thus ignoring a diverse range of hidden and less obvious forms of racism. CRT assists us to become 'colour-conscious' and challenge the underlying, less obvious forms of racism often embedded in our social structures (Delgado and Stefancic, 2007).

Delgado (2007) suggests also that in the United States advances in civil rights for 'blacks' often coincide with the self-interests of the white population and changing economic conditions: for example, the change of heart in the American legal system regarding desegregation in schools in 1954. Prior to this legislation, most cases had been lost or narrowly won. Closer analysis of the decision would suggest the Justice Department intervened and responded to pressure to have the United States be seen in a better light and improve its image in the Third World.

ACTIVITY

Consider your social work values and think of an example of how 'colour-blindness' could have an impact on these and how you would integrate 'colour-consciousness' into your practice.

Research is an example of the way in which CRT can be integrated to inform thinking in social work education, where it is acknowledged that teaching and curriculum design relating to cultural diversity has increased over the years. Daniel (2007) conducted research in the United States and referred to the CRT, which offered a sound conceptual framework from which to apply research findings, in this case with regard to minority students on a variety of higher education social work courses. Daniel suggests in his research there has been a lack of critical assessment of the academic and social experiences of ethnic minority students and there is a need to 'confront the inequalities that continue to undermine' (2007, p. 1) their professional development. Fifteen African-American and Latino students were interviewed and offered the opportunity to provide a critical insight into the issues they experienced. The results showed that these students felt marginalized, isolated and invisible, with administrators and staff unable to see minority students as individuals and the curriculum having very little relevance to their lives. CRT enabled Daniel to explore these issues, highlighting the concerning institutional structures, policies and practices that possibly contributed to racial and ethnic educational inequalities within colleges and universities and also exploring ways to make changes for the benefit of minority student socialization. CRT is continuously developing and recent world events have had an effect on the focus of supporting research for CRT. Dr Patricia Hill Collins from the University of Maryland suggests that, since 9/11, CRT has shown an increased interest in 'cultural studies and discourse analysis, encompassing work on areas as diverse as the body, ideologies and the significance of mass media and popular culture' (Collins, 2007, pp. 1, 2). As a student and practitioner, you will work with a diverse range of service users, many of whom will experience racism in one form or another.

Integrating Thompson's PCS model and the CRT into your practice will assist you with developing a deeper understanding of the issues of racism and cultural competency. The process will prepare you 'not only for ethnically sensitive practice, but also to challenge institutional and other forms of racism' (CCETSW, 1989, p. 10).

Working with families

Social workers need to understand the problem of racism and its impact on individuals, families and communities. One way of understanding racism in the lives of black and minority ethnic people is to consider black experiences and black perspectives. Singh (2000, pp. 14–15) defines these black perspectives as a basis upon which 'individual, group and collective aspirations can be developed and defined', providing a foundation on which to build 'a political and philosophical challenge to the hegemony of white European frames of thinking'. The experience of black service users according to Singh (2000, p. 11) has been characterized in four ways – the lack of 'access to positive social services' because of the assumption that black people 'look after their own'; social services being used to 'police' black service users in terms of immigration control; the use of stereotyping that contributes to a higher representation of black service users in the criminal justice system and being sectioned as being mentally ill; and finally the use of a 'black cultural pathology' to explain the problems of individuals and of families.

A central difficulty in addressing racism within our society and within our major institutions such as the NHS and police is that there is a continuous denial of racism as a structural disadvantage. The structural and institutional nature of racism was highlighted in the sociology section. Dominelli (2008, pp. 30–1) outlines eight strategies of avoidance in how people deal with racism–de-contextualization, denial, omission, the colour-blind approach, the dumping approach, the patronizing approach, avoidance and exaggeration.

Dominelli also highlights the inability of social workers to 'formulate collective strategies' that do not effectively have to choose between meeting the needs of the white service users and those of asylum seekers and refugees in a resource-limited situation, thus giving credence to the notion that some individuals are 'deserving' and others are 'undeserving' based on a racialized hierarchy. Ritchie (2008, p. 59) writes about this need to shift the focus 'on individual pathology to one based on the analysis of power' in the consideration of social problems and recognizes there are limited models of practice that would help social workers meet some of these radical goals, which include: 'reallocating resources to those who are most disadvantaged', 'building a community's capacity to care for itself' and 'disrupting institutional practices that actually create social inequality including charity work' (2008, p. 60). In essence, key black perspectives proponents like Dominelli, Ritchie and Singh highlight the need for social workers to address racism at its structural level, rather than personalizing it. The implications of this discussion move from the focus of how not only individuals, but also social and organized groups, and ultimately communities and society, structure their relationship with marginalized individuals and groups. The question and challenge posed here to social workers is whether they can be radical and activist in their professional approach to addressing structural inequality?

ACTIVITY

Following on from the point made above, how radical do you think social work could or should be in relation to addressing structural inequality?

Refugees and Asylum Seekers

Refugees and asylum seekers fleeing persecution provide a distinct set of challenges for social work. In the legal context, a person in the UK is classed as a refugee only when the Home Office has considered and accepted an individual's claim for asylum and as a result has given that person leave to stay in the UK with refugee status. If the individual is waiting on a decision from the Home Office, they are classed as an asylum seeker. The United Nations High Commission for Refugees (UNHR) estimated that in '2004 the UK hosted 298,854 people in need of international protection' (Patel and Kelley, 2006, p. 1). Figure 4.3 shows the numbers of asylum applications in the UK (33,960) in 2004 and the main countries of origin. Of those, it

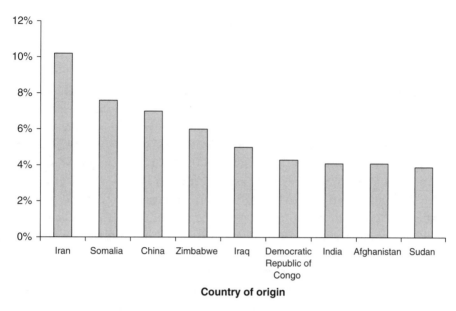

Figure 4.3   *Number of asylum seekers entering Britain by country of origin (2004)*

is estimated that there are 80,000 asylum-seeking children in schools in the UK, with approximately 120,000 children as refugees.

In 2002, under the Nationality, Immigration and Asylum Act 2002, for those refused asylum status the government removed any entitlement to social care services that are provided under the National Assistance Act 1948. Their entitlement to support from the National Asylum Support Service–this include limited social care, secondary and tertiary health care–was also cancelled. There are exceptions and in some cases local authorities have a duty to support asylum seekers if they have needs linked to a disability or mental health (especially after being detained for treatment), or have been looked after by the local authority, or are classed as unaccompanied asylum-seeking children (Patel and Kelley, 2006). Considering these factors and statistics, it is easy to appreciate that the needs of these groups are many. An understanding of the issues and problems which are commonly experienced by all cultures, such as language barriers, loneliness, isolation, mental health, housing issues and racial harassment, will provide the practitioner with a holistic view of their situation. A sound knowledge of relevant legislation, policy, procedure and theories would also ensure 'competence in the provision of services that are sensitive to clients' cultures and to differences among people and cultural groups' (NASW, 2008, p. 6).

For consideration

Since 9/11 and 7/7, the discourse of race and ethnicity has become more complex in that it is also bound up with religion. And in the wake of Islamophobia–an example of the 'new racism' outlined in the sociology focus–being Muslim raises questions about national loyalty and identity and individuals and a whole group of people are likely to be stereotyped (Ahmed, 2003, cited by Dominelli, 2008). Dominelli (2008, p. 43) states that after 11 September 2001, 'Muslims in the West have been redefined as terrorists rather than citizens. Religion and ethnicity have become politicized, culturalized and biologized to yield various forms of racialized profiling that work to their detriment'. Social work has a key role to play to mitigate against unfair and unjust discrimination. In a political climate where 'the otherness' is feared and is perceived to be subversive, it becomes more difficult, though more essential, to enter into such debates both at a national as well as at a local level. Such stereotyping and fears need to be *de*-constructed in the training of social work students so that they are not paralysed in their work as qualified practitioners in a political climate that can be both personally and professionally challenging and demanding.

There is no expectation that an individual or service provider is supposed to know all there is to know about every culture. However, there is a requirement for cultural competency and for health care organizations and educators to be proactive in the development of tools and curriculums to understand multicultural needs.

Lived Experience

In the lived experience a young Zimbabwean woman (Tatenda Govera) recounts her experiences of racism both in Zimbabwe and in the UK.

As you read the interview it would be useful to consider issues that have been discussed in the sociology and the social work focus. Doing so should help you relate what can seem quite abstract theories and concepts to individual people.

The following prompts should prove helpful in doing so:

- The sociology focus highlighted the importance of historical influences on the development of racist ideologies and ideas. Relate that discussion to Tatenda's experiences of living and growing up in Zimbabwe. Also, reflecting on why a knowledge of the history of how racist ideas came into being is important for understanding racism and ethnicity in contemporary society.

- Reflect on how racism has affected both Tatenda's job opportunities and her experiences of work in the UK.
- Refer back to the PCS model as outlined in the social work focus and apply it to the lived experience.

Having been born just a year before Southern Rhodesia gained its independence from the British colonialists to become Zimbabwe in 1980, I did not experience the institutional racism and overt discrimination that used to exist then, on a personal level. What I can relate to, however, is the aspect of structural oppression and the visible social divide that was prevalent when I lived in Zimbabwe. Very few blacks and whites mixed socially. Racism was perpetuated through 'exclusive whites only' clubs and private schools which charged exorbitant fees, thereby deliberately alienating the majority of black families who could not afford these. Whites effectively controlled the economy, they owned most of the big companies. Large pay gaps used to exist between black and white employees of similar pay grades. The social divide between blacks and whites was more pronounced in Zimbabwe than in Britain.

My experiences in Britain broadened my perspective of racial issues, in particular how racism manifests itself in every day life. While the United Kingdom has made enormous strides towards tackling overt discrimination, thanks to the enforcement of equal opportunity legislation, there is still a lot work needed in tackling 'sub-conscious' racism. Sub-conscious racism is not so obvious, to the extent that the perpetrator sometimes thinks they are doing the 'right' thing when often they are being racist. This is a form of racism which derives its existence from stereotyping ethnic minorities in an often derogatory compartmentalization, such as every Muslim is a terrorist, every black African is an asylum seeker, or every black Caribbean is a drug addict. Sadly, this phenomenon obtains in other areas of society such as recruitment and selection, the treatment of ethnic minority kids in schools and in general with how society deals with disadvantaged minority groups. The offshoot of sub-conscious racism is to blinker how social workers tackle abuse in ethnic minorities. For example, their judgment on what is acceptable and not acceptable might be prejudiced by someone's ethnicity. The challenge for the social worker is to understand Britain's multiculturalism, promote and celebrate differences, and ensure prejudices do not affect their professional conduct.

Despite various theorists highlighting that there is no scientific evidence to prove that some races are more intelligent than others, the sad reality is that, in some cases, individuals from ethnic minority groups grow up to believe misconceptions about the superiority of other races. Such social stigmas may create psychological barriers, which will impede career development amongst people belonging to ethnic minority groups. However, my personal experiences within the UK employment market tell a somewhat different story. I could not secure even a management trainee position despite having a Bachelor of Commerce Honours Degree in Management on my arrival in England. This is typical of many of my friends in possession of Law, Finance and Marketing degrees obtained from reputable United Kingdom universities. I therefore found myself working in care homes, which ultimately made me embark on a career change to enter a profession whereby I would be guaranteed a job upon qualification. The reality is, unless an ethnic minority is within critical shortage professions such as, nursing, social work and civil engineering, the chances of obtaining a good job are close to zero. It is also important to note the importance of geographical location when it comes to an acceptance of ethnic minorities within the employment sector. The further south in England one goes, the more opportunities there are for ethnic minorities.

Having worked in the health and social care sector for over six years, I have had a couple of experiences whereby I felt I was treated differently because of the colour of my skin. In one instance the service user I worked with was very vocal about her dislike for black people. Although she had learning difficulties such behaviour was not tolerated by management who were always quick to offer their reassurance by speaking to her and myself. Stereotypical thinking that ethnic minorities are not as competent in their roles is not an uncommon feature within the workplace. There were unfounded assumptions about my intelligence, as on many occasions people felt the need to explain even the most basic of instructions, like switching on a computer. I also often detected a lack of trust or belief, particularly from service users, about issues I would have relayed to them. They would sometimes seek verification on the very same subject from someone else, which I often found infuriating. A typical example occurred when I worked as a social work assistant within an adult social care team. I was allocated a particular case and therefore phoned the client to make an appointment for a home visit. The appointment was made without any indication of any concerns by the client. I was informed by our receptionist that the very same client had phoned the office to confirm my identity, as soon as they had finished speaking to me. Although one might argue that the client was only exercising caution, I do not believe they would have done this had it been someone without a foreign name and foreign accent.

It is interesting to note that within the six years I have worked in health and social care in a variety of settings, I have only encountered two service users belonging to ethnic minority groups in care homes. Whether this is as a result of the belief that blacks or Asians look after their own, or that they are simply not aware of the services available to them, I do not know. What I am certain of, however, is that there were more numbers of ethnic minorities, particularly blacks, within the mental health institutions I worked in, as well as the probation services, in comparison to care homes. This goes to show the over-representation of ethnic minorities within the criminal justice systems and under-representation in care.

As a social worker I have an important role to play in understanding the prejudices that befall ethnic minorities and how these affect their perception of the social service delivery system. These prejudices often create a reverse psychology amongst ethnic minorities which leads to frustration with the system, loneliness and feelings of despondency which present challenges in dealing with issues of abuse within ethnic minority communities. Having highlighted the implications of racial issues to social work practice, it is important for social workers to avoid stereotyping and maintaining prejudices about members of different ethnic groups. Social work as a profession must be at the forefront of embracing multiculturalism and should celebrate individual and ethnic differences without compromising the quality of service that is delivered.

Further Reading

For a useful introduction to many of the sociological aspects of race and ethnicity consult:
Pilkington, A. (2003) *Racial Disadvantage and Ethnic Diversity in Britain*. London: Palgrave.

For a more advanced text, the following by Bob Carter is recommended:
Carter, R. (2000) *Realism and Racism: Concepts of Race in Sociological Research*. London: Routledge.

5

Poverty and social exclusion

Donncha Marron, Jeremy Millar and Muzz McKinnon

Key themes

- Sociology examines how issues of poverty and social exclusion emerge.
- There are broadly two different perspectives on the causes of poverty and social exclusion: individual or structural.
- How social exclusion and poverty are conceptualized influences the type of action that is put in place to reduce or eradicate poverty and social exclusion.
- The development of social work is linked to an understanding of poverty and social exclusion.
- The political agenda has shaped the social work focus on poverty.

Keywords

poverty, moral underclass, social exclusion, inequality, resources, deserving, undeserving, value

Introduction

The impact of poverty and the processes of social exclusion impact significantly on a wide range of social work service users. It is essential for social workers to understand and critically explore the role poverty plays in disadvantaging and placing at risk many vulnerable people. This chapter looks to engage critically with these themes from a sociological theoretical perspective, to examine historically the development of social work policy and practice and, finally, to witness the lived experience of poverty and social exclusion through the eyes of one young person.

The sociological focus will address the significance and consequences of social upheaval on British society over the past 200 years. Competing explanations of the causes and remedies for poverty will be introduced, along with an examination of the concept of social exclusion and the social policies introduced to promote social inclusion. Links will be made to the emergence in the nineteenth century of social work as a response to the impoverished circumstances of many in the working classes, particularly children, older people and those individuals with chronic ill-health and disabilities. The response to these social problems from the emerging social work profession illustrates competing ideological perspectives on poverty and their subsequent influence on social work values and practice. This tension could be loosely characterized in terms of those who locate responsibility for poverty in the individual and those who take the view that the route out of poverty is through structural change in terms of the redistribution of wealth and more equitable access to resources. The lived experience described by Muzz, a young person with sixteen years of social work involvement in his life, points to the challenges faced by social workers in terms of hearing the voice of the service user and then intervening in a manner that alleviates poverty and promotes social inclusion. Muzz's testimony demonstrates that this is a complex task that identifies things that social work did well and not so well.

Sociology Focus

The interrelated concepts of poverty and social exclusion from a sociological perspective form the focus of this chapter. Of course, a lack of material resources and the expulsion of certain individuals and groups from meaningful participation within society can be seen to be long-standing issues in human experience. Sociologists, however, are concerned with examining how these issues emerge and take on a particular shape and meaning within different social contexts and at different periods of history.

Sociology, as an academic discipline and as a particular way of understanding human experience, was born out of attempts to understand the enormous and ongoing social changes that were wrought by the emergence of modern Western societies. This includes such processes as the European Enlightenment, political revolutions, the Industrial Revolution and urbanization. Yet, social change never ceases and continues today in processes such as globalization, changes in how goods and services are produced and in the growing recognition of risks such as global warming.

A sociological understanding of poverty and exclusion, therefore, involves conceptualizing how continuing social changes produce these phenomena by impacting upon the lives, experiences and opportunities of certain groups of individuals. But things are not so straightforward. A sociological perspective is also concerned with examining how the wider understanding of these concepts changes over time. Ideas like poverty and exclusion have no stable meaning. Such concepts are produced by relatively powerful groups, by social scientists (including sociologists) and governing authorities, in order to both understand and intervene in people's lives. Sociologists thus also seek to understand how concepts like poverty and exclusion are created, by whom and for what purpose.

DEFINITION

Poverty is often seen to exist in two forms. **Absolute poverty** refers to having limited access to the fundamental needs of clothing, shelter and food required to support life. This form of poverty is often evident in developing countries. **Relative poverty**, more characteristic of developed societies, denotes how certain individuals are able to meet their fundamental needs but at a level considerably below the prevailing standard of that particular society.

The Development of the Idea of Poverty

There have always been poor people, people without the resources, means or ability to provide sufficiently for their own material needs of food, clothing and shelter. The significance, consequences and meanings of poverty, however, are shaped by the social context within which poverty is experienced. The anthropologist Marshall Sahlins (1974) has argued that in small-scale societies, characterized by hunting and gathering rather than agricultural or industrial production, anything more than a meagre array of material possessions was actually a disadvantage in this nomadic form of social organization. Meanwhile Tawney (1938) shows how in pre-sixteenth century Europe, where societies were characterized by feudalism and the dominance of the Church, poverty had a special religious significance. It was believed that the poor were close to God and that it was the religious duty of those with property and wealth to give alms – material support – to those who were in need.

The social problem of poverty – the poor as a political issue – might be seen, then, as a key issue in the development of modern Western societies. Morris (1994, p. 34) highlights two significant events in sixteenth-century Europe which created large numbers of people without the means to provide for their own needs. One was the Enclosure Acts, which denied rural dwellers access to common land to supply their own food. The second was rising food prices as people, now displaced from agricultural production, moved in greater numbers to cities in search of work. Rising numbers of people, concentrated into cities and cut off from the means to meet their own basic needs, was to bring poverty to the fore as a problem for authorities. The big question was how social order was going to be maintained.

The first of the English Poor Laws established in 1601 levied a tax on property within specific communities to raise funds for distribution to those within that community unable to provide for themselves. These laws also established the idea of a poorhouse, or workhouse, where those who were elderly or infirm could be looked after and those who were fit and able were given work. However, in order to keep costs down and discourage people becoming a financial burden on the community, pay and conditions were made deliberately worse than for any freely available job. The overseers of the Poor Laws, those entrusted with their administration and the collection of revenue to fund them, imagined that they faced an important problem. How were they to tell the genuinely destitute from those who were relatively able but just unwilling to work? A distinction was thus drawn between the 'deserving' and 'undeserving' poor. The former, by virtue of fate, were held to be victims of circumstance and so could not be held responsible for their condition. The latter, however, because of some flaw, were understood to be more or less responsible for their poverty and so were relatively unworthy of community assistance. They were *paupers* rather than being merely poor, individuals whose perceived ineptitude, laziness or moral deficiency made them unable to provide for themselves or their families (Katz, 1990).

In the work of classical economists like Adam Smith (1723–1790), who laid considerable emphasis on individual self-interest, poverty was actually seen to be a good thing because it spurred individuals to produce and to work for wages in order to feed, clothe and house themselves (Procacci, 1991). The logical conclusion then, particularly to the philosopher Thomas Malthus (1766–1834), was that any help for the poor was a bad idea. Malthus was afraid that by granting recognition to poverty in terms of charity or state intervention, it would reduce the incentive for individuals to take care of themselves and work to meet

their own needs and those of their families (Morris, 1994). In consequence, attitudes towards the poor hardened.

In the latter part of the nineteenth century in Britain and elsewhere,
with the continued existence of groups of individuals in extreme poverty,
liberal theorists talked about the 'dangerous class' or the 'residuum', groups
of people that had somehow been left behind by society (Steadman Jones,
1984). They were conceived as being surplus to the requirements of the
developing industrial capitalist society of the time. Some writers even drew
upon Charles Darwin's (1809–1882) new ideas about evolution to argue
that poverty might be a hereditary condition, passed down from parents to
children. In being congregated into cities, the poor appeared as a permanent problem whose conditions and character posed a threat to the maintenance of social order and the very idea of social progress that a modern
society was supposed to represent (Malik, 1996; Procacci, 1991). This was
to make poverty a significant political issue for elite groups. In response,
workhouses were formalized, and their numbers expanded during the
nineteenth century in order to deal with the problem (Morris, 1994).
Private initiatives such as the Charity Organization Societies were also
established to provide targeted, coordinated intervention (Katz, 1996).
We will look at this forerunner of modern social work in more detail
later in the chapter.

At the end of the nineteenth century, as social scientists continued to
study the problem of poverty, it became increasingly clear to some that it
could not be explained purely by the features of individuals. In Charles
Booth's (1840–1916) studies of the residential areas of the poor in the
1880s, the first systematic effort to scientifically measure poverty, it was
evident to him that poverty had a strong environmental or social dimension
(Welshman, 2007). As capitalist economies boomed with the second industrial revolution, only to go into a severe and prolonged depression, large
numbers of workers were sucked into work and then expelled into mass
unemployment. To many it was evident that poverty could not be reduced
to mere individual disposition or misfortune but was caused by wider
economic and structural factors.

From the nineteenth century into the twentieth century workers and
employers began to establish cooperative systems of insurance, funded by
contributions from the workers themselves, which would provide payments to tide them through periods of unemployment or compensate
them for workplace accidents (Ewald, 1991). In the twentieth century this
led to the establishment of welfare states in Western countries where the

state, to a greater or less extent, took responsibility for administering protections to help keep individuals out of poverty and promoting a redistribution of wealth (Katz, 1996; Morris, 1994). This included not only unemployment payments but also old age pensions and a wider range of services such as health care and education. So, instead of the creation of moral distinctions between the 'deserving' and the 'undeserving' and the provision of charity or work to those afflicted by poverty, the principle was established that all individuals had an automatic right to be protected from the worst effects of poverty regardless of their circumstances. Because poverty was now believed to have structural rather than individual causes, the individual had a social right to protection and equal citizenship. In reality, however, the division of a deserving and undeserving poor, the moralization of poverty and 'blaming the victim', were never to disappear (Katz, 1990). It should also be borne in mind that what kind of 'welfare regime' a particular state adopted, and how it approached problems of poverty and equality, depended on that country's particular history (Esping-Anderson, 1990).

ACTIVITY

What does the above discussion of the history of poverty tell us about poverty? Is poverty a 'natural' part of society or is its existence the result of other processes?

The Moral Underclass

The idea of a group of individuals characterized by a continuous struggle to meet their own needs, and as somehow being morally, culturally and socially separate from the rest of society continues to inform contemporary understandings of poverty. In more recent years the argument about the existence of a distinctive 'underclass' as part of the wider class structure emerged in the work of some sociologists, like Anthony Giddens (1973). The idea of an 'underclass', though, is most associated with the work of controversial American policy analyst Charles Murray. The original publication on which his reputation is based was *Losing Ground*, an analysis of how black minorities had been marginalized into American inner-city ghettos in the 1970s and 1980s (Murray, 1984).

> ## DEFINITION
>
> **Underclass** – a concept developed by Murray (1984) referring to a group of people who rely on criminality for income, prefer not to work or to look for work and who exhibit high rates of lone motherhood. The underclass emerges as a consequence, he claims, of the welfare state destabilizing traditional ideas of work and family life.

Murray identified three factors as being important in defining an under-class: criminality, as a way of 'making a living' by preying on one's fellow citizens; persistent unemployment, with no desire or wish to look for work; and a high proportion of single mothers, women choosing to have children out of wedlock. He traced its origins to the 1960s when the American Federal government began to spend increasing amounts of money on wel-fare, housing and enhanced social security programmes in an attempt to alleviate poverty and ease racial inequality. Echoing nineteenth-century liberal thinkers like Thomas Malthus, Murray argued that well-meaning policy-makers had tried to help the poor when they should have left well alone. In doing so, they destroyed the desire, will and effort of certain sec-tions of the population to work. This then led to the formation of specific underclass communities cut adrift from the rest of society. These groups, he argued, were caught in a self-perpetuating 'culture of poverty' characterized by an acceptance of high crime and a loss of belief in the values of work and marriage. The welfare state, from this perspective, was not the solution to poverty, it was part of the problem (Young, 1999). Murray (1990, 1996, 2001) later argued that a similar, white underclass – defined by criminality, unemployment and lone parenthood – was becoming entrenched within Britain's urban centres.

Essentially, Charles Murray had presented an argument that the welfare state had interfered in the natural workings of society, destroying the link between hard work, discipline and rewards. By receiving 'something for nothing', he argued, the underclass would not now take any job offered to them. At the same time, women were being encouraged to become lone parents rather than find a husband. In consequence, not only was the work ethic destroyed but so was the stable two-parent family as a key vehicle for providing proper role models for children. This, Murray feared, would produce a vicious circle leading to the ever greater expansion of the underclass and its anti-social values.

Murray's perspective has been heavily criticized for its conservative justification of inequality. In other words, it blames individuals themselves for the inequality they experience and argues that any redistribution of wealth only serves to make the problem of poverty worse. Some have argued, therefore, that the underclass concept has not been developed in order to describe an objective social phenomenon. Rather, it functions as a stigmatizing label that blames the victims for their own misfortunes and ignores the wider economic and structural reasons behind poverty and unemployment (Bagguley and Mann, 1992; Bauman, 1998; Gans, 1995). Murray has also been criticized for his use of anecdotal evidence and spurious selection of official statistics to support his arguments (David, 1996). In fact, much evidence suggests that the members of the supposed underclass dislike living on welfare, would wish to take up employment if the opportunities were available and maintain common values with wider society (Gallie, 1994; Roberts, 2001).

ACTIVITY

Discuss Murray's perspective on poverty. Do you agree or disagree with what he says? Why do you think his ideas may be seen as controversial?

Other social scientists, while acknowledging the existence of an underclass, put forward alternative reasons for its emergence. American sociologist William Julius Wilson (1987, 1996) argues that certain black working-class inner-city communities have been profoundly affected by globalization and the decline in the manufacturing industry. These changes have had grave consequences for manual work opportunities in these 'ghettos'. While middle-class and secure working-class individuals have migrated to the suburbs for housing and jobs, certain disadvantaged or less skilled individuals remain rooted in the area leading to a concentration of poverty. Not only do those left behind endure a dearth of employment opportunities, they also now no longer enjoy the influence of other community role models, access to good quality education and training nor other forms of community support and amenity.

While acknowledging structural and economic factors in changing the nature of the environment of ghetto communities, Wilson argues that these negatively manifest themselves in the contraction of community organization and collective responsibility. There is also an expansion and intensification of crime and violence. These, according to Wilson, produce constraints and opportunities that have an effect upon the culture and the 'unique response and behaviour patterns' of ghetto inhabitants. In an environment with no jobs or insecure part-time employment, for instance, drug dealing represents an attractive source of good income and is seen to be acceptable, or at least understandable. Or given the wider unavailability of work, women prefer to become single mothers in order to claim welfare resources rather than work in low-paid jobs or get married to men who have few employment prospects.

The Concept of Social Exclusion

More recently, the concept of an underclass has been replaced within wider academic and policy analysis by 'social exclusion'. While the concept of an 'underclass' was developed within the United States and the United Kingdom, the term social exclusion manifests more continental European origins. In France in the 1970s, for instance, social exclusion was used to describe the position of those who suffered both from inadequate employment as well as a distancing from the protections offered by the welfare state (Pierson, 2002, p. 4). In one sense, it is quite similar to the idea of an underclass because it conceptualizes people as being cut off from the mainstream of society. However, it tends to have fewer moral connotations than the idea of an underclass. Meanwhile, unlike the concept of poverty, it tends to emphasize how individuals endure low social participation as well as inadequate material resources.

> **DEFINITION**
>
> Like the underclass, **social exclusion** refers to a group set apart from the rest of society. However, whereas the term underclass tends to emphasize the behaviour and morality that distinguish certain groups from the rest of society, the term **social exclusion** concentrates more on the social processes through which these groups become distinguished. However, there is no generally accepted definition of either of these concepts.

The concept of 'social exclusion' has received much attention from government and policy makers. It is used by the United Nations and also by the European Union to characterize disadvantage. With the election of the 'New Labour' government in 1997, a Social Exclusion Unit was established which sought to coordinate the efforts of all government departments in the fight against social exclusion. But what does this concept actually mean? Pierson (2002, p. 8) puts forward five dimensions that overlap in order to create the

5 dimensions of ↓ what social exclusion is

experience of social exclusion on the part of individuals and communities. These include: material poverty, a lack of employment opportunities, inadequate social supports (for example, the help of family, friends and acquaintances), local area or neighbourhood disadvantage (for example, badly maintained housing stock, high crime rates, a lack of community participation) and the unavailability of services (such as, community centres, supermarkets, insurance coverage). However, while all the definitions and understandings of the term social exclusion embody material and social disadvantage, there is no rigorously accepted definition. The concept remains rather vague, even 'bland' (Savage, 2002). Indeed, Pierson's categories of social exclusion resemble Wilson's structural understanding of the 'underclass' and there is no clear way to go about separating these concepts.

Ruth Levitas (2005) argues that the term 'social exclusion' poses a problematic concept for sociologists and others looking at poverty and social divisions. Like the concept of underclass, social exclusion represents the primary significant division in society as one that exists between an included majority and an excluded minority. In emphasizing the condition of those that are 'socially excluded' and formulating policies of inclusion, inequalities of wealth and power across society are effectively ignored or sidelined. Indeed, there is an interesting correlation between the simultaneous rise of social exclusion as a concept and the decline of the language and politics of social class as described in Chapter 2. Picking up on the conceptual vagueness of the term, she suggests that there are three major discourses of social exclusion. Discourse in this sense means a particular way of thinking about, and thus acting upon, social exclusion as a problem. These discourses are:

- A *redistributionist discourse* (RED). Developed from a social democratic political perspective, this discourse sees exclusion as a dynamic and multi-faceted concept. Inequality is understood to be structural, to have multiple dimensions that cause poverty and exclusion from a wider participation in society. Only significant transfers of wealth and investment in government services will reduce the problem.
- *Moral underclass discourse* (MUD). Developed from the New Right political perspective of the 1980s, this discourse corresponds to Murray's underclass perspective examined in the previous section. The socially excluded, in this sense, are understood to be culturally distinct and different from the rest of society. This ignores the wider inequality and conceptualizes welfare as a contributor, not a solution, to social exclusion.
- *Social Integrationist Discourse* (SID). Developed from a more European, Christian Democratic perspective and championed in European Union policies, this discourse conceptualizes exclusion as a lack of moral integration with the rest of society. The main route to integration is seen to be through paid work and so it ignores the wider class and gender inequality within the world of work as well as within the wider society.

These discourses might be summarized as follows: 'in RED they have no money, in SID they have no work, in MUD they have no morals' (Levitas, 2005, p. 27). Within Britain, since the election of the Labour government in 1997, she argues that the main way that the term social exclusion has been understood is through a shifting combination of MUD and SID. RED, in contrast, has been systematically sidelined. In doing so, Levitas believes that social exclusion can never be solved, as to do so would require a significant redistribution of wealth and a fundamental alteration in a society that otherwise actively produces inequality. Later in this chapter we will see the consequences of this SID and MUD policy emphasis on contemporary social work practice.

ACTIVITY

Which of the three discourses identified by Levitas would you regard as being the most effective in reducing or eliminating social exclusion? Why do you think RED has been ignored in social policy?

Other sociologists addressing the wider question of social inequality have pointed out that social exclusion has emerged as a consequence, not a side-effect, of key changes in contemporary capitalist society. David Byrne (2005) and Jock Young (1999, 2007) have argued that Britain and other Western societies have been strongly affected by globalization and have endured significant changes in how they produce goods and services. This has made many kinds of employment much more insecure, short term and badly paid compared with the past. At the same time, governments have deliberately reduced welfare entitlements and benefits, giving people no alternative but to take up such employment. In consequence, this creates a large minority who are 'socially excluded'. Yet, this group are not cut adrift from society through unemployment. They maintain a continued relationship to work, shifting between periods of time on benefits and in temporary, low-paid employment.

ACTIVITY

Do you agree with Byrne and Young about the causes of social exclusion in current society? What effects do you see globalization having where you are today?

From this perspective, exclusion is an active process and the socially excluded serve a useful purpose within the economy for the benefit of others. They can be employed at low wages whenever required and can then be made unemployed when economic conditions change and employers no longer require their services as workers. Their existence in and out of work also serves to keep wages low and working conditions inferior for large sections of the workforce. When they do work, they provide useful, low-cost services, like domestic work, for the affluent, secure middle class. Social exclusion is thus a *process* as much as it is an experience of inequality. It is an integral feature of contemporary society that affects large numbers of individuals rather than a simple, static label that can be applied to a small minority. The point that needs to be addressed here is not to make individuals more included. Rather, it is to end the inequality of power and wealth that gives rise to exclusion in the first place.

Social Work Focus

Understanding poverty, social exclusion and the role of social work

The development of social work and the role of social workers are closely linked to understandings of the impact of poverty and social exclusion on sections of our society. In this chapter links will be made to sociological explanations by way of a historical analysis of the development of social work and the lived experience of the poor and marginalized.

Up until the early part of the nineteenth century the concept of welfare provision was limited and any kind of recognizable social work intervention non-existent. It was to the local community that people turned to in times of need. The charitable giving of the parish through the Poor Laws was in effect a safety net for the poor in the early years of the Industrial Revolution.

Early industrial capitalists can be portrayed by history as fairly ruthless individuals who consistently placed profits over the well-being of their employees. Whilst this was predominantly the case, there were notable exceptions, and it was through the endeavours of these (mainly) men that we have become acquainted with the potential for social welfare intervention. These people were usually referred to as philanthropists.

Charitable giving applied the *less eligibility* principle, meaning that the support offered to an individual or family could be no better than that earned by the lowliest labourer working in the community. Underpinning this philosophy, as we saw earlier, was the categorization of the poor into 'deserving' and 'undeserving'. Those who were honest, hard-working types who had fallen on hard times through no fault of their own would be seen to be deserving of charity, whilst those deemed to be lacking in moral virtues and not industrious would be viewed as undeserving.

Children were generally exempt from this judgement. Instead they were often viewed as potential reforming influences on dissolute (immoral) parents. They would be removed from their family for their moral safety and educated in what were known as 'ragged' or industrial schools. The Victorian charitable bodies had a sense of rescuing innocent children before they became depraved by the immoral lifestyle of their parents, who had often fallen into alcohol dependency, criminality and prostitution (Abrams, 1998).

Nationally at this time debates were taking place between members of the establishment as to the best way forward in terms of the care and regulation of the poor. The guiding principles already mentioned included:

- the division of deserving and undeserving
- less eligibility
- the rescue of innocent children
- a moral education
- the development of industrious habits.

These debates were closely linked to the ideologies and political agendas of the industrial era. At this time, as we have discussed, the prevailing view of society was one in which the individual was very much responsible for the well-being of him- or herself and his or her family through hard work, piety and submission to the existing social order (Jones, cited in Adams et al., 2002).

ACTIVITY

Consider your own attitude towards poor people and the values and beliefs they are influenced by.

The roots of modern social work lie in the founding of the Charity Organization Society (COS) (Smith, 2002). Established in 1869, this British body looked to rationalize the disparate activities of the host of charitable bodies that had evolved out of philanthropic and religious activities aimed at alleviating the misery of the poor. The COS was concerned that this absence of a regulating mechanism enabled the poor to exploit the Poor Law system to sustain their lazy and feckless lifestyles. The prevailing view of those forming the COS was that each case needed to be investigated to ascertain whether they were 'deserving' of support or not. It is in this view that we can see the roots of the case work approach to social work. This case by case approach was underpinned by client contact, recording, file keeping and the sharing of information across relevant bodies to prevent the emerging system from being exploited by the 'cunning' poor (Jones, cited in Adams et al., 2002).

At end of the nineteenth century there were two contrasting perspectives on how the problem of poverty was to be treated. These can be categorized by the concepts of residual welfare and institutional welfare. Residual welfare was favoured by the capitalist classes. They viewed welfare as a safety net to be given only in extreme circumstances to those deemed as deserving. They saw a danger in offering welfare to all as it would interfere with the 'natural' operation of the free market and the incentive of individuals to take care of themselves and their families. Opposing this position was the newer and more progressive belief that welfare provision should be institutional and available to all according to need. Whereas the former laid an emphasis on the primacy of the individual in society as the author of their own fortune or misfortune, the latter perspective viewed society as a collective in which all worked together to achieve satisfactory outcomes for everyone.

ACTIVITY

Think about these two positions in relation to the lives of people living in poverty. Where do you think responsibility lies for improving conditions?

As we saw earlier, a growing awareness of the deep-rooted social causes of poverty was increasingly being highlighted in the latter part of the nineteenth century and the early years of the twentieth. Two key pieces of research in this area were undertaken by Seebohm Rowntree in York and Charles Booth in the slums of east London. These reports proposed that poverty and deprivation be addressed through structural changes to society, that is, improving housing, access to health care, employment and social activities. These ideas were also highlighted by bodies such as the Fabian Society. A critical watershed came in the shape of the 1905–9 Royal Commission on the Poor Laws. This Commission produced two reports, one representing the majority and the second the minority views of the committee members. The majority report, backed by the COS, advocated a reform of the Poor Laws in order to tighten these up in terms of target-ing the residual poor whilst the minority report favoured state intervention to improve housing, health and employment security. Had this minority option been pursued the country might have embraced the idea of the welfare state nearly forty years ahead of its implementation in 1948.

After the Second World War, and in the aftermath of the establishment of the welfare state, there was a drive to provide more qualified social workers. The focus, though, continued to be case work-orientated with the practice of social workers strongly shaped by innovations in psychodynamic theory. Whilst there was an increased awareness of the impact of poverty on families and children, the social work intervention tended to address the individual's perceived deficits rather than any structural factors that may have been con-tributing to the circumstances of neglect, abuse and ill-health.

In the 1970s there was a move within social work to focus on the effects of poverty and social exclusion in an attempt to be proactive as a develop-ing profession in addressing the oppressive structural factors that impacted on the families who came to the attention of social services. This was an overtly political agenda informed by a range of left wing, Marxist-influenced, ideological positions. Many practitioners looked to class strug-gles and the revolutionary movements of the 1960s for their inspiration.

ACTIVITY

The radical social work movement of the 1970s has been somewhat erased from history. It had its roots in the Fabian position discussed in the minority report at the turn of the twentieth century and looked to alleviate poverty through the institutional redistribution of wealth. Have a look at the manifesto of the radical social work position and think critically about the view of the social work role put forward. Go to www.radical.org.uk/barefoot/ and follow the links through recommended books and articles to the 'Case Con Manifesto'.

The impact of Thatcherism throughout the 1980s and 1990s aggres-sively challenged the social work focus on poverty and any sense of a col-lective response to the structural inequalities in society. The infamous mantra of Margaret Thatcher (the then Prime Minister) was that there was 'no such thing as society', only individuals. In the face of this prevailing New Right ideology, social work retreated from many of its radical and socially inclusive agendas. The previous focus on poverty and structural inequality became lost in disputes over excessive political correctness and the perceived growth of a morally degenerate underclass that we detailed earlier in the chapter. The responsibility for poverty once again rested squarely on the individual.

A further development from the New Right ideological agenda was the introduction of models of service provision that borrowed from the corporate business world. Examples of this would include the promotion of a mixed economy of care, with local government buying in services from voluntary organizations and increasingly from private companies. These organizations would go through a process of competitive tendering whereby they would attempt to offer a service that demonstrated the best value for money or, in the view of the critics of this approach, the cheapest provision. This new approach to the 'business' of social work required bureaucratic managerial systems that offered ways of measuring outcomes and quantifying successful outcomes.

There was a view from the political right wing that much of social work practice was poorly targeted and that it lacked an evidence base for specific interventions and their efficacy in remedying people's problems. Research was commissioned and adopted from the North American experience to shape social work into what has been termed by critics a technical, rational and procedural task (Adams, 2002). The understanding of structural inequality and its role in maintaining poverty and generating social exclusion became sidelined in social work. Arguably, negative press stories resulted in social work becoming increasingly focused on systems aimed at managing risk and demonstrating accountability and evidence-based interventions. This reactive risk-averse model of practice is perhaps most starkly illustrated by the developments in child protection. In the space of the last twenty years social work has moved away from the language of children and families teams, which offered proactive intervention in the lives of families experiencing difficulties and crisis, towards an almost exclusively child-protection focused agenda in which the majority of the work involves multi-agency investigations and compulsory measures of control.

The rise of New Labour and its 'Third Way' policy sought to address poverty once more but attempted to do so without abandoning the new managerialist and public/private partnership approaches to developing services brought in during the Thatcher years. In the current mixed economy of care the aim still is to target services at the residual poor whilst tweaking universal benefits to lift families out of poverty. The gulf between rich and poor continues to grow, however, and the life expectancy and health outcomes for the most impoverished communities in Britain are lower than for some of the world's developing countries. These striking findings were revealed in the World Health Organization's 2008 report, which identified the gulf in life expectancy in two areas of Glasgow, only 13 km apart, to be twenty-eight years.

The two central policy foci of New Labour that have had most relevance for social work in the twenty-first century are reducing child poverty and tackling social exclusion, a concept we analysed in some detail earlier. Supplementary to these policies is the ongoing focus on the findings of inquiries into the deaths of children who were in the care of a local authority. The most current of these at the time of writing is the case of Baby P (Lord Laming, 2009) in which, once again, the absence of good interdisciplinary communication between the various agencies involved contributed to Baby P falling through the child protection safety net.

The evolution of social work training over the last forty years has been considerable, resulting in the current honours degree combined with professional registration and a commitment to ongoing professional development for all social workers. There have been a range of reforms across other agencies, such as the National Health Service, the police and education, aimed at an improved assessment of need, risk and coordinated interventions in the lives of vulnerable people. However, despite the progress made in these areas tragedies such as the Baby P case continue to happen.

In analysing the possible reasons for this we can return to the debate that commenced at the beginning of the twentieth century as to whether society should invest in the universal provision of welfare measures to lift citizens out of poverty or should focus resources only on those who are in crisis and at major risk of harm. Those who favour the more radical agenda of a universal state provision of quality services for all would argue that the poor life outcomes associated with structural inequalities (such as a lack of finance, poor housing, poor health and education) could be alleviated by a wholesale redistribution of wealth and they would view the social work task as being to support this approach and ensure that those marginalized by society gain an equitable access to resources. This embodies what we earlier saw Ruth Levitas call 'RED', or the redistributive discourse on social exclusion. Those on the other side of the debate would argue that resources should be targeted only at those most in need of support and that access to resources must be through assessment and involve quality assurance practices to ensure that society receives value for money in terms of spending taxpayers' money. While concerned with social exclusion, this approach ignores the structural factors causing social exclusion in the first place.

ACTIVITY

There is a constant challenge to manage the tensions within social practice. On the one hand, there are the expectations of emancipatory social work values, in which we address inequalities and social exclusion by pro-actively supporting people's access to services in a non-judgemental, needs-led manner. On the other hand, we must work procedurally in a technical rational manner to act on the state's behalf as an agent of social control and prepare socially excluded people to accept the prevailing social norms. Compare attitudes in society today by reading newspapers of different political persuasions, for example, the *Guardian, Daily Mail* or *Sun*.

The reality for social work practice in the twenty-first century is one of engaging with individuals and communities who are, to lesser or greater degrees, experiencing social exclusion. By this we mean that their daily experience of life will be marked out by a range of obstacles blocking their way to a full participation in society.

Health and well-being are affected by factors such as diet (money to purchase healthy food), exercise (disposable income to join sports clubs, etc.), stress (living in dangerous neighbourhoods), illness (related to poor housing, damp and cold conditions), mental health (resulting from neglect and abuse) and substance misuse (a dependency on alcohol and illegal drugs).

People's life chances are also limited through a lack of educational opportunity, with schools under-resourced and pupils affected by issues at home, such as hunger, domestic strife and the absence of parental role models. For many children their poor educational experience is compounded by negative attitudes at home towards schooling, and this can then lead to difficulty in moving on to further and higher education.

The lack of investment in many of the areas that were home to the traditional industries, like shipbuilding in Glasgow and steel manufacture in Sheffield, has resulted in long-term and inter-generational patterns of unemployment, which, coupled with people unable to work through ill-health and disability, present considerable challenges in terms of social work intervention.

ACTIVITY

What is going on? Reflect back on this chapter and consider the sociological explanations of poverty and social exclusion along with the evolving role of social work's response to those affected by poverty and social exclusion.

(Continued)

(Continued)

- What function has social work fulfilled for society over the past one hundred years?
- How has it addressed issues of poverty and social exclusion at a structural level?
- How has it addressed these issues at a service user level?
- How has this chapter informed your own knowledge and values in respect of working with people affected by poverty and social exclusion?
- Where do you go from here?

Lived Experience

For the lived experience, Muzz, a young Scots person affected by family break-up, poverty, neglect and abuse resulting in admission to residential care, reflects on his own personal experiences of social exclusion and poverty.

As you read Muzz's story it would be useful to consider the issues that have been discussed in both the sociology and the social work focus. Doing so should help you relate what can seem quite abstract theories and concepts to individual people.

The following prompts should prove helpful:

- Reflect on which of the main theories outlined in the sociology focus best makes sense of Muzz's situation.
- Discuss how poverty affects and influences Muzz's agency in making decisions about himself, and what he will do both in the present and in the future.
- Consider how social work could influence the structural conditions that have created the poverty that Muzz has experienced.

I stayed [lived] with my dad. He was bringing up three kids on his own. He didn't have a lot of money. There was nothing for luxuries, things like new clothes and days out. Pocket money was limited, not as much as other kids. The electricity was on a meter thing and sometimes it was cut off. My granny helped out with money for Christmas, there was a separate fund. What we got looked like more than he had.

The flat was a one-bedroom, so my dad slept in the living room. It was top floor, a lot of stairs; my legs were quite small back then. A fair wind came into the house. It wasn't a warm house. There was a bunk bed for me and my brother and my sister slept on a Z-bed. Two guys and a girl in the same room, it was hard.

Social work was involved with us from the age of four. They were annoying really, asking questions and poking you. They gave us funds for clothes, school uniform and to go on school trips. They would take us out for meals and talk to us.

We were re-housed to a three-bedroom in another area. A lot bigger, upstairs downstairs. A garden to play in, the school over the back and a park with lots of kids in. I got a bike and went swimming. My dad got vouchers for the cinema. He was good at getting the best deals. He didn't have a lot of money but made sure we didn't go without.

Our school didn't have much school trips. It was a mixed school, all different kids, some whose parents worked; others didn't and had family problems as well. I remember going to school wearing 'trackie bottoms' with two stripes. People would say 'where's your third stripe?'. Obviously they weren't Adidas; the kids with brand name clothes dissed us. It was hard keeping up.

There were problems between my sister and my dad. She had had contact from my mum and the social workers were talking about us going into care. She called her up and asked to stay for a while, the stays built up and me and my brother were invited for the weekend. We went 'cos we didn't know what it was like to stay [live] with a mum. It was a difficult time and a cut-off point for my dad after we stayed for the weekend, so we didn't go back [to Dad]. We were pressurized, we were little kids and couldn't stand up for ourselves. It was emotional blackmail, 'here's a fiver, go to the shop and get some sweeties'

My parents, my stepfather, were always ahead of the game; he got us to lie to the social worker. We'd been briefed before to lie and we'd been threatened that we would be put in a home. If they [the social worker] ask; 'you are getting on fine. You get out all the time.' They were aware after a while. There were concerns, there were Children's Panels and that. When I stayed with my dad I never missed a day at school. When I stayed with my mum I missed half a year of school before she got us enrolled.

Money was still a problem; my stepfather was disabled, he got a load of money which he kept to himself. He had a drink problem, he'd buy a couple of crates of beer a day. There was abuse. We had marks on us. My mother was a gambler, a gambler that can't help buying crap. She was in the cheap shops spending a fortune. Things she didn't need, she doesn't use. We had to rely on social work; it wasn't like my dad's, he used money efficiently.

I eventually got sick of the abuse. It wasn't just physical it was vocal as well. There had been marks and that but I gave a little alibi. The social work could have listened. There was always arguing. I went to stay with neighbours for a weekend and then I went to the social work department and told them about the abuse and that. I was thirteen.

I can't remember, I think I went into foster care and then residential. It improved my life to a certain extent. It gave me some independence, to use washing machines to do tasks and that. There were a lot more activities, a lot more of a budget. I could afford to buy a haircut instead of a home chop. It never looks perfect getting a home chop. There was money for clothes; you could save it up and buy decent stuff. There was pocket money as well. I could get smokes and snacks. A lot of us smoked.

We went away on holiday to Scarborough, a holiday resort; we went there for a whole weekend. We went swimming and for walks along the beach. We got pushbikes; the children's home got a fund for pushbikes. They had a computer as well, there was money behind it. There was always food. There was always more food than you needed in case an emergency person came in. That happened a lot.

The social worker didn't visit as often, every three weeks. Thinking about it now, it could have been a lot closer together. I had a key worker who I got on with. I got access to the phone to call my parents. A lot of Children's Panels later I got to visit and stay with my dad. He doesn't like to dwell on the past. He gets stuck and he can't let it go. He's hurting himself by doing it.

It's costing me £52 [rent paid for him] per week to live in my flat. The benefits I get are £46 (in his pocket to meet all his living costs), there is the contribution to council tax of £36 per month and then there is your gas and electricity and your food. I need to get food for the dog as well.

You can get a crisis loan if you really need money. They've made it entirely difficult; you've got a four-hour wait from Edinburgh for a decision. They ask you before they start if you would commit suicide if they don't give the loan.

I have a budgeting problem like my mother. I try to save and then I spend it all at once. I get my dog food; I haven't been paying my rent. I have a wee bit of arrears. I get the money for two weeks, it lasts about a week. It would be better to get it weekly. I have to borrow money off my dad. He doesn't like loaning money but wouldn't see me going short. You can't go to the same people all the time. You borrow a bit off one person and a bit off another. You can't go back to the same person and ask them for more money. This is the reality of juggling money when on benefits.

If I had a job interview I couldn't get money for new clothes. Maybe if I didn't have a dog; Primark is cheap but to be honest with a dog I can't afford anything else. I struggle with electricity, it always works under the emergency. I go without power and I've used candles; I'm lucky I've got a guitar, I play my guitar and produce my own music.

The biggest challenge on little money is the price of food. I have to travel, get a bus, get my shopping, get a bus back. You really want to walk four miles with loads of shopping [irony].

Many of my friends are on courses. It's harder for me 'cos I'm twenty-one; the courses are for the ages of sixteen and twenty-one. Once you're twenty-one your life's basically over unless you can get a job and stand on your own two feet. Up until last year I got support but my worker left and I've not been allocated a new one. He helped me with the paperwork, applications, and there's no one to help me now. When I was younger I was skiving school and never got the best education. It's hard sometimes to go over some paperwork especially like big application forms.

In my area there are a lot of addicts. I would say I feel safe(ish), about as safe as anywhere in the city. There are facilities, a pool and a library. You need an access to leisure card to get in cheap.

If social workers had looked more closely into the background of the family, asked a few more questions and not looked to the parents and put more pressure on us kids to speak, I think things might have been better.

I would advise a new social worker just to listen, really listen, really listen, 'cos there's sometimes things that are hard to hear. The government are to blame for poverty, they should sort it out. Obviously money doesn't grow on trees but the budget that people get is nowhere near what it should be. Nearly everyone that doesn't work lives in poverty, pretty much.

Further Reading

For a discussion of various sociological and social policy issues of poverty and social exclu-
   sion, consult:
Hills, J. and Stewart, K. (eds) (2005) *A More Equal Society? New Labour, Poverty, Inequality and Exclusion (CASE Studies on Poverty, Place & Policy)*. Bristol: Policy Press.
Spicker, P. (2008) *Social Policy, Themes and Approaches*. Bristol: Policy Press.

6

Later Life

Emmanuelle Tulle and
Rory Lynch

Key themes

- Being older varies over time and place.
- The process of ageing concerns much more than inevitable biological change and is shaped by social processes and social constructions.
- Ageism affects many older people, denying them the opportunities and resources to fully participate in social life.
- The Third Age refers to the opportunities afforded by the economy, greater financial security and the welfare state for those older people who possess the resources to enjoy a period of self-realization and relative affluence in their retirement years.
- Conversely, for other people old age can be a period of inequality and poverty.
- The older person's life context must be taken into account.

Keywords

social construction, older age, Third Age, welfare state, ageism, poverty, inequality, person-centred social work

Introduction

The British population is becoming increasingly older as a demographic shift occurs that sees 15.6% of the population over the age of 65, and 1.9% over the age of 85 (ONS, 2005). Such a change in the age profile of society presents many exciting opportunities associated with having a section of the population rich in life experience and job skills. It also raises many challenges, in that more older people may require social work and other social services. Key issues surrounding ageing and being older in contemporary society are surveyed in this chapter, the central observation being that ageing is much more than simplistic notions of bodily change and a decline in mental faculties. What we focus on instead is how age is socially constructed in contemporary society, and how prevailing discourses of old age and unhelpful social structures affect and influence the lived experiences of older people. Sociology plays an important role in exposing how contemporary society constructs old age and the social structures that become barriers to older people leading full and meaningful lives. Building on those sociological insights, the social work focus, in turn, examines how social work can tackle the discriminatory and oppressive social structures in order to empower older people to take control of their lives. In the lived experience an older person reflects on his life, touching on many of the themes highlighted in the sociology focus and social work focus.

DEFINITION

In sociology the term **discourse** refers to the ways a particular subject is discussed and conceptualized by ordinary lay people, institutions (such as government) or by academics.

Sociology Focus

The sociological understanding of ageing differs from popular beliefs, which tend to hold ageing as solely concerned with a biological and physical decline. In common with many of the other topics in this book, ageing and the general experience of being older is another example of an aspect of life that is open to social construction. Here, an element of life may appear 'natural' but instead emerges out of particular social and cultural beliefs. In the social work focus we explore the ways in which the process of the social construction of ageing occurs and what role modern medicine, social welfare and social policy and the social sciences have played in socially marginalizing older people. We also investigate the issue of inequalities. Later life is indeed a risk factor for poverty and a period in life open to discrimination in relation to accessing services. As we age, we are at increasing risk of losing our cultural value, power and influence. In other words, age is a key factor that assists in predicting our experiences in society.

See Chapter 1 for more on social construction and the sociological imagination.

Sociology is about analysis but also about challenging commonsense assumptions about people, and to this end the chapter will provide you with the tools with which you can re-imagine the experience of later life critically, or, to put it another way, with which you can exercise the sociological imagination (Wright-Mills, 1959). Indeed, things do not have to be the way they are. Two crucial questions that will drive your own understandings of the issues raised in this chapter are: first, what are the structural features that guide our ability to make decisions about the conduct of our lives in our later years, and second, how can we rethink how we deal with older people in ways that will significantly alter the balance of power?

The Social Construction of Later Life

For more information on social construction see Chapter 1.

DEFINITION

Social construction refers to what may appear to be natural and unchanging and is actually the outcome of social, cultural and historical processes. The implication here is that aspects of life are not as fixed and certain as they may seem and are subject to considerable change over time and between different societies.

What does it mean that later life is 'socially constructed'? It refers to the historical and cultural variability of how later life is interpreted, represented, managed and experienced. In short, what it is to be old depends on where and in which historical period you happen to live. Being old in contemporary Britain is not the same as being old five hundred years ago in the same country or today in completely different cultures. Being an old woman is not the same as being an old man. Being ninety years old today is not the same as being ninety years old fifty years ago. Variability in what it means to be older is an important point to bear in mind at all times.

ACTIVITY

Discuss how ageing and the experiences of being older have changed over the past fifty or so years.

Before proceeding it is worth tackling the thorny and problematic issue of biological ageing, given that it is biological change that is commonly associated with ageing. We all age (it is not just the experience of the old), right from the moment we are born. This inescapable process means we will undergo all sorts of changes, some visible (such as gaining height), some felt (such as experiencing growing pains), some less visible (such as developing heart disease over a period of years). Some of these changes are not life-threatening but they may threaten our cultural position – think of the way wrinkles are portrayed in the popular press and the trouble to which some go to minimize or erase these bodily developments. These changes are not meaningful in themselves, unless they lead to an early death, for instance; the point is that what happens to our bodies is given *meaning* only in *social* and *cultural* contexts.

So why have biological readings and an emphasis on the physical manifestations of old age become so dominant? To answer that question some understanding of how perceptions of ageing have varied and developed over time is required.

See Chapter 1 for more on the importance of developing a historical perspective of social phenomena.

A short social history of ageing

In Antiquity, Greek, Roman and Egyptian societies mused about old age, on what it is and what to do about being older. For people then, being older was not only a combination of the physical signs, but also of the social aspects of growing and being old – for instance the loss of influence that might come with getting old. It was also debated whether old age itself was a disease. The physician Hippocrates thought, for example, that old age was akin to a pathological state arising out of an imbalance in the 'humours' and did not find anything useful or pleasant about being older. Cicero was more positive about old age. He viewed old age as a time of philosophical reflection, and he guarded against confusing old age and disease (Thane, 2000).

Some ancient societies such as the Spartans bestowed a great deal of power to older citizens by inviting them to govern the city.

In medieval Europe, people generally did not live long enough to become old! The fortunate few who did, mainly monks and wealthy merchants, filled their older years with reflection and contemplation. Some of the poor did survive to old age but we know very little of their circumstances as they do not figure in the historical record (Minois, 1989). What we know is that older widows of means were feared and derided because their material independence was seen as unnatural (Brogden, 2001). Older wealthy men did not attract such contempt although the reverence they might evoke was mostly linked to their wealth and the potential for a rich inheritance. We also know that those who were physically incapable were often shunned, and there is evidence in the past of acts of exclusion (Elias, 1985) and cruelty (Brogden, 2001) against the very old and the dying. The past therefore was not always the Golden Age of old age, as some have argued or commonly perceived.

The Medicalization of Old Age, or the emergence of modern old age

See Chapter 1 for more insights into modernity.

The emergence of modern social constructions of later life begins in the period of modernity, from around the end of the eighteenth century and the start of the nineteenth century. One of the principal elements of the social construction of older age is the advent of modern medicine, or bio-medicine. From the end of the eighteenth century, old age became medicalized, that is, it became the focus of attention of doctors who became experts in the ageing process. Such expertise was earned by dissecting bodies and by comparing the bodies of the old with those of the young. The findings from these dissections were published in volumes such as *Clinical Lectures on the Diseases of Old Age* (Charcot, 2009 [1881]), which promoted a distinct biology of ageing and made old age an object of scientific inquiry. These developments in medicine entailed a number of consequences for our perceptions of old age.

- Old age became perceived as a biological process first and foremost, to the exclusion of other indicators, and as a biologically distinctive part of the life of the biological organism, open to observation and description. The clinical signs of old age could be shown and described.
- Ageing and old age were constructed as a deviation from the norm, the norm being found in the functioning of young adults' cells, tissues, organs and systems.

- Old age was confirmed as the *precursor* to death (as opposed to death being part of life itself).
- Ageing was understood as inevitable decline towards malfunction, corruption and eventually death, and a biological decline was used to explain a psychological, social and intellectual decline.

ACTIVITY

Identify why medical interest in old age was, in many regards, a negative development for older people.

The creation of 'the elderly'

Until the creation of the welfare state in 1948, from the middle of the nineteenth century, older people were constructed by society as being either helpless, poor but thrifty and deserving, or as irresponsible, amoral, lacking in virtue and undeserving. Throughout the early years of the twentieth century, however, debates about pensions and retirement took place in reaction to older, punitive forms of welfare such as the Poor Law. The idea that retirement was a time of hard-earned rest, should be available to all, and that people should receive some financial support, emerged in this period. The development of a more positive orientation towards retirement culminated in retirement becoming compulsory in 1948, set at the age of 65 for men, irrespective of a person's physical ability.

In many respects the enactment of the welfare state was a great advance for older people, but it was not without its drawbacks. Beveridge (1942) stated in his welfare report that not too much should be lavished on the old, as children and workers should take precedence. Narratives of the dependent, non-productive older person who is a burden on society were never far from policy decisions. Indeed, to this day there has developed a deep anxiety among policy-makers about the proportion and associated costs of older people relative to the rest of the population. A gender issue in the welfare state construction of older people also exists. Women were perceived as physically more feeble than men and their retirement age was set earlier. According to Arber and Ginn (1993) the acceptance of women as being less able than men also fulfilled patriarchal needs (the needs of men in society). Women tend to marry men who are older than them and setting a retirement age five years earlier than for men means that few women will be working beyond their husband's retirement, thus preserving the male breadwinner model.

See Chapters 1 and 3 for further coverage of the concept of patriarchy.

The Third Age and the New Older Active Citizen

DEFINITION

The **Third Age** denotes a way of being older that is full of opportunity and a self-realization of life goals. Economic growth, financial security and the welfare state have all contributed to making such a phase in later life possible.

From the late 1970s a very different group of retirees, who had benefited from the welfare state and increased all-round affluence fuelled by low prices, has emerged. These new older people retired early, supported by generous early release deals and some personal savings, their apparent financial security underwritten by the welfare structure. They appeared to pave the way for a new form of retirement, based on leisure, choice, consumption, freedom of movement and good health, rather than poverty and dependency. These third agers also appeared to take rational decisions about their future, for instance selling large homes in a buoyant housing market to release equity and 'downsizing' to more age-appropriate accommodation (Tulle and Mooney, 2002). They could use the released equity to buy outright, and this new accommodation promised the management of disability risks.

Peter Laslett (1996) theorized the Third Age as a new model of retirement, referring to a new stage of life, unheard of before, tucked between the constraints and responsibilities of young adulthood and family formation and a Fourth Age of ill-health and disability. The Third Age is characterized by the potential for personal development expressed in acts of consumption and the take up of new forms of leisure activities. Gone were the days of narrow horizons, passivity, ill-health and cultural anonymity. Now it seemed possible to forge a new life and a new identity, being future-oriented, rather than sitting in a chair reminiscing fruitlessly about the past and waiting for death. We are all aware of the advertising which is targeted at these Third Agers: for example, savings plans, cruises, travel insurance, and goods of all sorts, including anti-ageing cosmetics. A new market for these goods added credence to the relevance and reality of the Third Age as a viable stage in people's lives. Laslett did not have any particular chronological age associated with the Third Age but, realistically, it would extend from the early fifties to the early seventies, when people were healthiest and best able to use their comfortable income to engage in consumption.

There is no doubt that the above model of active citizenship had struck a chord with many maturing people. Here was a chance to escape negative stereotypes of old age – old age as a time of decline, ill-health, helplessness and rolelessness. It was also a chance for policy-makers to minimize what was perceived as the *burden* of old age, that is, the costs incurred by national economies of supporting a growing proportion of older people. If all old people became Third Agers and supported themselves, then resources could be targeted towards those in greatest need.

Laslett's theory of the Third Age, whilst indeed acknowledging a changing cultural context in which we might envisage our old age, received some criticism. Jones et al. (2008), in a review of the Third Age model of ageing, conclude that being in the Third Age is not the result of sound individual financial planning, but of favourable cultural and structural conditions that enable the emergence of new aspirations and new identities. There are therefore dangers about reconstructing the later years as a time of affluence and new possibilities for all. Not everyone can be included in the new Third Age vision of old age and there remains the issue of discrimination or ageism, which is considered next.

ACTIVITY

Discuss whether or not all people can access and enjoy a Third Age in their lives. What impact could the 2009/2010 recession have on future generations of older people? Perhaps think ahead to your own retirement.

Discriminations and inequalities

Ageism

DEFINITION

Ageism is the consequence of negative discriminatory structural and personal beliefs and actions based on an individual's or group of people's (young or old) age. The consequences of ageism are visible in restriction or denial because of age-based prejudice and discrimination in access to services, employment and full social acceptance.

One barrier to enjoying an active Third Age is ageism. The term 'ageism' was first coined by Butler (1969) to denote discrimination against people because of their age. What makes ageism different from other forms of discrimination, such as racism or sexism, is that whilst our race and sex are unlikely to change (unless we resort to invasive and painful surgical procedures to have a sex change), almost all of us will certainly grow old. Ageism can be manifested in cultural terms, for instance, in relation to clothing. Twigg (2007) has noted that the choice of attractive clothing which is appropriate for the changing bodies of older women is very restricted indeed. Thus, unless they have the means to buy very expensive designer clothing which can be altered, and because of their price is often targeted at mature women, from their fifties onwards women have to choose between fitting their bodies into clothing designed for much younger body shapes or resorting to the drab, shapeless clothes which, perversely, are often associated with older women. The growing popularity of cosmetic enhancement, from creams and potions to surgery, is a manifestation of the corresponding unpopularity of looking and acting old.

In more material terms, ageism has been manifested in relation to employment. From the 1970s, older workers started experiencing more restricted employment opportunities than younger workers. As recently as the late 1990s they were also less likely to receive training at work (Phillipson, 1998), which fostered their construction as hostile to change and technology. Older workers are also more expensive because, particularly in white-collar jobs, they tend to have higher salaries. Therefore when companies wish to downsize, or make 'efficiency savings', they will tend to do so by offering voluntary redundancy or early retirement, which is a way of targeting older workers. The popular expression of 'getting rid of the dead wood' is often deployed to refer to the practice of rationalizing older workers out of the workforce and reinforces the construction of older people as inefficient and a barrier to progress. The loss of their experience and skills honed over years of service does not seem to figure in the balance sheets, however,

ACTIVITY

Discuss why ageism is not just bad for an individual person but also for society as a whole.

Inequalities

As we saw earlier in the chapter, since the nineteenth century old age has been constructed as a time of poverty and disease. Whilst those risks are indeed higher in later life than at other points in the lifecourse, they do not represent the entire experience of ageing and there are specific social processes that account for these risks being elevated and access to the Third Age being further restricted.

Poverty and income

According to 'Structured Dependency Theory' (Walker, 1980), older people are not inherently poor. They are made poor by welfare structures in capitalist societies that render people redundant and dependent on the state because of their age. Carol Estes (1979) also argues that making older people dependent on welfare is functional for capitalist societies. Not only is retirement a way of making room for a younger and cheaper workforce, it also creates a captive audience for what she calls the 'aging enterprise'. That is, health and social care professionals and associated bureaucracies exist precisely to 'service' older people.

There is some merit in dependency theory analysis. When we exit the labour market upon retirement, we receive the universal state pension (provided we have contributed enough years – see below). In 2007/8, about 95% of people received the full pension or part of it, and only 14% received an income from a private pension scheme. Despite tax breaks, private pensions are expensive and outside the reach of all but those with comfortable incomes. Fifty-nine per cent received some income from an employer's superannuation scheme (DWP, 2009), which requires both employer and employee to make a contribution, with the final pension calculated on the basis of the employee's final salary. Access to such a scheme is dependent on employers making one available and, when they do exist, recent trends have been towards running down these schemes, as, in periods of economic difficulties, they tend to be perceived as a barrier to business recovery. There are several notable examples of such 'final salary schemes' being closed off to new employees (e.g. Royal Mail and BP, but also some local authorities). The implications of these developments will be felt in thirty years. Thus, on retirement, whether or not we are willing to continue working, we become dependent on sources of income over which most of us have little control. Most of us also tend to experience a sharp drop in our standards of living when we retire. So we must rely on concessions and the services provided by an ever-increasing range of 'experts' to live reasonably comfortably.

Lifecourse

> **DEFINITION**
>
> **Lifecourse** refers to the narrative, events and transitions of a person's life. In contrast with the concept of lifecycle, with its biological connotations of fixed and inevitable stages, the concept of lifecourse suggests a more fluid and dynamic approach to understanding how people move through their lives.

Another, complementary, way of examining issues of inequalities in later life is to take a *lifecourse approach*. Indeed, income levels in later life tend to mirror a person's socio-economic position early in the lifecourse and during their working life. Thus, income inequalities in later life reflect not so much age discrimination as they do socio-economic and status inequalities throughout the lifecourse (Jones et al., 2008). Recently, despite failing to keep the bank afloat and subsequently losing his job over it, the CEO of a well-known Scottish bank commanded more favourable retirement terms than the cleaner of the same bank ever would, because a cleaner is typically employed on a temporary contract offering no security of employment and certainly no pension provision.

Gender inequalities in employment can also explain gender inequalities in retirement. Typically women in full-time occupations earn 17% less than men doing similar jobs. Women also have to contend with incomplete work careers and, consequently incomplete National Insurance or superannuation contributions, for which they will suffer when they retire, with lower annuities. Older cohorts of women already retired have also been discriminated against. When the welfare state was created in 1948, women were excluded from full National Insurance Contributions (NIC, also known as the Full Stamp) on the grounds that they were primarily homemakers who were dependent on their fathers or husbands as heads of households for their livelihood. Women who worked were advised to contribute a reduced rate of NIC (known as the Half Stamp). The consequence of an arrangement that did not favour women was that, on retirement, these women were left with a reduced pension, or missed out on one altogether, and had to rely on their husband's pension, which would be reduced on their husband's death. Many older women were therefore left to lead very precarious lives in often inadequate housing, saved only from abject poverty by frugal spending habits acquired during the Depression, the Second World War and the period of reconstruction which followed. Inevitably, these deficits are reproduced in later life: in 2007/8, single women pensioners' incomes represented 87% of single men pensioners' (DWP, 2009). The existence of notable gender inequality led Arber and Ginn (1995) to put forward the theory of the *feminization of old age,* arising from the observation that many of the problems we attribute to old age (poverty and dependency) are in fact the problems of old women created by the subordination of women throughout the lifecourse.

Finally, there is also evidence of race-based health inequalities. In the United States, black older people tend to experience worse health than white elders and when diagnosed with chronic heart disease their survival is inferior to that of white elders with the same conditions (Ferraro and Farmer, 1996). One particular explanation for the existence of inequalities in health is the *double jeopardy thesis*, according to which people of minority ethnic groups would suffer both race and age inequalities. Such a conclusion is not borne out by the authors' analysis. They opt instead for the *persistent health inequality thesis*, which emphasizes the continuation of disadvantage present early in the lifecourse. If anything, black people who survive into very old age may be as robust as their white age contemporaries. It is simply that there are fewer of them left. As we can see, the aforementioned thesis can also be used to explain the widening of inequalities in health.

> For greater detail on health inequalities see Chapter 9.

Implications for social work practice

We have set out a case for examining old age and ageing using the sociological imagination (Wright-Mills, 1959). This has enabled us to show that the 'problems' of old age have their roots in the kind of social organization we have set up and in the surrounding culture, rather than in old people themselves. Choosing to highlight bodily deterioration to the exclusion of the lifecourse and historical processes or the structural determinants of old age is a societal choice, not a universal 'fact'.

It is true that the bodily experience of ageing has to be addressed, but so have other factors. As we saw, ageism is a key organizing principle of how we as individuals, relatives, employers and service providers relate to older people. Gender and race discrimination issues are being addressed in other areas of life. Thus we must find approaches to social work interventions that challenge ageist practice, whilst attending to the varied and multiple needs of potential and actual service users.

This leaves us with a few dilemmas, but these are not insurmountable. How can we as practitioners attend to the needs of older people in ways that respect their uniqueness as individuals without forgetting the life-course and structural features that have affected their current situations? Thus, when addressing the challenges faced by older people we have to take account of all of the following factors. Their gender, their ethnicity, the historical and policy conditions they have encountered throughout their lives, will provide a context for the individual's experience. Their occupational history and the cultural conditions that prevail at the time of the social work encounter help provide an understanding and assessment of their financial situation. Their health and mobility, access to social networks and informal help, and their ability to negotiate access to formal services are likely to be essential factors. We also have to take account of the history of welfare and the principles that underpin it.

In sum, we need to pay heed to the prevailing cultural climate. As sociologists such as Featherstone and Hepworth (1995) and Higgs and Gilleard (2000) have shown, being old is not something that people will readily admit to in contemporary Western society. The Third Age was presented by Laslett (1996) as an escape from old age, that is from social ageing or ageist attitudes. It is now commonly stated that one is only as old as one feels, that old age is a state of mind, that youthfulness is what matters and there are numerous ways of 'combatting' this terrible thing that being old apparently is. Consumption gives us access to cosmetics, exercise, surgery, travel, nice clothes, all in an effort not to seem to be our age. Looking or feeling old is in danger of being constructed as a personal failure. Andrews (1999) has convincingly argued that it is another way of marginalizing those who are old and disabled. Encouraging people to feel young and to exercise choice masks the structural conditions that affect what kind of old age we are going to experience, as individuals and as groups of people.

Thus, whilst we are indeed individuals exercising agency, the scope of the decision-making we engage in is bounded by our cultural, historical and structural position (Tulle, 2004). This is a good point to move on to in the next section to explore how effective and sensitive social work practice can be crafted from the realization that we all stand at the meeting point between individual agency and structures.

Social work focus

The sociology focus provides vital insights for social workers in working with older people. Through the sociological imagination we can perceive the various inequalities and discriminations encountered by older people, and how society negatively constructs old age. Such perspectives inform social work practice and assist social workers in developing a value-based approach to their work. Social work is, after all, much more than simply instrumentally following technical procedures. It is about attempting to bring real change to service users' lives. Only by making visible the deeper issues that influence and condition older people can social workers understand not just what is required, but also why a certain type of service and interaction is required. Being able to do so is at the heart of person-centred social work.

Engaging in person-centred social work also means that social workers should consider the nature of oppressive practice, particularly in gerontological social work (Dalrymple and Burke, 2006). In practice terms this means the social work practitioner has to be able to reflect on the wider issues of structural oppression in terms of health, pensions and access to community services across the lifecourse (Victor, 2005). While the underpinning aspects of this work will be defined by the ethical and value base of social work practice with a focus on dignity and a non-judgmental approach, there also needs to be a more rigorous emphasis on individualization and person-centred working (Payne, 2005). Individualization seeks to view the older person in the framework of their total life experience, and how these experiences have impacted on and influenced the current coping capacity of the client. The wider framework can be related to issues of friends, family, support networks, work life experience and loss. Person-centred working refers to the way professional and empathic social workers are able to enter into the 'lifecourse' of the older person with a greater awareness and understanding of the uniqueness of the individual experience. It is particularly important for social workers to consider the impact of life experiences, as similar life experiences may result in very different senses of identity by different older people. In effect, the person-centred approach acknowledges the uniqueness of individuals within social work practice, against the backdrop of a more generic sociological perspective on the nature of age and ageing (Wilson et al., 2008). The focus of the person-centred approach should be on acknowledging the 'abilities', whilst recognizing the structural processes in which older people become 'disabled'.

Ageism

One very clear example identified in the sociology focus of a social norm that negatively impacts on older people is ageism. Language, in particular, is one medium where ageist attitudes are evident and where social workers can challenge oppressive and discriminatory attitudes. The term 'older people' in the eyes of a considerable number of older clients is an appropriate expression, as opposed to 'the elderly', which is full of negative connotations and is also very value laden. The word 'elderly' presupposes that there are generic older people who have similar characteristics and can be seen in the same light by the providers of services (Bond et al., 2007). The reality is that the term 'elderly' denies older people their sense of uniqueness which, incidentally, would be perceived as offensive among any other groups, particularly the young. So, if we consider that older people may be treated as an undifferentiated group by organizations, social and cultural structures, and social work itself, then we can make the assertion that older people will be treated less equitably than other groups within society. Such action is the definition of discrimination. Older people are viewed in the context of their chronological age as opposed to who and what they are as a cumulative consequence of their individual lifetime experience (Crawford and Walker, 2004). When social workers interact with older people, it is important to consider this as a baseline for ethical working, as this consideration is at the heart of a social work understanding of the nature of ageism.

Further problems associated with ageism may be exacerbated as social workers generally become involved in working with older people at a time when they experience greatest need, particularly in terms of health and welfare issues (Lymbery, 2007). Working with older people when they require the most support can result in social workers themselves making negative and false assumptions of older people based on *disability* as opposed to *ability*. Such assumptions result in ageism and ageist thinking and practice. To avoid slipping into stereotyped thinking requires that social work practitioners must be aware of the negative stereotypes that can prevail in relation to older people generally, that older people are less able, dependent, ill, lonely, poor and less engaged in what is going on in the world around them. These can be reinforced by media depictions of the vulnerability and incompetence of the older person with a focus on issues of protection. Social workers who 'buy into' these stereotypes do so at risk of reinforcing discriminatory practice generally (Crawford and Walker, 2004).

ACTIVITY

Think about older people you know, in your family, in your social network, or in work settings. To what extent are they regarded by younger adults as 'adult' and to what extent are they treated differently to other, younger adults?

Social work has to be aware of the nature of the social construction of age and gender as discussed in the sociology focus, specifically within value-driven practice. First, if we assume that this construction is associated with wider issues of perceived deviance within society, then we have to ask what impact this has on older people, and particularly women (Llewellyn et al., 2008). Social workers will already be familiar with the often negative stereotypes of older people within the media and a society that values youth and image highly. Older people may therefore be stigmatized within the stereotyping process and may be perceived as socially less acceptable than other groups. It is interesting to note here that the subtitle of Goffman's seminal (1968) sociological work *Stigma* is 'Notes on the management of spoiled identity', which is relevant for understanding how stereotypes can affect identity. Indeed, stereotyping may lead to the labelling of older people, particularly women, as somehow culturally redundant, which may have a dramatic effect on their capacity for coping, self-esteem and resilience in later life. Social work practitioners have a duty to address discrimination and oppression in its many forms as a foundation for understanding the wider issues of sexism, racism, disability and ageism (Thompson, 1993, 2007).

> For more information on stigma read Chapters 1 and 9.

> For more on Goffman see Chapter 1.

Labelling means that once people are constructed as deviant, they are much more likely to live up to this label, leaving themselves open to an even greater level of labelling in the future (Payne, 2005). When this happens older people may find themselves at the receiving end of discriminatory and oppressive practice at odds with ethical practice. Such experiences may alienate older people, affecting confidence and self-esteem. If the older person is blamed for their lack of engagement with society, it is possible to see a continuum of discrimination. It is therefore imperative that, as part of their professional practice, social work practitioners take full account of the wider expressed needs of older people as well as developing a sense of how society can impact on older people in an oppressive way.

It is also generally assumed that as people approach older age they will start to 'disengage' from society as a natural and normal part of the lifecourse, a preparation for death. This process tends to rest on the belief that all older people wish to withdraw from society at a similar point in the lifecourse. The reality is that disengagement is a social construct which, as we saw earlier, can be functional for managing the labour market. It also exerts unwarranted control over older people (Llewellyn et al., 2008). The irony is that at a time when older people may be perceived as socially redundant, they may be fully engaged in their developing roles of grand-parents, carers and volunteers or pursuing other life goals as the Third Age approach to understanding older people suggests. From a social work per-spective we also need to address how assumed disengagement may lead to feelings of isolation by older people. It may also be the case that those older people who appear more disengaged may have been isolated throughout their lives and are in need of the specific understanding of social work intervention to support and facilitate an engagement with their peers and community, particularly in their declining years (Stuart-Hamilton, 2006).

Gender

Social workers cannot be 'gender neutral' in their assessment of the needs of individuals. In the sociology focus we discussed how the social structure of gender negatively influences older age. As a consequence of gender ine-qualities social workers have to recognize or appreciate the additional pres-sures on older women. Some older women may still be expected to carry out caring and coping roles in the face of persistent and long-term poverty or social expectations. This expression of inequality is a denial of the civil and human rights of older women, and addressing it should be at the heart of social work understanding of discriminatory and oppressive practice.

> Consider also Chapter 2 on Gender.

Empowering older people

As social workers we have not only to recognize the value of all people as persons and citizens but also be fully aware of the tension between auton-omy and protection: empowerment within the social work context means supporting and encouraging older people to engage in decision-making in relation to the services that impact on them. Doing so ensures that older people are afforded the greatest opportunity to make their own decisions about their current and future welfare and to promote, as far as possible, the potential for independent living.

How, therefore, may social workers approach ensuring the independence of older people? To achieve this we advocate an approach to understanding older people at the *micro* level within the context of their individual ageing rather than as a burden on resources within a population ageing narrative. According to the latter, older people are perceived only in the context of the resources needed to meet these needs rather than as individuals with a rich life history and a potential for contribution. Life history can also be recreated through life story interviews where older people are able to recount those aspects of their lived experience they feel are the most significant. Accessing and hearing what service users regard as being their most significant moments allows the social work practitioner to be closer to the reality of that experience and to demonstrate what it is to be 'humane, empathic, sensitive and understanding' (Atkinson,1998) within social work practice.

Being empathic is particularly important when we consider the societal dimension of the body itself. Being empathic means paying attention to how older people deal with ill-health and disability. It means that younger social workers must put themselves in the place of older service users by recognizing that they too will age. Lastly it means reconstructing the later years as a time, potentially, for consolidation and growth (Bond et al., 2007), rather than decline and deviance.

ACTIVITY

Consider how older people are depicted on film and television. Consider how you would feel if sexually active older people were portrayed in the same way as sexually active younger people.

In an economic climate where there are competing demands for resources, older people are viewed less as contributors to society and more as recipients, irrespective of the contribution they have made over their life course. Social workers need to have a well-developed sense of what users of services really need and want, and this can only be accessed through service user participation and involvement within the process of service development (Ray et al., 2009). Practitioners need to encourage and support older people to take part in debates about how to identify needs. Such a dialogue is particularly important in relation to older people in care settings, a population group that has already experienced the loss of community support, family, economic independence. People in care settings may, however, still have a meaning-ful role to play within society (Payne et al., 2000). By engaging in dia-logue the social work role may start as one of advocacy, but should develop, where possible, into one of encouraging a more proactive approach to independent decision-making and living.

A note of caution: social workers, however well intentioned, can assume that providing older people with a forum to express their views is enough, without taking into consideration the power dynamics at play within society. So, for instance, older people may be further disadvan-taged and discriminated against if they are expected to take part in debates and fora that may mirror and reinforce those wider social inequal-ities. It is therefore necessary for social workers to ensure that older peo-ple are supported throughout the *process* of meetings and agendas with their often confusing professional language. Anything less than this may result in the older person being treated more as a passive recipient of care and support, as opposed to a person who is involved within the inclusive and collaborative process (Vincent, 1999). In effect this means that older people in general are the people who are best able to identify their own needs and develop their decision-making capacity, and it is the social work role to support this process. Doing so is at the heart of the person-centred social work we discussed at the top of the social work focus.

Lived Experience

Here Richard Longstreet reflects on his experiences of being an older person. In the interview below he summarizes the experiences that have shaped his world-view, the role and place of older people in society and how he relates to the services he receives. As you read the interview it would be useful to consider the issues that have been discussed in both the sociology and the social work focus. Doing so should help you relate what can seem quite abstract theories and concepts to individual people.

The following prompts should prove helpful:

- Reflect on how Richard portrays himself as either supporting or challenging wider contemporary social perceptions and social constructions of older people.
- Consider issues of ageism in relation to Richard. Does he acknowledge its pres-ence in society and how does he respond to ageism when he encounters it? How do his reactions to ageism inform us about the tensions that exist between social structures and individual agency?

- How has his own lifecourse affected his attitudes to both society in general and to the services he receives? Do Richard's attitudes to life seem similar to your own or are there generational differences?
- How could you as a social worker enlist someone like Richard to challenge the wider social inequalities and negative stereotyping that impact on the lives of older people?
- Richard is a white working-class male, in what ways could his experiences and current situation be different, if he were a woman, of a different social class or from an ethnic minority?

Q. Hello, Richard. Can you tell me something of your background?

A. I am seventy-five years of age. I was born in Glasgow in 1934 and as a child I can remember war being declared and the concerns of my parents and what the future would bring. My father worked in the docks as a protected industry and was living in Glasgow when the docks were bombed during the war. I had two brothers and sisters, although one of my brothers has since died, and I keep in fairly regular contact with my other siblings who are still based in the Glasgow area. I trained in engineering when I finished school as this was one of the main occupations open to me although I would have liked to get away from home and this type of work and to get more educational qualifications. I served my apprenticeship in this trade and went to work in the Merchant Marine as a ship's engineer. I married a local girl in my twenties and soon after left for my first trip abroad. Over the course of the following years I travelled to Singapore, Mumbai and most of the main shipping ports throughout the world. This meant I travelled most of my working life and it was difficult to settle when I was back on shore. This had an impact on my relationship with my wife and we divorced while I was still working away.

Q. What impact did this career have on your life and what do you think you learned from this?

A. It was a very diverse and interesting career in the Merchant Marine lasting over forty years. This work had taken me to most of the major ports and seafaring nations of the world. From my point of view the plus side of this was that I experienced a range of people and cultures that I would not have otherwise experienced and I feel that this has impacted significantly on the person I am today. It has made me able to see the different sides of an argument and I believe that this has evolved through living with diverse groups of people throughout my working life. I believe these life experiences have made me independent in my thinking although I do acknowledge that travelling has had an adverse affect on my family relationships. I am well versed in a range of subjects from politics and history and I both learned from and utilized this within my working experience overseas.

Q. This interview is related to the relationship between social work practice and the wider issues of how people may be treated and perceived within society. How do you feel old age has impacted on you?

A. I view my age as an accumulation of years rather than any predicator of a decline. In reality I am as busy now as I was during my more formal working life and I have found new areas of interest in gardening which have not only provided me with a productive outlet but also with a sense of pride in my achievement in this area.

Q. What do you think when you see old age categorized in terms of disability, a lack of independence and a lack of contribution to the wider community?

A. I am always puzzled by this negative image of older people as I do not feel I have ever been discriminated against because of my age. I have a lot of friends who are younger than me and I am sure they do not think of me in terms of my age. Even if I did experience this age discrimination I would see that as an area that I could and would address myself. I think too many people give up in old age and assume that they no longer have a role to play. I don't think like that and I still have plenty to say and to contribute.

Q. In general do you think that older people are treated differently from younger people in society?

A. I realize that society treats people who are thirty-five differently from those who are seventy-five but that is not a view that I share. I feel about fifty and I have not stopped trying to become and remain involved within the farming community I live in. I am regularly asked to help out by local farmers and that indicates to me that I am being asked because of my skills as opposed to my age! I think that ageing is very much in the mind and that if you stay active and are able to contribute then there is no reason why someone should be treated differently because of their age.

Q. What would you say are some of the positive and negative aspects of ageing?

A. Some of the negative aspects are related to physical decline. I have arthritis and last year I developed a deep vein thrombosis and this has impacted on the amount of physical work I can do. The speed isn't there any more and I can't run for a bus. Prior to that, I was a regular hill-walker and cyclist – well into my seventies. Irrespective of my age I take a personal responsibility for my health and try to do everything in moderation. I don't smoke, drink moderately in a social way and I take care of my diet. On a more positive note I no longer have those responsibilities that I had when I had younger children, although I now have a formal role of grandfather in the lives of my grandchildren. I also have more time to think about things and pursue my interest in the history of farming as well as attending music and theatre evenings in my local community.

Q. How do you think you are perceived by the wider community as an older person?

A. I don't think I am treated any differently, as local people are still asking me to do the same things they did fifteen or twenty years ago. This involves physical labour, which I think they would not ask if they considered me too old. I am also included in any events that take place and I have no sense that this is related to my old age or otherwise.

Q. Do you think you are treated differently by younger people because of your old age?

A.   I do not tend to have a lot of contact with younger people in the wider community – more neighbours and children and grandchildren of neighbours. Most of my contact with younger people is with my own grandchildren, who tend to see me in a different light from years ago. They view me differently from their parents and confide more in me. I particularly value this relationship with younger people where I am able to offer my experience and knowledge. I think this is an important role for older people and the contribution they can make to the next generation can often be underestimated.

Q.   How are your current needs being met and how do you think these will be met in the future?

A.   At present I am very satisfied with the services I receive, particularly in relation to medical services and my ability to travel. This has made me feel independent and that I am still able to meet friends and to live independently. I realize that I am not inclined to complain about services because of my background and 'making do'. I don't know what my future needs will be but I would like to see more commitments made for older people services in general as I think older people are not catered for by politicians in the way that other groups are. It seems strange to me that after a lifetime of accumulating knowledge and experience that there is suddenly an arbitrary age where people are expected to retire irrespective of their personal needs and wishes. I worry that if I am not able to look after myself in the future that there will not be the services there to support me. I would also like more information on how to access these services and how I should go about this. Nevertheless I am well now and I have no fears for the future.

Further Reading

Gilleard, C. and Higgs, P. (2005) *Contexts of Ageing: Class, Cohort and Community*. London: Polity Press.

Hockey, J. and James, A. (2003) *Social Identities Across the Lifecourse*. Basingstoke: Palgrave MacMillan.

7

Health

Chris Yuill, Rob Mackay
and Angie Mutch

Key themes

- Health is much more than diet and exercise. Social processes such as class, gender and ethnicity have a profound influence on health.
- The medical model of health stresses a reductionist and health-professional-centred understanding of health.
- The social model stresses a multidimensional approach to health.
- Mental distress is commonly experienced in the UK. It is, however, subject to social stigma.

Keywords

medical model of health, social model of health, stigma, mental health, class, gender, ethnicity

Introduction

Sociology Focus

Health is a very important issue in everyone's lives. Having good health, both mentally and physically, can make a substantial difference to what we can do, in terms of both our work and our social lives, and is crucially important for our overall happiness and well-being. Social workers are often involved with people who have poor health in a variety of ways, whether this is in assessing someone's needs or coordinating and providing elements of social support or care. In some respects 'health' may appear to be a fairly straightforward enough concept to understand. For many people health is seen as simply the absence of disease, feeling fit, eating well and so on, and when something goes wrong then the medical profession will be there to sort out the problem. What this chapter outlines, however, is that health is in reality much more complex than the above sketch would indicate. The main message here states that the causes and experiences of health and illness frequently owe more to social processes rather than biological and medical processes. Indeed, for many of the people with whom social workers are involved, it is the social aspects and social processes surrounding their health problems that are the cause of the most worry and problems.

Three important themes are explored in this sociological account of health. First, the medical and social models of health and illness are compared and contrasted. This indicates different approaches to conceptualizing health. The medical model offers a conventional perspective of health and medicine, while the social model parallels the social work concerns of holism and placing clients' needs and wishes at the core of practice. Second, developing on from a central tenet of the social model that health is distributed unequally across society, attention falls on three key areas of health inequality: class, ethnicity and gender. In keeping with the theme of this chapter, it is social processes as opposed to medical or biological concerns that are causal for these inequalities. Third, and finally, the focus moves to considering how health issues (in this case mental health and mental distress) can be subject to prejudicial attitudes. Once the sociological content has been outlined the social work section contextualizes the above themes for social work practice, before the final section gives voice to someone who has experienced the social impact of mental ill-health.

Sociology Focus

Medical and social models of health

The introduction above alluded to a particular perception of health that informs everyday discourses on and perceptions of health. In many respects this characterization of health and illness is similar to one that sociologists term the *medical model*. This is the dominant perspective of health in most Western societies and accords a privileged role to the perception of the science of biomedicine, its perspectives and practitioners. While biomedicine and the medical model display many strengths in terms of providing cures for a whole range of diseases and illness, they also exhibit other features and characteristics that are less helpful, which include (Nettleton, 1995, p. 5):

1. *Mind–body dualism.* In biomedicine the body and mind are regarded as quite separate entities and it is the biological body that is of prime importance in this framework. The body here refers to the physical, biological body while the mind refers to personal identity and the sense of self. By bringing the body to the fore in this way the medical model removes the subjectivity of the person who is ill. This can mean in practice not appreciating the ill or distressed person's needs, wishes and particular circumstances.
2. *Mechanical metaphor.* The body is likened to a machine or an engine and the doctor or surgeon is akin to a mechanic or engineer required to follow predetermined laws and procedures that can 'fix' anything that is 'broken'.
3. *Technological imperative.* In terms of treating someone, then technology in the form of pharmaceuticals or cutting-edge devices and machines offers the best way forward.
4. *Reductionist.* All aspects of health are reduced to the level of the biological.
5. *Doctrine of specific aetiology.* There is a set and identifiable cause of every disease. This usually implies a specific pathogen or trauma that has occurred at the biological level.
6. *Specialist voice.* Only the views and perspectives of the medical practitioner are valid and there are no other voices or people eligible to put forward views on health and the causes of ill-health.

A more rounded and holistic view of health is presented in the *social model* of health. Here health is understood as emerging out of the society in which a person finds him- or herself. It is social as opposed to medical and biological forces that predominate.

1. *Holism.* Instead of separating the mind and body the two are seen as crucially interwoven. This means understanding how both the biological aspects of an illness and the social situation and personal circumstances of someone interconnect and how these affect each other. This element is the most important in the social model as it guides an understanding of health in its fullest, richest and most complete sense.
2. *Social aspects.* Health is highly patterned by class, gender and ethnicity. Not to diminish the role of individual agency and choice, but much of our health is strongly conditioned by our social location. These social processes exert both subtle and quite overt influences over levels of control, access to resources, and the ability to enact decisions. In society generally the inequalities that exist with class, gender and ethnicity are also evident in health. Substantial and enduring health inequalities exist in relation to these processes and are explored in greater depth below.
3. *Lay perspectives.* It is not just experts that possess knowledge about health and healing. Ordinary people can also have extensive knowledge based on their own experiences as well as that of peers and their wider community and culture. In

some cases, such as chronic illness, for instance, ordinary people can have quite extensive in-depth knowledge of a condition that is greatly affecting their life.

4. *Participation and partnership.* Relationships between health or social care professional and service user are much more equal and participative. The professional may possess specialist knowledge, but how it is actualized and deployed depends on a consultation and agreement with the service user

---

DEFINITIONS

The **medical model** refers to a perspective on health that emphasizes biology and the medical profession, while the **social model** refers to a perspective on health that emphasizes a wider social and cultural, and more inclusive approach in understanding health.

The above exploration of differing and opposing models of health is not an abstract discussion or an attempt at empty theorizing. As will be evident later in this chapter, how health is conceptualized has an overwhelming bearing on how the care someone receives is organized and how various health and social care professionals relate to their service users.

ACTIVITY

Social work practice best fits which of the above models? What is the reasoning behind your answer?

Exploring health inequalities

The section above drew attention to the different ways in which health can be conceptualized. One of the key messages contained in the social model of health is that poor health is not a random occurrence, but rather is socially patterned by class, gender and ethnicity. This section further examines these health inequalities, indicating the extent and various explanations of each. It is also worth noting that often the issues raised in the previous chapters on class, gender and ethnicity appear and are relevant again here. The other forms of inequalities (for example, power, economics and status) explored in those chapters often have an indirect or direct influence in conditioning and affecting health.

Class and health inequality

For more on class see Chapter 2.

The differences in morbidity and early mortality between the social classes are highly significant. In the UK, for instance, a man from social class V can expect on average to live 7.5 years less than a male from class I. Between women the difference is slightly less, at five years (Hattersly, 2005). Also, both men and women from social classes IV and V will on average experience more ill-health, limiting illness and self-report poor health more often than their peers in social classes I and II. It is not only in the UK that these trends and inequalities exist. They are also to be found occurring on a global scale. A recent WHO report (CSDH, 2008) identified that whether in industrial Western countries or in so-called developing nations, class differences were similarly highly apparent. Class, when it comes to health, definitely still matters and one's class position has a considerable bearing on one's length and quality of life.

What is also notable about these trends is that they have been in existence for some time. In fact, many of the earliest attempts, dating back to the Victorian era, which sought to explore how health differed across social classes, came to similar conclusions that working people disproportionately suffered poor health, while in more recent times the Black Report (Black et al., 1980) and the Acheson Inquiry (Acheson, 1998) pointed to the same conclusion, that a negative relationship exists between class and health.

The statistics and the conclusions alluded to above are in themselves very thought-provoking, in addition to being very useful for outlining and describing the many iniquities of the contemporary health landscape we inhabit. They do not, however, necessarily tell us *why* these differences both occur and are persistent (if not worsening in some cases) across time. To that end we are required to turn to the theoretical work that attempts to offer an explanation in addition to the descriptions outlined above. There have been many theories advanced in the past. The aforementioned Black Report, for instance, published in 1980, famously identified four different possible causes of health inequalities (cultural, material, artefact and social selection), which in turn provided much of the basis of sociological research into health inequalities during the 1980s and 1990s. Recently, however, two different (and in many ways competing) explanations have come to the fore and these will be outlined next.

The psycho-social approach

The psycho-social approach places an emphasis on psychological reactions to social situations, hence the term 'psycho-social'. In the case of health, this is the emotional experiences of living in a society with high relative inequality rather than a reference to absolute standards of wealth. Wilkinson (1996), a leading advocate of the psycho-social approach, argues that a society which exhibits sizeable gaps between the rich and poor results in those who are poor being subjected to a variety of negative emotions (shame, stress and so on) that will impact on their health. Those negative emotions 'translate' into bad health by engaging the body's stress systems. In doing so the bodily systems responsible for the immune system and other health-related functions are, in turn, switched off. If the negative emotions carry on for a protracted period of time, as they often do in contemporary society, then health suffers.

Societies and communities that exhibit less of a gap and more social cohesion, on the other hand, are healthier. Social cohesion refers to the bonds and interactions between people, allowing those who need help or assistance to access either material or emotional support. The negative emotional experiences are lessened or ameliorated by that contact and support.

The town of Roseto in Pennsylvania provides a useful case study of the psycho-social approach. Italian immigrants founded the community of Roseto in the late 1890s. From the 1960s onwards it was noted by medical and sociological researchers that the town exhibited high levels of good health, with notable low levels of heart disease. What was especially interesting and, in many ways, surprising at the time, was that diet and exercise were not significant factors in the good health of the community. Neither was affluence; the majority of the community were not much above the poverty line. The critical reason for the Rosetans' good health was to be found in how they lived as a community, with strong social bonds, an emphasis on community values and general other directedness. Notably, as the community became more 'Americanized', more individualistic and less community-orientated from the mid-1960s onwards the health advantage Rosteo enjoyed became increasingly eroded.

DEFINITIONS

In reference to health inequalities the **psycho-social** approach focuses on the emotional responses to living in an unequal and fragmented society, while the **neo-material** approach draws attention to the deeper structural forces of capitalism and its uneven distribution of resources (adequate housing and health care) as being responsible for the enduring patterns of inequality in class morbidity and mortality.

The neo-material approach

The neo–material approach places its emphasis on the structural and material causes of health inequalities. This approach has, in many respects, come about as a critical reaction towards the psycho-social approach. The focus here is very much on what is seen to be the deeper causes of fragmentation and inequality in society, something that neo-materialists, such as Lynch et al. (2000), claim that the psycho-social approach is inadequate in doing. While not dismissing that there is a psycho-social approach, the neo-material approach claims that we must dig much deeper into the causes of class and health inequality and identify the social, political and economic processes that create the fragmentation of society and the poor health of so many people. Central to their argument is that governments' adopting neo-liberalism (a political ideology that promotes a highly capitalist free market) have corroded society, creating a small but highly wealthy social elite, while running down important resources such as housing, education and health care for the wider, but especially poorer, sections of the population. We can therefore only truly understand why health inequalities occur by reference to how capitalism creates and perpetuates all forms of inequalities in contemporary society.

ACTIVITY

Which of the above approaches do you think best understands the causes of health inequality?

Ethnicity and health inequality

For more on ethnicity see Chapter 4.

The health of people from various ethnic minority groups on a variety of measures tends to be poor. Nazroo (1997, p. 32) found that, for instance, one in three people from an ethnic minority reported less than good health or were experiencing long-standing illness or were registered with a disability. Often the health of ethnic minority groups is worse than that of white British people as indicated in Figure 7.1 below.

There have been many reasons advanced as to why this pattern of ethnic inequality occurs. Older explanations were built on theories of genetic or cultural causality. This implies that there is something 'wrong' or 'deficient' in (1) the actual biological make-up of ethnic minority groups or (2) in their

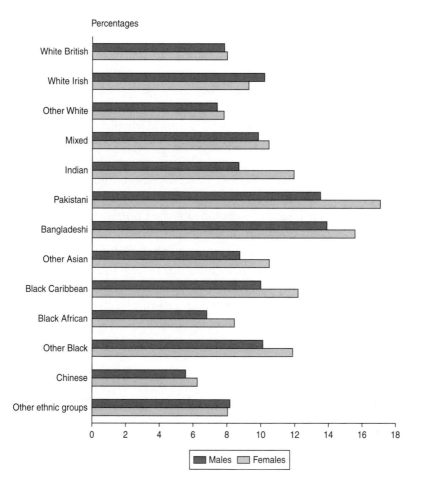

Figure 7.1 *Age standardised 'not good' health rates: by ethnic group and sex, April 2001, England & Wales (ONS, 2004). Reproduced under the terms of the Click-Use Licence.*

culture that predisposes people from ethnic groups to greater ill-health. Such explanations have not stood the test of time. Though no doubt unintentional, biological explanations echoed racist notions of non–white people being the biological other and inferior to white people. These notions existed in previous eras when science tended to support rather than disprove, false notions of white superiority, while the cultural explanation lapsed into 'victim blaming', where it was the ethnic minority's culture that was seen as faulty – such as their culture having a diet high in too many 'bad' foods, for example. This perspective could also imply that the ethnic minority culture, this time instead of their biological make–up, was also somehow inferior in comparison to white culture.

Again, if one thinks of dietary culture, the UK's ethnic majority diet is hardly an exemplar of sensible eating! Secondly, cultural explanations stereotyped ethnic cultures as a static 'shopping list' of features (for example, diet, dress and customs) unchanging over time and between generations.

Currently, explanations of ethnic health inequalities have usefully moved away from the genetic and cultural explanations outlined above. The focus is, instead, on the more social process of racism (particularly the lived experiences of racism) as being the crucial process in shaping and conditioning the health of people from ethnic minorities. Various pieces of research, for example, in the UK (Karlsen and Nazroo, 2002, 2004), the United States (Krieger et al., 2005) and in New Zealand (Harris et al., 2006), support this explanation of the lived experience of racism that is the underlying process that leads people from different ethnic groups to experience different levels of health. The racism identified in these studies ranged from verbal or physical abuse to dealing with the consequences of institutional racism. Importantly, both indirect and direct forms of racism had a negative effect on health. Sometimes the anticipation or fear of being subjected to racism and the anxiety, stress and worry that creates are enough to lead to ill-health.

ACTIVITY

Why do you think the anticipation of racism possibly affects the health of people from ethnic minority groups?

Gender and health inequality

For more on gender see Chapter 3.

Unlike the sections on class and ethnicity, this section is less clear-cut in certain respects. Conventional sociological wisdom held that gender and health inequalities could be neatly summarized with the phrase 'men die and women suffer'. Why this aphorism does not hold quite so true currently relates to some important shifts and changes that have occurred in the gender relations in society that shape and influence men and women's health. However we are still far away from the fundamental changes that would witness equality between the genders, for instance, gains have been made that have narrowed some of the inequalities between men and women.

It may be more useful to consider how contemporary discourses of masculinities and femininities condition and shape the health of men and women.

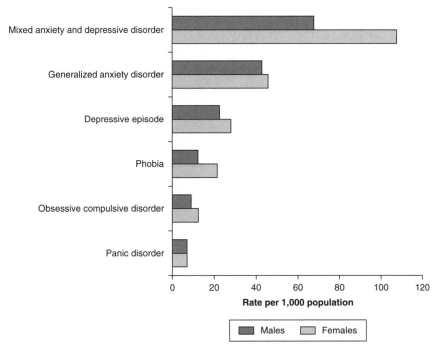

Figure 7.2 *Weekly prevalence of neurotic disorders: by sexes, 2000.*
Source: ONS (2006) Reproduced under the terms of the Click-Use Licence.

Ideas of hegemonic masculinity can ironically negatively impact on health. This is evident when men discuss health or admit to having health problems. Dominant masculine discourses require men to be fit, healthy and not to admit to weakness in public and to health professionals. When it comes to mental distress then having to live up to social expectations of what it is to be a man can pose difficulties in revealing depression, for example (Emslie et al., 2006).

ACTIVITY

Who do you think exemplifies the stereotypically fit and healthy male in today's societies? What media sources exist that may put young men under pressure to conform to certain aspects of hegemonic masculinity?

Mental Distress and Well-being

The previous sections in this chapter have discussed health very broadly in terms of both physical and mental distress. Focusing on mental distress more directly, we can note a very interesting contradiction: despite the high-levels of mental distress (see Figure 7.2), in society people with mental distress issues often face a very negative and unsympathetic societal reaction. Somewhere around 1 in 6 people are currently diagnosed with a mental illness. The actual figure may be much higher as not all people who experience mental suffering seek help and therefore go unrecorded.

Despite the commonness of mental distress, this condition still attracts considerable social stigma. People experiencing mental distress frequently report that they find the negative imagery and perceptions surrounding their condition just as problematic, if not more so, as managing and experiencing the symptoms of mental ill-health.

The 'Counting the Cost' survey carried out by Baker and MacPherson (2000) for the mental distress charity MIND highlighted the extent of the problems that stigma creates. Often people with mental distress were labelled with disparaging and offensive terms of abuse, such as 'schizo' or 'nutter'. This can lead to a lowering of self-esteem for those on the receiving end and can also prevent people seeking the help they require or expressing how they are feeling to others in case of a negative reaction.

ACTIVITY

Why do you think so much negative imagery is attached to mental distress? Identify portrayals of mental ill-health in the media and popular culture and decide whether these images provide positive or negative depictions of mental illness.

For more on Goffman, micro-sociological approaches and symbolic interactionism see Chapter 1.

The sociological theory of 'stigma' provides insights into this situation. Developed by Erving Goffman in 1968, the theory focuses on the micro-sociological order of society and how people rehearse, mediate and enact their day-to-day interactions. For some people, however, these daily encounters are fraught with risk and danger, as some aspect of their identity may be considered to be a stigma – an attribute that potentially prevents them for being fully accepted by others. They acquire what is termed a 'spoiled identity'. Social life from this sociological perspective is very much a stage on which we perform our identity and sense of self. In order to do so, people have to engage in thoughtful reflection (effectively rehearsing how they wish to appear to others) about how they present themselves to others and how they may do so in a manner that will be widely accepted. There are some traits, characteristics and past life events that we all may possess that potentially could jeopardize that successful enactment of self. Often people manipulate such 'problematic' attributes and pieces of information so as they do not disrupt their outward presentation of self.

There are, though, certain attributes that are especially 'problematic' for society. Examples of these include disability, drug and alcohol misuse, sexuality, a criminal record and mental distress. It should not be taken that these are considered to be intrinsically or essentially deviant. In fact, in his writings Goffman was very much on the side of people who had been rejected, sidelined and stigmatized by society. Deviance here is seen as a *relative* concept depending on the situation and the people involved, and does not imply any moral judgement of someone with a disability or a criminal record, for example.

ACTIVITY

As a social worker in what ways could your clients be stigmatized?

DEFINITION

As developed by Erving Goffman, the theory of **stigma** refers to the process of how people are excluded from full social acceptance due to certain aspects of their body, personality or life-narrative being potentially regarded as socially 'problematic' and how they respond to that exclusion by managing information about themselves so as to effect some form of acceptance.

Those who possess an attribute that is potentially stigmatizing can find themselves either rejected or marginalized by society. This prospect of rejection and exclusion from society can prompt people into actions that Goffman terms 'passing'. Here, the person with a potential stigma attempts to hide or disguise that stigma. Doing so involves engaging in sometimes quite elaborate routines and creating narratives that avoid making the stigma visible.

One should be wary about drawing pessimistic conclusions from the above sketch of stigma. Historically, people with spoiled identities have overcome stigma. The Gay Rights movement from the 1960s onwards is a good example of how a previously stigmatized group can alter social attitudes.

In the UK we can see mental distress service user groups actively campaigning against the negative stereotyping of mental suffering. Though, as Ferguson (2003) suggests, the social position of people who have experienced mental distress may be best improved by parallel campaigning alongside other groups, such as trade unionists, in reducing other forms of social inequality and discrimination.

The sociology of health indicates that health is much more than simply biology or diet and exercise. It is social processes of class, ethnicity and gender that we are required to explore in order to properly understand health in its fullest, widest and deepest sense.

Social Work Focus

Understanding Health Inequalities and Stigma

It is an inevitable part of a social worker's job that he or she will have frequent contact with people who are experiencing poor health. The reason for poor health, as we explored in the sociology focus, is often as a consequence of wider health and social inequalities. People may also have contact with a social worker because of their experiences of the negative social reactions brought about by the stigma related to physical illness or mental distress. Social workers are, as such, involved in health matters in a variety of ways, either providing very practical support or tackling prejudice and discrimination. One common example of the practical support social workers provide is evident in care management. As an activity, being a care manager involves the monitoring and coordinating of a community care package. The social worker here would have the responsibility of ensuring that service users receive the best possible care that is tailored to meet their needs by drawing on reports from health professionals and any other needs or wishes identified by the service user – though often financial considerations will limit what can actually be achieved.

What any social worker should be aware of is how important sociological perspectives can be in assisting effective social work practice in relation to health. Considerable overlap exists, for example, between the social model of health outlined in the sociology focus and many core social work values, and in how social workers approach the wide array of health and social issues that face service users. Both stress the importance of working with people on a partnership basis, understanding that different viewpoints exist and the crucial importance of social context in framing and influencing people's lives. The social model therefore appears to be a 'natural home' for the belief systems of social workers, where social work values should lead to respecting the uniqueness of each individual, alongside a commitment to social justice.

By adopting the social model of health, social workers will also differentiate themselves from other professionals and professional bodies. It provides social workers with a distinct perspective that informs and implies certain courses of action that will go beyond, for example, seeing health problems as being amenable to drug therapies or the outcome of lifestyle choices. The social model also urges us not to 'blame the victim' but to identify the social causes of their problems and thereby establish effective strategies to tackle those problems. By also understanding the importance of the social context of health, knowledge of anti-discriminatory practice and anti-oppressive practice can be more firmly embedded into social work practice.

In order to explore the relationship between sociology and social work in relation to health, the bulk of the social work focus is on social work and mental distress and the critical role that sociology plays in strengthening social work practice.

Social Work and Mental Distress

It will be apparent from the sociology focus that many people in contemporary society experience mental distress and mental suffering. Many of those who do experience mental distress may have an encounter with a social worker, whether in a hospital or community setting. Contact with a social worker may arise for a number of reasons ranging from complex relationship issues to issues relating to the management of basic day-to-day activities. The social worker is a member of a multi-disciplinary team normally involving psychiatrists, psychologists, mental health nurses (hospital and community), occupational therapists and general practitioners. This team is commonly referred to as the 'Community Mental Health Team' and is responsible for the clinical care and treatment of the individual patient. These team members are required to have a knowledge of mental disorders. Just because different people work in a team does not, however, necessarily entail that they share the same perspectives on understanding mental health and illness, and what are the most effective or suitable modes of treatment.

The reason for knowledge of mental health being contested is that different professional groups are influenced by different models of health. As stated in the introductory chapter, how one conceptualizes an issue within social work and sociology is highly important. The way in which an issue, such as mental health, is understood guides the actions, therapy and support that professionals provide. The two competing understandings in this instance are the medical and social models of mental health. Both are very similar to the more general medical and social models of health outlined in the sociology focus. As the discussion below indicates, each perspective leads to quite different approaches in therapy, support and care.

The medical or biological model of mental illness (Hothersall et al., 2008; Rogers and Pilgrim, 2005) is the dominant perspective in the UK and its influence can be observed in the terminology used in mental health laws and policy papers. The medical model of mental health asserts that certain human behaviours are that of an illness or disorder. Scientific principles inform this model and suggest the causes of mental illness are related to organic and biochemical factors. By conceptualizing mental health as an illness or disorder, which is biological in origin, then the type of treatment that follows will be medically orientated, often involving drug treatments. For example, the service user contributor points out she was treated with drugs whilst detained in hospital as opposed to other forms of treatment.

The social model of mental distress (Tew, 2005) is the perspective that a person's behaviour is understood within the framework of their social context. As such, the social model offers a holistic view of the lived experience. Doing so requires that all aspects of somebody's life, including relationships, sexuality, ethnicity, health, employment, housing and spirituality, are taken into account and respected. The focus on respect and holism within the social model implies that the person or service user is accorded a central role in the social work relationship and can therefore be described as an expert on their own situation, who can, in turn, inform the social worker as to what is or is not appropriate for their needs and situation. By locating an understanding of human behaviour at a societal level, the social model also identifies that power and the effects of stigma and discrimination are important concepts, which condition and shape the lived experience of mental distress. Finally, within the social model of mental illness, the preferred modes of treatment include talking therapies and approaches which assist an individual to understand which changes may be made to the context of their life within the community and wider society in which they live.

The social model also advocates that political campaigning or activity by a social movement is necessary to challenge and transform oppression and discrimination. Since the 1970s in the UK there has been a significant mental health service users movement which, even while taking many different organizational forms, has essentially asserted the right of service users to have a voice as to their needs and to influence services both at an individual and collective level. For some individuals and organizations (for example, Survivors Speak Out), campaigning extends to articulating a different way of understanding their experiences with concepts and language that are removed from those of psychiatry.

Stigma, the discrimination of people experiencing mental distress and the PCS model

DEFINITION

Thompson's **PCS** model (1993, 2006) identifies that discrimination and oppression occur in the three inter-related spheres of the personal, cultural and structural. Attention is importantly taken away from discrimination and oppression being purely the outcome of individual attitudes and is placed in a wider context of deeper and more powerful social and cultural contexts.

In the sociology focus we explored how certain illnesses can lead to an individual or group of people becoming stigmatized and thereby be subjected to discrimination and oppression. People with mental health problems can be especially vulnerable to the negative experiences of stigma. Discrimination and oppression are importantly more than just the opinions of individual 'bigots', or the views of uncaring or unpleasant people. An understanding of discrimination and oppression must properly locate them as outcomes of social and cultural processes.

Thompson (1993, 2007) has created an especially relevant model that assists social workers to locate discrimination and oppression within these social and political processes. It is called the PCS model, due to its drawing attention to the inter–relationship of the personal (P), cultural (C) and structural (S) elements of discrimination and oppression. The PCS model operates on the sociological premise that we may be individuals, but we are so only in the context of a wider society and culture. How the society and culture in which we live is shaped, its values and norms, its prejudices and structural inequalities (class, gender and ethnicity, for example), influences and informs our individual attitudes and behaviours. Again, it must be underscored that prejudice, discrimination and oppression are not reducible to the ideas of individuals but are fundamentally the properties of specific social and cultural arrangements. Sociology is crucial here in its ability to unlock and explore those social and cultural arrangements. So, in many respects, the structural level is the most important level in the model, as it foregrounds and strongly influences the inner cultural and personal levels.

See also Chapter 4 for application of the PCS model.

So how do all the parts of the PCS model fit together and how does one element exert an influence on the others? Thompson (2007) points to the critical role that ideology plays in doing so. Ideology provides a justification for the dominant ideas of a particular society and maintains the various social structures and inequalities of that society. So, for example, in contemporary British society capitalist ideology maintains that we need managers to run our businesses. It is also important to note that ideology, as a concept, does not simply refer to ideas, but also to how ideas shape people's lives and becomes the weft-and-weave of an everyday common-sense understanding of social relationships. Such social relationships between people, and between people and institutions, can therefore come to be seen as 'natural', even though they are instances of social construction, and therefore do not have to be that way. What sociology can provide, as we discussed in the opening chapter, is a critique of ideology that can highlight the inequalities it can mask.

Thompson (2007) in his most recent work has warned, however, against the misuse of his model, and care should be taken as to how the PCS is mobilized in attempting to analyse a particular issue. There is, he observes, a tendency to use the PCS model in an oversimplistic, if not reductionist, way. There is nothing automatic about how the levels of the model speak to each other, for example. Just because an oppressive or discriminatory value is bound up in the structural levels of society this does not mean that everyone at a personal level will mindlessly follow this. The PCS model also does not – and neither was it intended to by Thompson – provide an 'instant' and exact analysis but rather acts as a *guide* for deeper reflection on social work practice when dealing with the challenges and contradictions of what is a highly complex and contradictory world.

Since the PCS model draws heavily on our sociological knowledge of society, it can therefore provide a useful and real example of how sociology can inform social work practice, the importance of which is useful in relation to anti-discriminatory and anti-oppressive practice. Unlike the concept of 'non-discriminatory practice', there is an active meaning attached to 'anti-discriminatory practice' with a clearly understood professional responsibility to identify, and actively *challenge*, acts that are discriminatory in their effect (Scottish Social Service Council Code of Practice, 2005). Through the application of the PCS model, it is possible to evaluate aspects of practice more systematically. The PCS model is more fully outlined below, illustrated by a reference to mental distress.

ACTIVITY

What for you would be the difference between being non-discriminatory and being anti-discriminatory in your practice?

Personal

This aspect of the PCS model refers to situations that occur at the personal level that involve the social worker in practice. A possible situation may be that a service user with a history of mental illness has been unsuccessful with a job application and is of the opinion that this failure is because he/she had disclosed their medical history. Such discrimination on the grounds of mental illness falls within the scope of the Disability Discrimination Act (DDA) 1995. Such actions are illegal, and there are legal recourses to challenge acts of discrimination. The example points to the positive use of legislation to protect and promote the legal rights of people. Sometimes what is highlighted by the DDA 1995 is the way that mental health legislation can be experienced as oppressive, such as the use of compulsory treatment orders. However, anti-discrimination legislation in this context can also be experienced as empowering (Dalrymple and Burke, 2006), in that not only is an injustice addressed but also the service user can experience a real sense of being recognized as a citizen. Some of the benefits of being Sectioned (made subject to the statutory provisions of mental health legislation) are explored in the lived experience focus. It is for this reason that social work students will receive a considerable amount of training in the law. Knowledge of the law can then be used by social workers to inform and advise service users as to what is meant by discrimination and how a recourse by the law may be achieved. The role of professional advocacy in social work is also highlighted here, and how social workers can use their position to put the case for their service user to other professionals or those in authority positions.

ACTIVITY

Read Chapter 8 on disability for further information on advocacy.

Another very important aspect to be aware of at the personal level of the PCS model is the significance of the impact of stigma, as outlined in the sociology focus, on the person. A key task of the social worker is, through conversation with the service user and others, to preserve and promote the person's self-determination and control over their life. In practice doing so requires a great deal of sensitivity. Attitudes of service users may range from mental illness being something you do not speak about with friends and colleagues, to mental illness being just like any other illness and it is best to be open about it. Another consideration is that a person may take their diagnosis too literally and so may, over a period of time, behave in ways that will conform to the stereotype of a schizophrenic, for example.

Cultural

The cultural aspect of the PCS model refers to how dominant social values are created and maintained, often through the use of stereotypes perpetuated in all aspects of culture, whether in the media, in films or in children's stories, for instance. Language is the key medium for transmitting these values because language is never neutral and frequently refers to power relationships in wider society. As we noted in the sociology focus, there are many negative cultural representations of mental illness and people who experience mental distress. The symbolic associations are with evil or danger on one hand, or with people who are just weak-willed and need to 'pull themselves together'. A straightforward implication, therefore, is that social workers need to avoid language that may be devaluing or judgemental, and should always try to adopt respectful and inclusive language. In the lived experience we explore one example of a social worker who was judgemental of a service user's abilities. She was deemed to be too weak and incapable of fulfilling her role as a parent on the basis that she had a mental illness.

ACTIVITY

Again, look at Chapter 8 on disability for a discussion of the importance of language in describing and classifying forms of oppression and discrimination in society.

Social networking is relevant here by way of informing service users and their families as to local and national anti-stigma groups and organizations (such as See Me Scotland). This approach involves various strands of activity that are aimed at challenging negative and inaccurate stereotypes whilst at the same time promoting the message to the whole population that these issues could affect any one of us. One activity, for example, has been to provide guidance to the National Union of Journalists and newspaper editors as to responsible way of reporting events that might involve persons with mental illness.

Structural

This is referring to socio-political processes that take place at national and local level. Although this may appear distant from day-to-day practice, it is arguably the very structures and procedures adopted by agencies that impact on the processes used by social workers and these *may* have the effect of creating an unequal effect. Therefore what is being described is sometimes called institutionalized discrimination. What does this mean? Help with this comes from the MacPherson Report (1999), which was the result of an Inquiry that was held into the racist murder of Stephen Lawrence. The report developed a definition of 'institutionalized racism' which was as follows:

> The collective failure of an organization to provide an appropriate and professional service to people because of their colour, culture or ethnic origin. It can be seen or detected in processes, attitudes and behaviour which amount to discrimination through unwitting prejudice, ignorance, thoughtlessness, and racist stereotyping which disadvantages minority ethnic people. (MacPherson, 1999)

ACTIVITY

Consider the above definition of institutional racism. Then reflect on the systems operated by professionals and service providing agencies in the mental health field. Do you think there is a similarity with regard to 'processes, attitudes and behaviours' that could create a form of institutional discrimination against people experiencing mental distress?

Some concrete examples of institutionalized discrimination in relation to health generally will include the operation of eligibility criteria; these may privilege the situation of some social groups over other social groups. Or an unwitting assumption may be made that in the course of carrying out an assessment of need that informal female carers will assume the major caring role for a relative. As a result of that value-laden assumption, the view is taken by agencies that formal services do not require to be financed and provided as the work is being done already and, effectively, for free.

In relation to mental distress we can see that the operation of the benefits system also works in a way that locks people into the status of being a 'psychiatric case'. For example, to continue to receive invalidity benefit requires a person to be medically assessed and in this situation to provide evidence of symptoms of mental distress. This may be in sharp contrast to progress being made towards an independent life and so this institutional check may impede the process of personal recovery.

Implications for Social Work Practice

What the above discussion of the PCS model strongly indicates is that social workers have to address wider social and cultural processes. Adopting a rights-based approach whereby the well-being and civil rights of a client are safeguarded is therefore a suitable response for meeting this challenge. A rights-based approach is also congruent with the Code of Practice underscoring the need for social workers to have not only core legal knowledge, but also an understanding as to how this can positively benefit their client (Dalrymple and Burke, 2006). For example, mental distress falls within the scope of the Disability Discrimination Act 1995 and so discrimination imposed on a person with an identified mental illness is an illegal act, and as such is open to challenge. As part of the practice process, a social worker can be both pro-active and challenging.

Anti-stigma work is a significant professional activity and can be carried out in relation to each of the three levels–personal, cultural and structural–as identified in the PCS model outlined above. It is important to recognize the impact of stigma on the person and so a key task is to work to preserve the 'personhood' of the service user through enhancing personal agency. Sociological knowledge is so useful as, by drawing on the works of Goffman and others, this provides real insight into the personal experiences of those subject to a stigmatizing process, as indicated in the previous sociology focus.

Respectful conversations with the person in which a sensitive use of language is important can be one method for reducing the effects of stigma with an individual client. The distinction between the person and 'the mental health problem' is made at all times, and so, by avoiding the phrase 'your depression' and referring to 'the depression', opportunities can

The British Association of Social Workers (2002), in its Code of Practice, sets out five principles:

- Human dignity and worth.
- Social justice.
- Service to humanity.
- Integrity.
- Competence.

The Code of Practice for registered social service workers in the UK (SSSC) requires that social service workers must:

1 Protect the rights and promote the interests of service users and carers.
2 Strive to establish and maintain the trust and confidence of service users and carers.
3 Promote the independence of service users while protecting them as far as possible from danger or harm.
4 Respect the rights of service users while seeking to ensure that their behaviour does not harm themselves or other people.
5 Uphold public trust and confidence in social services.
6 Be accountable for the quality of their work and take responsibility for maintaining and improving their knowledge and skills.

Figure 7.3   *Key ethical and value statements for social workers*

be created for the person to consider how they can exert influence over the problem. Social workers are also ideally located within and across organizations to mediate and to promote a culturally-appropriate message through the use of positive symbolic language.

The promotion of social networking (Hothersall et al., 2008) is relevant to consider here as social workers should have up-to-date information about local and national anti-stigma groups. This information can easily be shared with service users and carers. However, there is more to it than that, and a social worker can also enable people to access these supports and resources whether these be local meetings or joining in with an online community. Such activities help to create social cohesion through the building of social capital. In the sociology focus the work of Wilkinson indicated the potential positive effects of being involved in a cohesive society or community. To do this we need to understand the nature of empowerment (Mackay, 2007) through an identification of the barriers and then supporting people to exert control and take appropriate actions.

Social work values and ethics

You might be wondering why social work places such stress on ethical and value statements, as summarized in Figure 7.3. If you refer ahead to the service user's contribution and the experiences she relates, then we can begin to understand why ethics and values are of such importance. Her comments are significant when she reflects on the different impacts that two social workers have made upon her and comments: 'your role of being a social worker can give you much power, but remember that power should not be wielded as a threat'.

ACTIVITY

Reflect on this statement. Look up the Code of Practice for social service workers and identify those requirements that relate to the exercise of professional authority and power.

The service user's statement is a timely reminder that, as social workers, we need to exercise authority in a purposeful and sensitive manner that does not remove from people a sense of autonomy and self-determination. Adopting a partnership approach to the service users and carers we work with provides the means by which this ambition can be met. This process involves social workers in orientating themselves not as experts but as active listeners with a knowledge as to how professional and organizational systems operate. And by contributing to a collaborative process in which the service user can gain confidence by telling and sharing stories with an accepting listener the service user can find their own voice and can also be supported to make sense of their experience at different levels (Mackay, 2007). Further to this point, the service user contributor comments that with the second social worker her confidence grew as a result of his 'non-judgemental approach'. By acting in such a non-judgemental manner social workers can initiate processes that can lead to a service user experiencing a greater level of control and thus becoming able to take charge of their journey into well-being.

Working in partnership also involves effective conversations with *the service user* about the diagnosis, in which the person can be supported to be well informed about the diagnosis and what this might mean. The use of booklets and reliable websites is most useful here. This method can be a useful basis to explore with the person the meaning they ascribe to the diagnosis and how this might impact on their own self-perception, and is often influenced by the stigma attached to particular diagnoses, such as 'Schizophrenia' and 'Borderline Personality Disorder'.

The implications for social work practice include adopting the value position of offering authentic respect to the person and making a commitment to collaborating with partner agencies and fellow professionals. It is necessary that a social worker understands the psychiatric language not only to follow the conversation but also to contribute to inter-disciplinary discussions. This adoption of technical language does not mean that a social worker has to mimic psychiatry when working within this area. Indeed a social worker can know the psychiatric language without necessarily subscribing wholly to this medical paradigm, the issues of which were discussed in the sociology focus.

Lived Experience

The following account is from a woman who has experienced mental distress over a number of years. She lives independently and maintains her contact with psychiatric services. Here she shares her experiences of hearing voices and the severe impact this has had upon her. She offers reflections on her experiences of being detained in hospital and also her encounters with social work.

As you read her account it would be useful to consider the issues that have been discussed in both the sociology and the social work focus. Doing so should help you relate what can seem quite abstract theories and concepts to individual people.

The following prompts should prove helpful:

- Reflect on which of the main sociological theories best makes sense of her experiences.
- Reflect on why social workers need to abide by a strict ethical code when working with people who are experiencing some form of mental illness.
- Identify which of the health and social care professionals follow either the medical or social models of health.
- Discuss why society may hold negative images about mental distress and illness.

I knew the night before what I must do! The monster spoke clearly to me. I heard its every word. It puzzled me though, because no one else seemed to hear him – only me! I couldn't understand that – it made no sense to me! He wanted to kill my son – and no one could hear his threats except me. I love my son! I love my son more than life itself, and so, I knew what I had to do. The monster had to be destroyed, and, since the monster was inside my head, then it meant that I had to die. I had to die so that my son could live!

And so, I left the ward, and began my journey to the end. It was strange; I felt no fear, only an immense feeling of nothingness. My struggle was to end. I was going to kill this cruel, evil tormentor. I was going to save my son, and save my soul!

The journey was a blur. I seemed to be walking on auto-pilot. One moment I was on the ward, the next I was at the pier. The pier had a small lighthouse at the end – far out to sea, and surrounded by plenty of rocks. There would be no mistake, and it felt good! The monster spoke to me – 'Yes, this is what you must do. If you do not do this, I will kill your son!' The pier was protected by a gate, surrounded by barbed wire; obviously put there to stop people going onto the pier! Ha! Did they really think they could stop me! I climbed the gate – I felt no pain! And then I walked to the end of the pier. The waves crashed below me. What a relief to finally be here. The monster told me that if I jumped it would leave me forever. My son would no longer be in danger! And so I jumped! And I felt the pain; the intense searing pain of bones breaking! And I was drowning; I couldn't stand – my back and leg were broken! I could only swallow the water as it slowly dragged me to an endless sleep!

And then there was nothing! The voice was defeated! Nothing, until I woke up, surrounded by monitors, wires and drips. I was in hospital! And then I heard him again! The monster spoke to me again! He laughed at me! He laughed and mocked me! 'Ha ... did you really think you could escape me?'

And I thought that I had truly died to all hope!

Being Sectioned

I was lying in the spinal bed, having been admitted to hospital after my suicide attempt, when two men in suits arrived. They asked me who I was, and when I answered, they told me that they were from the Sheriff Court, and that they were presenting me with documents called a Section 18.

They then told me that this meant that I was confined to hospital and the care of my consultant for six months. Not only would this prevent my ability to discharge myself from hospital, it would also mean that I could be given treatments, e.g. drugs, against my will.

The above sounds, and was, at times, a traumatic experience for me. There were indeed times when I was forcibly given drugs against my will, which I found frightening. However, there were actually many benefits from being Sectioned, which may sound surprising!

First, the Section gave me a sense of safety. It meant that the staff could take care of me, when I was clearly unable to look after myself. I was still hearing voices telling me to kill myself, but being Sectioned meant that I couldn't leave, and the ward, being a locked ward, offered me little chance to kill myself there.

The Section also meant that I was ill, and slowly, as my psychosis subsided, I began to understand that I had been very, very ill. Ill enough to want to die! Although I didn't always like taking them, the medication had been helping, and as the 'fog' cleared from my brain, I began to see that life was worth living again. Had I not been on the Section, I would have been free to leave the hospital, and would most likely have committed suicide. The Section afforded me the chance of recovery.

In all, I spent 11 months on Section.

Social Work Encounters

My first encounter with social workers came about as a concern about how and where my son would be cared for. He had initially been staying in the hospital with me, but this was no longer deemed appropriate, due to the high number of patients on the ward. There were concerns about his safety there.

My first encounter with social work, with its emphasis on my child's safety, left me feeling traumatized and emotionally bruised. I was highly suspicious of social work in general, and also very scared; scared of the power that social work wielded. At any time social workers could decide to take my child away from me and that left me feeling powerless.

However, he [the social worker] was replaced a few months later and the second social worker could not have been more different. He was supportive and right from the outset said that his role was to support and enable me as a mother who happened to have mental health difficulties. He organized, once I left hospital, for my son and I to attend a local Family Centre. There my son got nursery care, whilst I attended classes on parenting skills. Having been in hospital for a year, this was very helpful. Through his non-judgemental approach and support, I felt empowered and my confidence began to grow. So much so that, as my fears of losing my son began to decrease, I felt able to ask for more help when I felt my mental health was deteriorating!

For social work students reading this, I would ask that you consider the differences in approach of the two social workers I was involved with. It is vital that you first see and understand your clients as people before a condition such as mental illness.

Your role of being a social worker can give you much power, but remember that that power should not be wielded as some kind of threat. Rather, by enabling your client to work with you, a much better relationship, and thus a better outcome, can be achieved.

Further Reading

Useful introductory texts on the sociology of health are as follows:

Barry, A-M. and Yuill, C. (2008) *Understanding the Sociology of Health: An Introduction*. London: SAGE.
Nettleton, S. (1995) *The Sociology of Health and Illness*. Cambridge: Polity Press.

More specific social work material can be found in the following:

Hothersall, S., Maas-Lowit, M. and Golightley, M. (2008) *Social Work and Mental Health in Scotland*. Exeter: Learning Matters.

8
Disability

Chris Yuill, Colin Keenan and
Frankie McLean

Key themes

- Disability is experienced by many people in society.
- How disability is conceptualized directly influences social work practice.
- The causes of disability are to be found in social attitudes and a denial of social justice, though this does not exclude individual physical and psychological suffering.
- Disabled people have many identities and do not solely perceive themselves as being 'disabled'.
- Social workers have to negotiate the tensions of providing support for an individual but not **individualizing** the socially created problems disabled people encounter.

Keywords

Social model of disability, medical model of disability, disabled people, identity

Introduction

There are many people with some form of disability or life-limiting illness in the United Kingdom, and working with disabled people, carers, extended family and support services is a major activity of social work. Problems associated with disability may often be very visible to people generally, but often, especially to those who are able-bodied, the problems may be less obvious or apparent, or indeed, hidden. To a disabled person there are challenges to be met possibly, on, a surprising number of fronts.

The complexities of defining and conceptualizing disability form the main focus of this chapter. Various debates concerning the causes and experiences of disability are outlined, but the fundamental point that underscores this chapter is that disability is not simply a negative state of physical difference. Disability should instead be regarded as a multi-dimensional concept that applies to many different levels of human existence. Having an understanding of disability as a concept is vitally important for social workers working with disabled people. It is from how a situation or relationship is understood that working relationships are built and the form and delivery of services is shaped.

Terminology

Words and names are not neutral entities, and a whole series of power relationships can evolve when particular names or certain expressions are applied often to minority social groups. For example, Bauman (1989) discusses how in the Second World War one technique the Nazis developed to demonize Jewish people was to describe them as subhuman, and how in the Vietnam War American soldiers invoked racist terminology to refer to Vietnamese people. The effect of engaging in reordering people's status, he argues, is to reduce the humanity of that group. In doing so, the diminution or belittling of the target or minority group can sanction a transgression of, or allow, as it were, others to transgress their rights as human beings and permit(s) a range of violence. This process creates an 'othering', whereby a group of people cease to become part of society, and, in turn, become the enemy, the excluded and not to be trusted or accepted and treated with disdain. As the French philosopher Foucault maintained, power is often applied through the categorizing and naming of groups that makes them visible. Once made visible by having a category applied to them, a minority can be open to social marginalization.

The negative labelling of disability, and the consequences that flow from it, are why vigorous disputes exist around the terminology used to describe disabled people with disabilities. It is not an empty exercise in 'political correctness', but rather an important and serious move to redress some of the discrimination facing people with disabilities. In the past, terms such as 'cripple', 'handicapped' or 'retarded' have been used in both official and everyday discourses. As such, their effect is to reorder people with disabilities as 'the other', as a group who are not worthy of acceptance or full social inclusion. A certain dehumanizing is also inherent within these terms, as notions of individuality or personhood are absent. Instead an undifferentiated catch-all category that reduces the varied experiences of disability to a homogeneous block of the social other is advanced.

The terms being used in this chapter are 'disabled person' and 'people with disabilities'. These maintain the human or 'person' aspect of disability, while not losing sight of the reason why this particular group of people is discriminated against.

ACTIVITY

Identify other words or expressions that possess implicit power relationships denoting the inferiority of a particular group of people.

Sociology Focus

Conceptualizing Disability

Until fairly recently the standard approach to discussing approaches in understanding disability would have centred on the differences between what were termed 'the medical model of disability' and 'the social model of disability'. The essential difference between the two is that the former depicts disability as being located in the individual and understandable only in the context of a medical and biological framework, while the latter posits disability as emerging out of the discriminatory and prejudicial attitudes of society with social justice being necessary to bring about equal participation for people with disabilities. There has been a discussion and attempt of late to refine this dualistic approach in order to develop a more nuanced understanding of the dynamics and experience of disability. What those developments are will make better sense once the two models mentioned above are outlined in greater detail below.

DEFINITION

The **medical model of disability** refers to a negative understanding of disability that focuses on physical difference and individualizes problems. The **social model of disability** conversely locates disability as emerging out of discriminatory social attitudes and a lack of social justice.

The medical model of disability perceives this as being a personal tragedy with disability being the result of deformed and damaged limbs. The disabled person is therefore in a fairly helpless position and reliant upon the intervention of health and social care professionals in order to realize an acceptable standard of living. As such, this approach to disability is heavily medicalized, with all the dimensions of disability reduced to the biological and physical.

The social model, on the other hand, stresses that disability emerges out of social prejudice, discrimination and a lack of social justice. Disability is, therefore, located within society and not in the individual. An important element of the social model is the distinction made between *impairment* and *disability* and how those terms are defined. The Union of the Physically Impaired Against Segregation (UPIAS) (1976, pp. 3–4) provide a useful example of a social model rendering of impairment and disability:

> **Impairment:** Lacking part or all of a limb, or having a defective limb, organ or mechanism of the body.
>
> **Disability:** The disadvantage or restriction of activity caused by a contemporary social organization which takes no or little account of people who have physical impairments and thus excludes them from participation in the mainstream of social activities.

What should be immediately apparent in the above definition is that there is no direct linkage made between impairment and disability – the former does not lead to the latter. Instead, what is disabling is the societal reaction to impairment. This is an important and thought-provoking point to make. Disability now resides in society and not in the person. To improve the social position of a person with disabilities it is not they who have to change and adapt, it is society that has to change and transform prevailing negative attitudes and other barriers that exclude disabled people from exercising their full participation in society. By decoupling impairment from disability the social model has made an important conceptual and political shift away from traditional and individualized accounts of disability evident in the medical model of disability.

ACTIVITY

Why do you think it is important to place disability in a wider social context?

It is useful to explore further the discrimination and prejudice experienced by disabled people. One notable and negative aspect of modern society is the existence of various forms of prejudice, discrimination and oppression. Racism, sexism and sectarianism are examples of these processes, where people are treated in a certain way on the false grounds that skin colour, gender or religious heritage implies a lower or inferior social status. To this list we can add 'disablism', the oppression of people with some form of physical 'difference'. This form of oppression, as with the other forms just mentioned, often emerges in an individual's actions and beliefs, but critically it is structural in origin.

This reference to 'disablism' being structural in origin means that negative beliefs about people with a disability are bound up in all aspects of society and are much deeper than simply people's bad attitudes. Those attitudes are supported by negative cultural depictions of disabled people (the popular belief that disabled people are somehow 'inferior' or different to able-bodied people) and the discrimination that disabled people encounter in the workplace and in the built environment. Ultimately, though, they reside in the uneven access to material resources and expressions of power.

The built environment provides a very clear case of the disabling barriers that people with disabilities encounter in their lives. The barriers that disabled people have to negotiate and which create their exclusion are not just an inconvenience. They are also a denial of civil liberties and social justice. Parallels can be drawn with exclusionary societies such as apartheid-era South Africa where black people were denied access to certain buildings and public spaces such as parks and beaches. There is nothing natural or inevitable about the physical built space which we inhabit and in which we go about our daily lives. The way in which buildings and streets come into being is the outcome of decisions made by present and past generations. Acknowledging this understanding of how the built environment has developed leads to two important observations. First, the current built environment represents ingrained social and cultural attitudes and prejudices concerning disabled people. They were not considered in the planning and building of previous buildings and public spaces and as such are excluded from accessing such environments today. Second, if the built environment is the outcome of people's past and present decisions, then future decisions can reshape the built environment, making it barrier-free and fully accessible. A call for a totally inclusive environment should not be thought of as simply being restricted to ramps and railings and other instances of adaption, but rather as a total re-think of the built environment, where a variety of users and not just able-bodied people have their needs represented and acted upon (Imrie, 1996, 2006).

Many of the popular objections to barrier-free housing, such as building or conversion costs or the demand for them, can be easily dismissed. Costs are minimal and demand may be low due to the extent of the exclusion deterring disabled people from using public buildings and spaces in the first place.

ACTIVITY

Think about the buildings you frequently use. How accessible for people with disabilities are they? What could be done to make them more accessible?

There are also many examples of the negative stereotyping of disabled people in 'popular' and 'high' culture. Possessing some form of physical difference is a common technique of denoting that a character is evil or dangerous, for example. This approach is evident in many children's fairy tales, and especially so in the original Brothers Grimm versions, from which many of today's tales are derived. Wicked witches and characters such as Rumpelstiltskin are often 'deformed' or 'hunchbacked'. One could also argue that the association between physical difference and being evil remains today. The classic James Bond villain Blofeld is facially scarred, for example. Even though there was probably no deliberate intention to provide negative stereotypes of people with disabilities, what is important is that there is a cultural association with bodily difference and being apart from good society.

ACTIVITY

Identify other examples of negative stereotyping in popular culture.

Updating the social model?

Various commentators have recently been re-evaluating the social model of disability, but not in order to dismiss it or to reverse the social model's main insight that social discrimination is integral to an understanding of

the causes of disability. It is, rather, to refine and further explore not just
the structural elements of disability, but also the personal experiences of
disability. The reasons for this current disquiet are to be found in the gen-
esis of the social model of disability as a concept. Its roots lie in the disability movement of the 1960s and early 1970s. This time is significant as other
oppressed minority groups, such as women, ethnic minorities, and gay and
lesbian people, were self-organizing in an attempt to gain greater equality
and win fundamental civil rights. One has to appreciate that many of the
rights that we currently take for granted are actually historically quite
recent. Because of his skin colour, the father of Barak Obama, for example,
may have been barred from entering certain restaurants in the 1950s in
Washington DC, the city where his son was inaugurated as President in
2008 nearly sixty years later. Without the political agitation of certain
militant groups in the 1960s and early 1970s, the barriers that prevented
black people, women and other groups from enjoying the rights they currently possess may never have been realized. As such, the social model
shares much with other political movements, and their ideologies and
understandings of the world were forged in this political turbulent time.
The main similarity according to Tom Shakespeare (2006) is a tendency to
engage in polemic. At the time this approach was perfectly valid, if not
highly necessary in advancing emancipatory agendas. In terms of disability
the main polemical point that was advanced was that disability was social
and not physical in cause. Having that point central to the message greatly
advanced the social position of disabled people. The causes of disability
could therefore be overcome not by the interventions of the medical
establishment but by a raft of legislation that outlawed discrimination in
housing, employment and in society generally. This approach to disability
is evident in legislation such as the Disability Discrimination Act, though
doubts have been raised as to how effective such legislation is in practice.

As such the social model of disability was a massive step forward (and
one very far from completion in many respects!) for people with disabilities.
Politically then, the social model was highly effective. As a sociological tool,
or as a concept for fully understanding, it requires further refinement,
though without abandoning the central premise of locating disability in its
social context. One consequence of the political focus of the social model
was that the personal aspects of disability, and the subjective experiences
and cultural interpretations of impairment and disability, were given little
or secondary attention. This lack of attention on these elements of disability has arguably served to inhibit the social model from reaching a full and
complete understanding of disability. Tom Shakespeare (2006), for example,

has raised the important, but highly problematic, issue of the biological and physical basis of disability and why considering it is necessary in order to acknowledge some linkage between impairment and disability. He, and Williams (1999) also, have both claimed that the emphasis on the social aspects of disability ignores the fact that, as with all people, those with a disability are embodied physical beings. As such humans experience emotions, pain and joy. It is that capacity individually to feel pain and suffering that is absent in the social model. By allowing the body back in, so to speak, this does not concede to the medical model of disability that physical impairment is causal in disability. As Williams has argued, the body is social as well as biological; much of what we do with our bodies (for example, projecting and performing our sense of self) can only be understood with reference to social processes.

ACTIVITY

Discuss the advantages and disadvantages of the social model of disability.

It is therefore perhaps more useful to perceive disability as emerging out of a range of multi-dimensional processes that are primarily social and cultural but also physical and biological. However one may conceive disability, it is clear from current debates that a succinct and all-embracing model that encompasses all aspects of disability has yet to be formulated, but meanwhile the fundamental case that disability is much more than simply a biological difference and 'defect' is inescapable.

Disability and Identity

One recent turn in disability studies has been to examine issues of identity for disabled people, that is, what it means to be disabled and also how having a disability relates to other aspects of identity and the self. The wider sociological material on identity to be found in the work of Giddens (1991) or Jenkins (2008), for example, highlights the same point—that identities are not singular but plural and fluid not static. This observation means that we can be many different 'selves' both in our daily lives and throughout our lives and that we can occupy and perform many different identities depending on the context and situation. At this moment, one aspect of your identity may be that of a student, but you will also have an identity that relates to your gender, ethnicity, cultural tastes and so on. Identities are the outcome of two processes. On one hand, there are influences beyond our immediate control such as where we live, our ethnic heritage or our social class, and on the other hand there are the choices we make in deciding our tastes and what we want to do. Both processes influence each other and what becomes our individual identity emerges out of those two processes.

Atkin et al. (2002) provide a useful example of the nuances and subtleties of disabled people and identity, which expands on the issues outlined above. A multiplicity of identities was found in their work with young South Asian deaf people. Having a disability was definitely one element of the young people's identity in that they perceived themselves as being disabled but their sense of who they were did not stop there. They also articulated the complexities of British and Asian national and cultural identities, as is common throughout the Asian community in the UK, regardless of having a disability or otherwise. And like other people they also identified themselves with youth cultures.

A useful lesson for social workers here is that disabled people do not perceive themselves as possessing and as being preoccupied with nothing but a disabled identity. It is but one aspect of their identity among many others. Olney and Brockelman (2003) have also found that identity exists in relation to the environment or situation in which people find themselves. People with disabilities may perceive themselves as disabled in one context but not in another. A student may perceive him/herself as disabled by the lack of support, but not in another situation where it is not needed. The availability and access to resources can in itself be of major significance to whether people see themselves as disabled or not.

ACTIVITY

Reflect on your own identity. In what ways has your identity more than just one aspect to it?

Disability is a common way of being for many people in society. What is incontrovertible about disability is that much that is causal in creating disability is to be found in the social and not in biological 'defects'. Social attitudes, prejudice and discrimination all create a society that is not accepting of a body that does not accord with that depicted in able-bodied discourses. As a consequence, disabled people are marginalized and excluded from society, for example, either located in poorly paid employment or not employed at all. This situation is not simply a state of affairs that is unfortunate or regrettable, but is actually also a denial of civil liberties and human rights. The social model of understanding of disability has made a great contribution in advancing a positive agenda for disabled people that shifts the causes away from individual bodies to societal failings. Much of what would bring about positive change for people with disabilities lies in reversing those social failings and building a fully inclusive society.

Social Work Focus

The previous sociology section has emphasized the fundamental social basis of disability, which is that disability is not purely to do with the limbs and bodies of people with disabilities being somehow 'different', and that it is not only at a biological level that disability can be understood and conceptualized. However, by accepting that disability is social, we create a potential tension for social work practice. As the introductory chapter explored, social work is often carried out on an individual basis, where the social worker spends time working one-to-one with a client. If one accepts that disability is social in origin and not to do with a biological 'misfortune', then working with individuals is at odds with this approach. At worst, by working individually with a person with disabilities, the social worker could inadvertently replicate the processes and attitudes that are causal of disability in the first place. By interacting with the disabled person as if the problems and issues that face the disabled person are the disabled person's problem, the potential consequence is that the disabled person must adapt and change, not society. This problematic tension forms a substantial theme for the rest of this chapter as it examines the interactions between social work and disabled people.

Given the extent of the barriers and obstacles that society creates for people with disabilities, social workers may be called upon to provide and offer support and assistance. Quite often such social work involvement is also offered as much for those around the person with the disability, such as parents or informal caregivers, as for the person him- or herself. People who provide support and care for disabled people often face difficult circumstances themselves, such as poverty and a reduced income, because they give up their time to look after someone else.

The following examples illustrate some of the circumstances in which a social work intervention may be offered:

- Where there are social or structural barriers that make it difficult for disabled people to live their lives as they would want. Such barriers may be financial, social, including problems with the built environment, emotional or any combination, and, in such circumstances, the service user may engage the assistance of an advocate.
- Where someone with a disability is receiving a service that is not related to disability, for example, because of a court appearance the service user is referred as part of the criminal justice system, or a referral has been made because of child care or protection needs. A profoundly deaf service user may require a specialist service for interpreting purposes in such situations.
- Where the experience of living within a disabling society creates challenges or problems. For example, facing exclusion or experiencing stigma on a daily basis may produce emotional reactions such as depression, relationship difficulties and more. Stigma may be experienced by both the disabled person and the carer, and Hobdell et al. (2007) found that parents, particularly mothers, of children with epilepsy experienced a stigma that was attached to the diagnosis of epilepsy itself.
- Where a major change in family or social circumstances dictates a change in living arrangements, for example someone with learning difficulties who has lived with his/her parents is now at a point where the parents are unable to continue to ensure the levels of safety or support they previously have and different living arrangements need to be considered, or a significant carer dies.

There are three levels (individual, structural and political) on which a social worker may offer support and engage with the requests from a disabled person. These are outlined below and the tension identified earlier between individual (medical model) and social approaches is highlighted throughout.

First, at an individual level, social workers may be involved with interventions of a potentially therapeutic nature that may seek to assist a disabled person to cope with the emotional damage created by living in a disabling society. As recent debates concerning the social model of disability have indicated, the presence of suffering and emotional distress is very real, a consequence of being excluded by society or of impairment. While such an intervention may be justified on the basis of addressing and attempting to reduce an emotional upset, the basis of the intervention may also be helping to sustain a medical model approach to disability, which may simply perpetuate society's stigmatizing attitudes. In effect, this may reinforce the perception that disability is to do with the impaired body of the disabled person. In this respect, it is very important that, as social workers, we do not perpetuate structural inequalities by adopting 'theoretically, narrow interpretations of the problems faced by individual service users' (Fraser and Matthews, 2008, p. 47) and as Woodcock and Tregaskis (2008, p. 66) state, 'social workers need to recognize how their preconceived notions and cultural experiences shape their view of impairment'. This comment underscores why models of disability are vital and why a discussion of models of disability encountered in the sociology section is fundamental to social work practice. There is always a strong link between theory and practice. It is never enough simply to know what to do, it is vital to know and understand *why* one is doing it.

ACTIVITY

Reflect on what the different approaches to disability have made you think about disability. Has your thinking on the subject changed in any way?

Second, it is important that social workers consider the impact of structural and societal factors. Over the past forty years, social work practice has developed an awareness that working with each service user on an individual basis potentially results in the problems being seen as existing within the individual. Again, doing so runs the risk of lapsing into a medical model approach, which ignores the critical influence of wider social attitudes. Implicitly, therefore, by focusing only on the individual it is almost as if the individual is being made to carry responsibilities that are actually based more on structural inequalities within society (Banks, 2001). Principles of empowerment and advocacy are central to work with disabled people in addressing issues of access and entitlement.

DEFINITION

Empowerment refers to the process of ensuring that service users have the opportunity and balance of support to put forward views, to make choices and take decisions, while **advocacy** concerns the support given to service users, including direct intervention, which may include putting forward views and making statements on behalf of service users.

Third, there is a political dimension to the handling of complex issues surrounding the disempowerment and oppression of disabled people. The commitment of social workers to an anti-oppressive approach to practice may lead to a desire to lobby for legislative change and for the development of services organized by the users themselves (Dominelli, 2008). In this case, the question arises as to how far social workers employed within local government organizations are able to engage in a basic challenge to existing political structures. Political activity may place the social worker in difficult legal and contractual positions, and this indicates some of the problems of adopting a fully radical approach to social work.

ACTIVITY

What more radical steps could be taken to tackle the problems experienced by disabled people?

Advocacy

Social work practice incorporates the concepts of advocacy and empowerment. Advocacy is based on ensuring that an individual's rights or interests are expressed, either by the individual or someone or some group representing him or her. Basically, the individual has a difficulty caused by some external factor that requires an assertive challenge. Brandon et al. (1995) highlighted the link between advocacy and the social model of understanding disability, because the process of ensuring that rights and interests are upheld tends to locate the source of difficulty within society or social structures and not in the individual. At this point it is useful to consider advocacy in greater depth.

Many health professionals, lay people or volunteers, organizations in the not-for-profit sector and sometimes service users themselves are actively involved in advocacy in a variety of ways. At its core, advocacy is concerned with the inter-relationship of representation and power. Representation involves acting on behalf of someone (or a body of people) who, for whatever reason, experiences difficulty in, or encounters barriers to, expressing his or her needs, rights or grievances to, or about, a more powerful person or institution. Many different people and groups within the health and social care landscape will use advocacy services or act as advocates, including people with disabilities, people with learning difficulties, mental health users and people with specific chronic conditions.

This need for representation is unfortunately necessary because of the many different, diffuse and complex power imbalances that exist in health and social care. Health and social care professionals hold power by virtue of some of the following factors. All professional groups have a unique knowledge base. The more esoteric or specialist that knowledge base is, the more powerful they can be, as it is only they who can claim unique insights into the causes and cures of certain phenomena. The gatekeeping role of most health and social care professionals serves as another source of power. It is up to a professional to decide whether or not someone is eligible to gain access to certain types of treatment or care. There is also a legal dimension. Health professionals have certain abilities supported by legislation to act in a manner that may be against the wishes of an individual. An obvious, but perhaps extreme, example is the right which psychiatrists hold to place someone in hospital (commonly referred to as Sectioning) on grounds of an individual's mental health posing a threat to that person or others. Social workers must guard against negative professional stereotyping: in executing these powers, professionals are not intrinsically malevolent and are not enacting those powers out of malice or a disregard for the people who seek their help.

The above outline of advocacy captures much of what the concept and the practice are about. As with other concepts in health studies, however, it is always far from being neatly defined and clear-cut. This situation exists, in part, due to the varied nature of advocacy. Many different forms of advocacy exist. Each form possesses its own distinctive advantages and disadvantages, using distinct social actors from volunteering or professional backgrounds, with or without specialist training or skills, or the resources of a large organization to support their work.

The mental health charity MIND (Kelley, 2005) and Mackay (2007) have usefully identified the main forms that advocacy can take. These include, but are not restricted to, the following:

- **Self-advocacy:** where the person represents themselves and advances their own issues with and to another party.
- **Group advocacy:** as the title implies, this form of advocacy exists on a collective basis. Individuals combine with others who share some form of commonality or a common purpose. Claims and representation here are made on behalf of the group.
- **Peer advocacy:** this can be an equal form of advocacy as it involves someone who has had direct experience of a particular service representing someone who is currently using that service.
- **Professional, or paid advocacy:** as with other areas of the not-for-profit sector, there has been a professionalization of services, with advocates being trained and salaried by national charities, or independent organizations, for example.
- **Citizen advocacy:** involves a member of a local community being trained to assist someone else in their community. This support is often on a long-term basis.

The rise in advocacy in all its forms needs to be seen in relation to wider changes and processes in society. Fundamentally, the idea and practice of advocacy existing at all are dependent on the models of liberal citizenship that exist in Western nations. An essential feature of Western democracies is that people are no longer posited as passive subjects of a feudal monarch, who must unquestioningly obey their superiors, but rather as active citizens of a state who possess certain rights that are incumbent on the state to uphold and protect. The idea, then, of being able to speak out for oneself or on behalf of someone else emerges from this democratic impulse.

The particular growth of advocacy during the 1980s and onwards is further reflected in the public ideologies of the Conservative and Labour parties during their terms of office (Redley and Weinberg, 2007). The Conservatives throughout the 1980s and early 1990s sought to diminish the state as much as possible, emphasizing individual self-help and self-reliance instead. This approach is evident in policies such as *Patient First*. Key to this policy was an ambition to redefine people who used health and social care services as consumers of health and social care services as opposed to being patients in a hospital or long-term care institution. A noticeable power shift between user and professional is inherent within this move. Regarding, and acting towards, someone as a consumer entails quite a different type of relationship than that which one may have with a patient. The former is imbued with notions of the individual being an active participant in the process with the professional providing a service for them. The latter indicates a passivity where the individual follows what the professional tells them. Such a move to reordering patients as consumers was part of wider social trends in the 1980s, which saw the emergence of an avowedly more consumerist society in Britain.

The Labour party was also keen to promote a more rights–based agenda for health and social care service users. They eschewed the more consumerist aspects of Conservative policy and instead preferred to develop a partnership approach. Users of state services were to input and identify their needs in the development and provision of the services made available to them. Both perspectives offer a slightly different emphasis, but they both acknowledge the importance of 'allowing in' and giving space and importance to the service user or consumer voice.

The self-activity of certain campaign groups also has to be recognized. Disabled people have been actively involved in campaigning for social justice in order to redress many of the social barriers that have excluded people with disabilities from being full members of society. The right to speak on one's own behalf and to participate in equal relationships with professionals were key demands of disability rights activists (see Oliver, 1990; Swain et al., 2005).

The advantages of advocacy have been implicit in the discussion above, the prime advantage being that advocacy allows for people or groups of people to express their needs and wishes. This though does not mean that advocacy, as with any development in health and social care, is without its challenges or issues. Advocacy can set out a quite radical agenda, calling for a redressing of power relationships within a variety of professional and service user encounters. In practice these ambitions are not necessarily fully realized, and professionals, whether on an individual or group basis, can seek to resist or dilute the implications of working in an environment where advocacy exists. For example, the call by some professionals for greater equality and participation can become rhetorical. Lip-service is paid to the ideals, but in practice nothing really changes. Powerful professional groups can adopt the language of being supportive of the interests and rights of their users, ticking the appropriate boxes, but not fully relinquishing their power and status.

Overall, the emergence of advocacy represents an important, but not yet absolute, shift in power in the health and social care landscape between service users and professionals. It is an acknowledgement that professional power is not always inherently positive in its practice and decisions, and that the voice of the individual or the groups who work with a professional have to be heeded and taken into account. As such, advocacy accords with the social model of health. The reasons for the rise of advocacy are to be found by referring to wider and deeper structures and processes in society. Advocacy emerges from democratic principles but its current form has been shaped by political ideology, the self-action of social movements and the rise of a consumerist society.

Empowerment

Empowerment and advocacy may be linked, but they are not the same concept by different names. Empowerment is a key principle of current social work practice and has been defined as 'the capacity of individuals, groups and/or communities to take control of their circumstances, exercise power and achieve their own goals' (Adams, 2008, p. 17). Such a concept fits the social model of disability but directly confronts the medical model. Self-advocacy may well empower the individual or group, whereas professional advocacy may be helpful, but not necessarily empowering. Some organizations that employ social workers may be wholly committed to the principle of empowerment, while others may pay lip-service to the principle, but may also be threatened by the implication of the service user having more power than the representative of the organization.

Range of impact

The disabling attitudes and barriers of society do not impact solely on a persons with disabilities. People with disabilities have families, and the negative impulses of society can cause problems and pose issues for the wider family. This has the potential seriously to alter the quality of life for more people than just for the person who has the disability. Children can face significant difficulties if they have a parent or sibling who is a disabled person. It is impossible to identify every potential issue they may have to confront but according to Barnardo's there are about 175,000 children in the UK who have had to take on significant caring responsibilities for a parent (Barnardo's, 2006).

The following is an excerpt from Emma's account of her experience:

> When my mum is ill, I have to lock all the doors and we are not allowed to answer the phone because she thinks somebody is trying to hurt us and stuff. ... I'm supporting mum. Sometimes I do get a bit annoyed. ... When I follow her to the doctors I wait in the waiting room. I take her but then she has to go in by herself because she goes in and talks and does not want to upset me. I check her medication when she's got home or when she's feeling ill and times like that I have to go and get them personally and make sure she takes them and watch her. (Aldridge and Sharpe, 2007: 13)

In such circumstances it is clearly very difficult for Emma, faced with her mother's mental distress, to lead the life that other young teenagers do. At her age involvement with her peer group is a natural and necessary part of her social and emotional development. She is going to find it hard to maintain the contact with her peers that others do. That already raises the potential for her to be marginalized. If she does not find some peer group to fit in with, she may become a scapegoat by virtue of non-conformity and from being marginalized she may find herself more actively excluded and stigmatized. She may very well need the support that a Young Carers Group can offer. Groupwork may lead to political action, while individual work and advocacy may assist Emma in coping with her current situation. In social work practice there may be no absolutely right or wrong approach, but each intervention must have a clear purpose.

Lived experience

For the lived experience, Frankie McLean, a young man with a hearing impairment, reflects on his experiences as a disabled person, both as a student and as a social worker.

As you read the lived experience it would be useful to consider the issues that have been discussed in both the sociology and the social work focus. Doing so should help you relate what can seem quite abstract theories and concepts to individual people.

The following prompts should prove helpful:

- Reflect on one of the main themes of this chapter concerning balancing the need to interact with disabled people on an individual basis, while not losing sight of the structural causes of disability.
- Discuss which of the sociological theories of disability best explains what is described below.
- Consider how social workers could challenge the structural causes of disability.
- Reflect on advocacy in relation to what is communicated about disability below.

The label 'disabled' can mean many different things and encompass a diverse range of labels. People's experiences of disability and the nature and extent of the barriers that people with disabilities experience in society can vary, and different societies and cultures can differ in their treatment of certain groups. For example, in some countries in the world it is illegal for deaf people to drive, while in others it is perfectly legal!

While de-individualization can be helpful in appreciating general experiences and understanding the very basic needs of particular groups, there is a need to individualize and treat each individual as unique with their own distinct needs that could very well differ from another person who may appear to have the same disability. For instance, the autistic spectrum encompasses a wide range of labels and conditions; ditto for deafness, blindness, physical disabilities and so on. 'A physically disabled man' may get around in a wheelchair, or walk with a limp and struggle with stairs. 'An autistic boy' may dislike eye contact and recoil at physical contact, or he may have poor social development and awkwardness. 'A deaf woman' may mean someone using British Sign Language as her first language, or a woman who wears hearing aids and uses lip-reading and speech to communicate. These are mere examples of a wide range of possibilities. Individualization, therefore, is very important and it would be advisable not to make assumptions. Each person needs to be assessed in their own right, as a unique human being. Bear in mind that some people may not agree with a particular label placed on them, or the label may be wrong – it is the writer's experience that issues with the 'learning disability' label are commonplace and professionals can be quick to label people. Labels can stick, particularly if they are formally recorded, which may then pose problems for the individual at a later time if the label is wrong or inappropriate.

Attitudes play a considerable role in the barriers that people with disabilities face. The 'majority rules' – and since people with disabilities are in the minority with needs and/or features that are not shared by the majority, their needs can be overlooked or ignored. Imagine a society where everybody used sign language – deaf people who use sign language would thus not be disabled on the grounds of their language. It is important to keep an open mind and adopt anti-oppressive practice as the norm, identifying where oppression occurs and challenging it. Not everyone can be wholly knowledgeable about every disability – so if in doubt, ask (appropriately and sensitively, of course!). Being open and honest, admitting to gaps in knowledge, is the best way to appreciate each individual and learn more about him or her. Muddling through and making mistakes or assumptions will not facilitate a good working relationship, and people will usually respond better to situations where they are more involved.

Being patronizing can be as bad as displaying outright, blatant discrimination. There are many other facets to a person other than just the disability, and it is important that maximum possible independence is promoted and the person's abilities and personality respected. Patronizing attitudes can be disempowering and disrespectful, taking away many of the individual's attributes and shifting the focus on to the disability. Mr Smith could be a forty-year-old man who has worked nearly most of his life and is happily married with three children ... and who happens to make use of a wheelchair to get around. To perceive Mr Smith as a 'poor disabled, wheelchair-bound man' does not do justice to his successful career and family life. People with disabilities are perfectly capable of contributing to society in many meaningful ways, and many will do so while others may want to but may also be prevented or discouraged from doing so due to barriers. If everyone were the same, the world would be a very boring place – we should embrace, even celebrate, the diversity of the human population.

There are various policy initiatives and legislation that exist to protect the rights of people with disabilities. The Disability Discrimination Act (DDA) is a good example. However, there are loopholes and, again, attitudes can still play a great part in how the legislation is enacted in real life. The DDA states that 'reasonable adjustments' must be taken – the interpretation of what is 'reasonable' and what is not is key. Adjustments may or may not require resources, and where resources are needed this often means money. Finances are a powerful structural component of the very fabric of today's society. For example, employing a support worker or sign language interpreter can be costly, particularly as this is an ongoing as opposed to a one-off cost. It could be (and frequently is) claimed that this cost is not reasonable, therefore circumventing the DDA. While there are sources of funding available, they may be inadequate or certain criteria might not be met and therefore attitudes do matter a great deal. One university may (legally) refuse to admit a deaf student to a degree course due to the sheer costs involved in paying for a sign language interpreter throughout the duration of the student's six month intensive work placement, but another university may feel obliged to admit that student on the basis of their academic ability, regardless of the costs. If long-term change is to be elicited, and attitudes challenged, there is an acute need to look beyond the financial implications and adopt a long-term view, slowly influencing and changing traditional views and ways of working. The scenario given of the deaf student is a real life example, and the university that accepted the student should be congratulated on its obvious long-term view and readiness to consider the need to challenge society's attitudes despite an obvious financial expense. There needs to be more of this happening if positive change is to come about.

We have spoken of the need to challenge oppression in society (which includes patronizing attitudes) and to keep an open mind. However, it is a fact that some people with disabilities can be quick to take advantage of their disability and use it for unscrupulous purposes. While it is very true that people with disabilities experience disadvantages, in some cases the disability may have little bearing on certain events. For example, it may be argued that a criminal offender who persists in offending should not be allowed to escape the criminal justice system simply because they have a disability. Conversely, it could be argued that society has made that person a criminal because of the disability, and putting them in the criminal justice system would be overly harsh and further oppress them. There is no right or wrong view here, but it clearly works both ways and until people start to question and challenge structural oppression this uncertainty, and unfairness, will persist.

It is also fair to say that many people with disabilities are able to be independent – indeed, many *are* – and more than capable of managing their own lives. Just because they have a disability this does not always necessarily equate to a need for support or 'help', That said, some people with disabilities do need support, in which case they should be involved as far as possible and the support should be at an appropriate level. The 'care versus control' debate is particularly relevant in this case and worth keeping in mind. Having a disability can be extremely isolating and people with disabilities may enjoy the support/care and attention. Whether this is a good thing or not is yet another question that is open to debate. Mention should also be given here to carers – caring for a person with a disability can be hard work, and if it becomes too stressful then the carer may resent the disability, and perhaps subsequently the person. The focus in this case may be to try to minimize the impact of the disability on all those involved as far as possible.

There is clearly a wide range of issues associated with disability. Only a few have been touched upon here, in relatively small detail, the word 'may' has been used frequently, and no clear answers have been given. As social workers, it is important for us to see each individual we come across as being exactly that – individual. We have to be ready to question and challenge preconceptions and fixated, traditional ways; it is only through this that long-term change can be elicited and social justice become more of a reality. One size most certainly does not fit all.

Further reading

A good all-round coverage on contemporary disability issues can be found in:
Shakespeare, T. (2006) *Disability Rights and Wrongs*. London: Routledge.

While a coverage of social work issues can be found in:
Adams, R. (2008) *Empowerment, Participation and Social Work*. London: Palgrave Macmillan.

9

Crime and Society

**Chris Thorpe and
Mike Shepherd**

Key themes

- Ideas of what constitutes crime and what acts are classified as being deviant vary across time and culture.
- Sociological perspectives of crime largely attempt a value-free approach.
- The reasons for committing acts that are seen to be of a criminal nature are largely the result of structural process as opposed to individual psychology or individual 'wickedness'.
- Distinct patterns exist in who commits crime and who are the 'victims' of crime.
- Social work in criminal justice settings is both a political and a moral activity.
- Social work intervention must be realistically aware of an offender's environment.
- The concept of 'social capital' has a major impact on the potential effectiveness of social work intervention.

Keywords

crime, deviance, inequality, structure, value-free, social construction, social capital, criminogenic needs

Introduction

In modern Western societies, the social reality of crime is an inescapable part of everyday life. Vast amounts of resources in the form of time, money and government policy are devoted to trying to manage crime. Because of the prominence of crime for governments, and the very often destructive consequences that criminal behaviour has for individuals and communities, it should come as no surprise that the subject has a long and prominent tradition within sociology. This chapter examines three key topics in the sociology of crime. First, it delineates the most influential theoretical approaches to crime utilized by sociologists. Emphasized here are the ways in which sociological thinking about crime focuses upon the role of broader, and often 'hidden', social structural forces as being essential for understanding why people engage in criminal behaviour. Second, by considering the broader social processes rather than individual psychological factors, the question of why certain types of individuals are more likely to act in ways that are criminal is tackled. Third, and finally, the chapter draws attention to the socially constructed nature of crime and the processes by which individuals as well as certain behaviours come to be viewed and labelled as 'criminal'.

Sociology Focus

Sociological ways of thinking about crime and criminal behaviour differ and are distinct from those of other behavioural scientific disciplines such as psychology, criminology and psychiatry. Whereas, generally speaking, these disciplines take individuals and their unique personality attributes as the starting point for analysis, sociological accounts of crime by contrast concentrate on the social component of an individual's character and behaviour. There are four distinct attributes of sociological accounts of crime and criminal behaviour that differentiate and distinguish the discipline from those just mentioned.

- First, in keeping with sociology's general approach to the objects it studies, sociological theories of crime are *objective*. So whilst acknowledging that crime is real and can effect people's lives in very negative ways, nevertheless sociologists will try to adopt a 'value-free' approach to the study of criminal behaviour.
- Second, and following on from the point above, it is also the case that sociologists are not necessarily concerned with eradicating the *social problem* of crime. It is the job of government officials and policy-makers to decide how best to utilize the findings of sociologists in order to tackle crime.
- Third, sociological theories of crime examine the extent to which *social variables* such as social class location, gender, ethnicity, age, etc. affect the likelihood that an individual will be disposed to commit crime. The point to emphasize here is that people are largely only 'semi-consciously' aware of the social component of their individual actions. It is exactly this element of their behaviour that is of most analytical interest to the sociologist.

- Fourth, central to the sociological apprehension of crime is the view that no behaviour is *inherently* criminal. In other words, what is understood and perceived as 'criminal' is something that varies from one society to another and changes over time – another example of how much in society is the result of social construction. So, for example, smoking marijuana is illegal in Britain because it is classified by the government as a class C drug. In Amsterdam in the Netherlands, by contrast, it is legal to smoke marijuana in certain circumstances.

DEFINITION

Social construction refers to how an everyday aspect of life may be experienced as being 'natural' and as having always existed in the way that it currently does, when instead it is the outcome of particular cultural, social and historical processes existing in a specific society at a particular point in time. This implies that what we accept as normal and natural today was not seen that way by past societies nor will it necessarily be seen that way by future societies.

ACTIVITY

Discuss your reaction to how sociology approaches the study of crime and deviance. What does the sociological approach to crime and deviance have in common with social work approaches to crime and deviance?

Theorizing crime

In researching crime and criminal behaviour, sociologists employ a variety of theories and conceptual tools in order to direct, manage and focus their analyses. There exist a number of influential theories that have been devised in order to try to understand in greater depth how and why crime occurs within society.

Functionalist accounts of crime

Functionalism and functionalist theories concentrate on the ways in which social phenomena and institutions *function* within society. Originating in the work of the founding French sociologist Emile Durkheim, functionalist accounts of crime and social deviance examine the social function that crime plays in the overall maintenance and reproduction of social life. Contrary to commonsense views, Durkheim held that crime was an essential part of any 'healthy' functioning society, providing that the amount of crime did not reach a level that he referred to as 'pathological'. Such a view was justified by Durkheim on the logic of the following four functionalist criteria. First, crime and criminal behaviour stand as a yardstick or gauge against which society measures its sense of moral consensus and shared values. Second, in spite of its destructive consequences, crime increases social solidarity by clarifying and sharpening in people's minds those moral sentiments and shared values that underpin their collective exist-ence. Crime further enhances social solidarity by provoking a common moral reaction from people, who, in denouncing certain forms of behaviour, reaffirm their shared sense of what is right and wrong. Third, crime can often be understood as what Durkheim referred to as 'an anticipation of the morality of the future'. In other words, if society is too rigid and not responsive to changes in the attitudes and ways of living that are characteristic of particular social groups, certain 'criminal' acts might actually be symbolic of a shift in public attitude towards a hitherto unrecognized social problem.

Interactionist and labelling theories

Whereas functionalist perspectives concentrate on the social functions of crime and deviance more generally, labelling perspectives focus on indi-viduals and the social processes by which they come to be identified, understood and labelled as 'criminal'. Central to labelling theories of crime is the notion of 'selfhood' as learnt and acquired by individuals from an early age (Aggleton, 1987 p. 51; Blumer, 1969). As individuals, it is argued, we acquire a sense of self-identity and individuality through our interactions with 'significant others' such as parents and our immediate family, and later on through wider social interactions in the form of school, peer groups, work and so forth (Cooley, 1909). Over time and through our interactions with an ever-widening number and type of people, individuals learn to think about themselves from the 'point of view' of others, enabling them to anticipate and regulate which courses of action are most likely to meet with approval, or more negatively, disap-proval. On this view, individuals internalize the normative values and roles of society which in turn intimately shape the ways in which they see and think about themselves.

A useful example, following Becker (1953), is the adolescent who takes up marijuana smoking. In doing so he commits an act of what is termed 'primary deviance' (Lemert, 1952). As a one-off act, smoking marijuana has no significant influence on his self-perception – the adolescent does not imagine himself as a criminal. If, however, he were to smoke marijuana more frequently until he were eventually apprehended by the police, then this would constitute an act of 'secondary deviance'. Repeated episodes of smoking marijuana and contact with the police may cause him to re-evaluate his sense of self, such that he would begin to think of himself as a criminal. This gradual but definite socially mediated process, whereby the individual's sense of self is transformed as they embark upon a 'deviant career', illustrates that becoming a criminal is something that is learned and takes place over time.

Marxist approaches to crime and New Left theories

The fundamental premise of Marxist and New Left approaches is that it is the structure of modern society itself (specifically modern *capitalist* society) that is the essential root cause of crime (Downes and Rock, 2003; Lea, 2002). For Marx, the defining feature of modern capitalist society was the wholly uneven distribution of material and economic resources, namely property and money, across society, to the extent that a very large percentage of the total social wealth is concentrated in the hands of a very small ruling class. The repercussions of this stark social inequality are that the vast majority of people in society, the working classes, are able to acquire only very little money and very few material possessions. Marxist theories of crime, therefore, emphasize the notion that the social structure itself, namely the class lines along which society is organized, dispose people from the working classes and those below them to commit crime, because they cannot achieve a decent standard of living via legitimate means.

Furthermore, Marxist theories of crime argue that far from representing the will of the people, the state, in fact, serves in the interests of the ruling class, typically because it is the same members of the ruling class that are most likely to occupy positions of power as politicians and government officials. For Marx, this meant that the entire political and legal systems are designed in, and reflect the image of, the interests of the ruling class, and their concern to preserve their wealth and status within society. The role of the criminal justice system and the police then is to ensure that the great majority of society, the working class, is deterred from trying to take back what is theirs by right as the direct product of their own labour.

ACTIVITY

Assess the above sociological perspectives on crime and deviance, identifying the advantages and disadvantages. In what ways do these perspectives make you think about crime and deviance differently?

The social distribution of crime

Whilst criminal behaviour can nearly always be attributed to the willed actions of individuals, almost all crime contains a social component. Depending on the basis of a wide range of social variables, research indicates that certain categories of individuals or social groups are more or less likely to engage in criminal behaviour. In analysing the social distribution of crime the main social factors concerning sociologists are socio–economic (class) status, gender, ethnicity and age.

More information on social class can be found in Chapter 2, and on gender in Chapter 3.

Social class and crime

The relationship between an individual's socio-economic status, or social class position, and their propensity towards crime is a particularly important one for sociologists. It is a widely held assumption in society that people of a lower social-class standing are more likely to commit crime, a belief that tends to be supported by research, both in the form of qualitative interviews with offenders as well as more quantitatively based surveys (Croall, 1998). Whilst, at first appearance, official statistics would appear to suggest a very strong link between social class location and crime, there are various points that need to be looked at before any concrete conclusions can be drawn.

First, it is important to consider that offenders with different class backgrounds are treated and handled very differently by the police and agents of the criminal justice system. In spite of the official rhetoric, not all individuals are dealt with by the legal system in the same way, a situation that can occur at two levels. At one level, if an offender appears to be of working-class origin – perhaps the individual has a strong local accent, dresses in a certain manner, and is already known to the police – then the police and other law enforcement groups may be more likely to make judgements about, and project social stereotypes onto, the moral character of the individual (Aggleton, 1987; Piliavin and Briar, 1964).

At another level, differences in social-class location can be directly translated into differences in the type of crime committed by individuals. So, in parts of inner Manchester, for example, car crime is one of the biggest problems confronted by police on a daily basis, and the perpetrators of car crimes are characteristically of a working-class background (the example of car crime is a good one because it illustrates how differences in material wealth dispose individuals towards certain types of crime). Simply, the chances of a middle-class youth stealing a car are considerably less, because either their parents may have bought them their own car, or they might be in a position to borrow their parents' car.

Conversely, it is not surprising that certain types of financial crime – such as money laundering or fraud – are more likely to be committed by middle-class offenders because certain types of jobs, such as banking or finance accounting, require a degree of education and professional training beyond that of most working-class individuals.

Further pursuing the relationship between differences in types of crime and social class location is the fact that the legal system tends to take a sterner view of acquisitive crimes such as burglary, mugging, or theft, crimes associated with the working class, than it does of 'impersonal' and more middle-class crimes like tax evasion, embezzlement and fraud (Lawson and Heaton, 1999, p. 232). In this very short overview, I have highlighted a few of the main ways in which social-class location is thought to influence an individual propensity towards criminal behaviour. As Croall (1998, p. 100) quite rightly notes, any empirically sensitive and worthwhile discussion of the links between socio-economic status and crime must 'recognize the different offending patterns of different classes'.

Gender and crime

Men, as opposed to women, are more likely to fit with lay-perceptions of a criminal. But do reality and the research reflect this image? According to Pollack (1961), writing almost fifty years ago, women commit more crime than official statistics would have us believe. Moreover, of those crimes that are carried out against men, a large majority go unreported, because men are too embarrassed to report them because of their supposedly dominant status within society. Crimes such as a prostitute stealing her male client's money, or domestic violence where the male is the victim, comprise good examples of such crimes. It is fair to say that the division of criminal labour in society is indeed gendered to the extent that women are less likely to commit crimes including murder, serious violence and corporate crime, but more likely to be convicted for prostitution. Where women do commit crime it is more likely to be for offences such as theft, receiving stolen goods and forgery (Croall, 1998, p. 138). That women are regarded as biologically disposed to be more 'submissive' than men, and thus overall generally more vulnerable, is something that, although highly contested, nevertheless appears to influence crime statistics. Coleman and Moynihan (1996), for example, found evidence that suggested retail managers might be less likely to pursue a prosecution against a woman where that woman was either elderly or pregnant.

Proponents of social control theory argue that the reason why girls commit less crime than boys is because they are subject to a higher degree of social control. Because of their alleged 'vulnerability' girls are more likely to be chaperoned by their parents than boys and are subject to greater control in terms of their use of leisure time. It could further be argued that, as adults, women are still more likely to spend more time in the domestic sphere and thus simply will have less access to or an opportunity for committing crime (McRobbie and Garber, 1976). Critics of such views, however, are quick to point out that these arguments rest upon strong gender stereotypes, and they also point out that it would be very difficult empirically to validate such claims. Thus, whilst gender and crime are clearly related, the extent to which gender alone shapes individual propensities towards criminal behaviour is highly contested, and perhaps a far more analytically insightful way to think about gender is to add to it other variables, such as age.

Age and crime

Age is a highly significant variable when considering the propensity to crime, particularly in relation to young people, defined as individuals between the ages of 16 and 24. According to official statistics (see Figure 9.1), young people are highly likely to commit crime, but, as always, the key issue for the sociologist of crime is whether or not such a statistic really does mean that young people are in some way innately more criminal or whether there are other social and cultural variables that must also be considered.

That young people seem fundamentally more disposed to commit crime seems highly unlikely, and sociologists working in this area cite a number of arguments to defend this position, such as the public nature of much youth crime, as well as the recurrent fears about moral degeneracy that are projected onto young people by the wider society. For these reasons many sociologists are keen to re-align the parameters of the debate about young people and crime in such a way that this acknowledges the fact that young people are far more likely to be the victims rather than the perpetrators of crime.

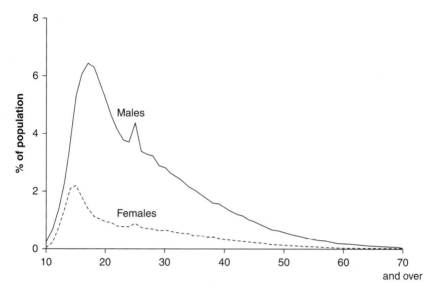

Figure 9.1 *Offenders as a percentage of the population by sex and age, 2007 (England and Wales) (ONS, 2009b, p. 135, from Office for Criminal Justice Reform, Ministry of Justice)*
Reproduced under the terms of the Click-Use Licence.

Notes:
1 People found guilty of, or cautioned for, indictable offences in 2007.
2 Age 25 includes those offenders for whom age is not known.

Crime and ethnicity

In the history of the study of crime and criminal behaviour, the links between ethnicity and age have featured prominently. Official crime figures and statistics do not record the 'race' or ethnicity of offenders, so information comes from a variety of sources, such as police reports and prison statistics which, although informative at one level, are also very limited. Because such a small proportion of offenders end up in prison, prison rates cannot be taken as representative (Croall, 1998). In part the reason for the lack of information about 'race' and ethnicity is related to the difficulty in defining such terms when carrying out research. Bearing these limitations in mind, research would indicate that black people are statistically over-represented throughout the criminal justice system whereas Asians are typically under-represented (see Table 9.1).

Sociological explanations for the over-representation of ethnic minorities in crime statistics can be understood at a number of levels: first, prejudice and discrimination can and do occur, especially when whole ethnic groups

TABLE 9.1   *Prison population of British nationals: by sex and ethnic group, 2006 (England and Wales)*

Ethnic group	Males	Females	All
White	80.8	82.7	80.9
Mixed	2.7	4.1	2.8
Asian or Asian British	4.9	2.0	4.8
Black or Black British	10.6	10.0	10.6
Chinese of other ethnic group	0.2	0.4	0.2
Total (=100%) (thousands)	62.7	3.4	66.2

Source: Office for National Statistics, 2008: 131
Reproduced under the terms of the Click-Use Licence.

are referred to in monolithic terms such as 'blacks' or 'Muslims', to which negative attributes are attached. Since the events of September 11 in 2001, for example, Muslims in Western nations such as Britain and the United States have increasingly protested against what they perceive as ethnic prejudice directed towards them on the part of the media and law enforcement agencies. Second, institutional discrimination may play a role, as in the example of the failure of the police to recruit candidates from a variety of ethnic backgrounds. Third, racism and a racist criminal justice system could be a factor, where racism is attributable to individual judges, police officers, etc. Fourth, the criminalization of whole ethnic groups is another important explanatory mechanism, as in the example of the 'demonization' of black youths in the early 1970s in England in relation to muggings (Cohen, 2002 [1973]; Goode and Ben-Yehuda, 1994).

ACTIVITY

In what ways does the patterning of crime mirror wider social inequalities? Given the patterning of crime and deviance, what does that suggest to you about what issues and social processes may be exerting an influence on a social work client in the criminal justice system?

Social Work Focus

The location of Criminal Justice Social Work Services as part of the wider system of local government provision enables councils to adopt a robust evidence based approach to working with offenders towards reducing offending while at the same time promoting the social inclusion of offenders through strong community provision. (ADSW Statement of Values, 2003)

The first part of this chapter has attempted to explain crime from a sociological perspective. This section will focus on social work practice with offenders, examining the extent to which social workers can respond effectively to the challenges of addressing sociological influences on crime.

Social work is one part of the criminal justice system, but there are a number of other stakeholders in this system who do not necessarily share the values of social workers. Those stakeholders include:

- The police, who are responsible for investigating crime, public order, crime prevention and who liaise with other agencies involved in public safety. The police also have significant contact with victims and witnesses. The police will present information to the court in respect of offences that may lead to a conviction being secured.
- The legal profession both prosecutes and defends criminals in the courts. The prosecution legal team seek to secure a conviction on the basis of evidence and motivation. The defence legal team act on behalf of the offender either to prove their innocence, or, where guilt is admitted or found, to mitigate on the offender's behalf to secure a lighter sentence.
- The judiciary, which will hear cases, and, if guilt is established, pass sentence. The judiciary are independent, and a judge, sheriff or magistrate may use his or her discretion in the disposal of cases and impose a variety of sentences as he or she sees fit. The courts themselves have a number of officers and clerks working to process offenders through the system.
- The prison service, which manages the incarceration of offenders securely and humanely, undertakes rehabilitative work with prisoners and prepares them for release.
- Government and the legislature, which determine what constitutes a criminal act. Legislation and the policy on crime can be influenced by evidence from research, ideology, public opinion and a range of social, cultural and human rights and, occasionally, economic factors.
- A number of ancillary agencies such as victim support, witness support, drug and alcohol support agencies, and the voluntary sector have an interest in the criminal justice system and will routinely be working with offenders and the victims of crime (Mooney and Scott, 2005).

Earlier in this chapter we raised the issue of the social distribution of crime, thinking about age, gender, ethnicity and socio-economic status. The criminal justice system tends, on the whole, not to place wealthy or white-collar criminals under the supervision of social work departments. Though society's economic losses from white-collar crime are far in excess of those from housebreakings, shopliftings and benefit frauds, white-collar crime is born out of social and economic advantage rather than the 'social problems' of poverty, deprivation, unemployment, etc. Significant economic malpractice or fraud is more likely to be addressed by the imposition of a financial penalty or imprisonment, with the perpetrator

SOCIOLOGY FOR SOCIAL WORK

TABLE 9.2   *Crimes recorded by the police in the UK: by type of offence, 2007/8*

	England & Wales(%)	Scotland(%)	Northern Ireland(%)
Theft and handling stolen goods	36	33	23
Theft from vehicles	9	4	3
Theft of vehicles	3	3	3
Criminal damage	21	31	28
Violence against the person [a]	19	3	27
Burglary	12	7	11
Drugs offences	5	11	3
Fraud and forgery	3	2	3
Robbery	2	1	1
Sexual offences	1	1	2
Other offences [b]	1	12	3
All notifiable offences (=100%) (thousands)	4,951	386	108

[a] Data for Scotland are serious assaults only. Those for England, Wales and Northern Ireland are all assaults including those that cause no physical injury.
[b] Northern Ireland includes 'offences against the state'. Scotland excludes 'offending while on bail'.
Source: ONS, 2009, p. 128 from Home office; Scottish Government; Police Service of Northern Ireland

seldom deemed to be in need of the community-based support and guidance social work traditionally provides. Social work predominantly receives and treats those who commit the crimes that society most fears – robbery, assault, drugs, etc. Additionally, a general overview of crime in the UK reveals that both the perpetrators and the victims of the type of crimes most commonly disposed of in the courts reflect a lower socio-economic status (Home Office, 2009). Reiman (1979) suggests that there could be said to be an economic bias in the system, and that the law and the courts defend an unjust social order and sustain an image that crime is the preserve of the poor.

Types of Crime

Crimes of dishonesty, such as housebreaking and shoplifting, are nearly half of the overall total, with their numbers having decreased each year since 1998/99. Other crimes include the handling of offensive weapons, drug crimes and breaches of bail conditions (Table 9.2).

Reflecting this view, it might be helpful to consider who forms the largest group of convicted offenders in the UK. It is composed of young males between the ages of seventeen and twenty-five, as indicated in Figure 9.1 in the sociology focus. Typically, individuals in this group will possess 'criminogenic needs', that is, those needs that are met by committing crime, some of which reflect sociological interpretations of crime. These may include poverty, inadequate accommodation, poor family relationships, limited educational qualifications, limited work skills and/or a poor employment record, a susceptibility to negative peer influences, difficulties with drugs and alcohol, limited social skills and anti-social attitudes to law and order. These needs locate the individual offender within the context of structural elements of society where identities and actions are moulded by the collective. The individual is perceived as being less in control and less self-determinant than one might imagine (Smith and Natalier, 2005).

As social workers we want to try to understand what has happened in the lives of these young people to lead them to deviate from the norm and to become involved in offending behaviour. Some may be well known in their local communities and may already have been labelled as individuals to be avoided. To this extent a degree of social ostracization will be meted out by the community, and offenders can easily become isolated from their normative peer associations. More entrenched offenders may, therefore, seek out others like themselves and form new relationships, finding a renewed sense of 'community' in a deviant identity and subculture. These offenders are often found to invest heavily in and be co-dependent on social groups of other offenders (Braithwaite, 1989).

Assessments and interventions undertaken with offenders necessitate an acknowledgement that social work in the criminal justice system is a political activity, with statutory social workers bound by the legislative and policy frameworks. It is also a moral activity, with a set of standards and codes of practice that determine the values and ethics of practice. Most often our role is determined by a court or a parole board with terms and conditions of supervision and compliance which must be adhered to. The social worker must, however, balance the expectations of the sentencer with the needs of the offender. The social work role, therefore, becomes one of both support and control. There is something of a dilemma within the sociological context of crime, in that society expects convicted offenders to accept an individual responsibility for confronting the consequences of their actions and to make changes to their behaviour (Mcguire, 1995), while core social work values and evidence from practice accept that this cannot be achieved unless a number of other basic unmet needs are addressed.

An offender's first contact with criminal justice social work will likely be at the request of the Court for a background report (known in Scotland as a Social Enquiry Report, and in England and Wales as a Pre-Sentence Report). This contains a range of factual information, analysis, comment and advice on the disposal of the case. The worker is tasked with assisting the court to apply an appropriate sentence. Not only will the worker address issues pertaining to the commission of the offence and offending behaviour, but also social factors, such as finance, family relationships, education, training, employment, accommodation, lifestyle, physical and mental health, risk of self-harm and substance misuse. The assessments undertaken during this pre-sentence period, before the offender returns to court to hear his or her fate, will allow the worker an opportunity to develop a sense of the offender in the wider context of the environment he or she inhabits and to present the whole person to the sentencer.

For all that offenders are expected to take responsibility for addressing their individual behaviour, intervention programmes need to be realistic about the social and economic environment in which individual offenders live. What opportunities actually exist for offenders to move forward into meaningful occupations? What provision is there for appropriate housing not located in an area of deprivation with high crime rates and endemic drug use? Simply placing an offender on a Probation Order (known in England and Wales as a Community Rehabilitation Order) is no guarantee of long-term change. Offending behaviour is most often thought of as a cycle, and there are multiple factors in the process of 'desistance' from crime (Ward and Maruna, 2007), including resilience, maturation and social bonds, which add to the complexity of rehabilitation. For example, the informal social order of the workplace or the college classroom encourages conformity. 'It has to be seen in a context of where the factors associated with offending are embedded in a person's background, upbringing and social experience' (Crow, 2007, p. 78). In this respect social work operates in the criminal justice system with a clear social inclusion agenda.

> It is important that politicians do not separate out the individual 'responsibility' component from the component of community well-being, which as well as recognising the importance of community safety also implies efforts on behalf of the community towards the social inclusion of offenders. (Moore and Whyte, 1998, p. 19)

Social work in the criminal justice system is, therefore, an influential force in creating the conditions, or at least the potential, for desistance in an individual's experiential cycle of offending. Much of 'what works' with offenders incorporates a cognitive-behavioural approach, which suggests that criminal behaviour is learned and can be explained by social learning theories, which historically derive from clinical psychology. Cognitive-behavioural therapy, which is used extensively in offender management programmes, responds to the notion that offenders have poor problem solving skills, are compulsive and do not think consequentially. Psychological studies have shown that offenders may have an 'external locus of control' (Crow, 2007), which means they have a belief that their behaviour is controlled by external forces (an idea sympathetic to the sociological understanding of crime and deviance). Because of this, they struggle to assume individual responsibility for their own behaviour. Programmes that focus on reasoning, behaviour modification and victim awareness are successful because they also focus on restructuring offenders' thought processes in order to control behaviour, alongside the social worker modelling or promoting socially acceptable attitudes for offenders (Ross and Fabiano, 1985; Vennard et al., 1997).

Work with offenders is primarily about reducing the risk of reoffending. In community-based social work the emphasis remains on a rehabilitative approach, which explicitly addresses criminogenic needs. Of course, it is often unrealistic to expect someone to desist from crime if the social and economic aspects of their lifestyle leave them rooted in poverty. Nevertheless, the prevailing ideological climate dictates that offenders be confronted by the consequences of their actions. Those consequences can impact upon not only on any victim of crime but also on the offenders themselves, their families and the community. Much of the work undertaken during the supervision of offenders explores offenders' thinking and how their motivation to offend may elicit a short-term gain, but a longer-term loss, in terms of the damaging consequences of anti-social behaviour. Just as crime itself is a social construct so, to an extent, is an offender's justification for their crimes. The social worker is tasked with a forensic deconstructing of offenders' reasons for committing offences and then with assisting offenders cognitively to reconstruct their thinking patterns, their attitudes and beliefs about themselves and the world around them. This work draws on offenders' intrinsic personal capital and a willingness to engage in a collaborative working relationship to foster change. In a sociological context, the concept of social capital is also important:

> The emphasis in Scottish legislation on the primary duty of social work services to 'promote social welfare' (Social Work (Scotland) Act 1968, Section 12) is to a large extent in keeping with emerging thinking on social capital, social integration and desistance. (McNeill and Whyte, 2007, p. 177)

Social capital refers to social networks and the benefits that can accrue to offenders as a result of their existence in the communities in which they live. Offenders who have access to social capital can be empowered to conform to the values and normative behaviours of the community. Unfortunately, social capital can also bind the offender to a community of low socio-economic potential in which there is no 'bridge' to new networks that might offer a pathway to improved life chances. More seriously, where social capital is absent and offenders are marginalized even in their own communities, there is, as mentioned earlier, a retrenchment into anti-social attitudes and behaviours amongst pro-criminal groups.

Recent studies have shown that social work can play a part in engaging more effectively than at present with this notion of social capital. The results suggest that probation work can use a strengths-based approach to assist the offender to build better relationships with families and communities, and seek new networks. Some argue that social workers could even practise a form of indirect probation work by engaging themselves with an offender's social networks in order to enhance social capital (McNeill and Whyte, 2007). Whether this is practicable for all is as yet unknown. What is known is that communities of poor socio-economic potential, and with low levels of social cohesion, will continue to produce generations of offenders, and that a risk/needs approach alone may manage offenders, but will not necessarily provide the stimulus for long-term change. Sociological factors that facilitate crime are prevalent in communities lacking good educational facilities, poor employment prospects and inadequate housing. If these conditions persist then the cognitive and behavioural interventions, the skills training, problem solving techniques and the pro-social modelling are likely to be diluted in their effectiveness.

With prison costs high in the UK and elsewhere, Ross (2008) suggests a form of 'justice reinvestment', citing research by Houchin (2005), which noted that the probability of imprisonment increases with increasing deprivation. In 2003 a quarter of all prisoners in Scotland's jails came from just over 50 of the 1,222 council wards. Ross argues for a redistribution of imprisonment costs across the demographic concentrations of high crime areas to invest in regeneration, improving drug treatment facilities, health and mental health programmes, employment training, after school programmes and infrastructure improvements.

Recent policy initiatives from the Scottish Government (*Fast, Fair and Flexible Justice*, Scottish Government, 2008) make clear its commitment to promote the reintegration of offenders and 'to promote across the public sector the need to address the social and health needs of offenders'. It posits a desire for an effective 'joining up' at local and community level and recognizes that criminal justice interventions alone cannot achieve the outcomes necessary and that wider joint action is required 'to really make a difference to offenders – accessing and sustaining suitable housing, improving skills and accessing training/employment, addressing issues of physical and mental health'. Equally, current policy acknowledges structural and societal considerations by demanding that the offender 'pay back' for the harm done through swift, rigorous and effective penalties that meet the needs of the community and the victim while also allowing the offender to utilize support to effect personal and lasting change. This policy chimes with the situation in England and Wales, with the Home Secretary recently describing how 'The government is committed to a swift, fair and effective justice system that is seen to work for all' (Ministry of Justice, 2009), and with offenders being seen to pay back to the community for the damage or harm caused, and the community itself having a say in what form this 'community payback' should take.

Lived Experience

For the lived experience, a social worker (who wishes to remain anonymous), has worked in criminal justice and reflects on her experiences of working with offenders and ex-offenders. In the passage below she summarizes her observations on working in the criminal justice sector.

As you read the interview it would be useful to consider the issues that have been discussed in both the sociology and the social work focus. Doing so should help you relate what can seem quite abstract theories and concepts to individual people.

The following prompts should prove helpful:

- Reflect on one of the main themes of this chapter that crime is not wholly explicable by reference to 'bad' people, but rather that social structure plays a crucial role in the lives of people who commit crime.
- Discuss which of the sociological theories of crime best explains what is described below.
- Consider why people who have engaged in criminal activity have to deal with issues of stigma.
- Identify the steps that could be taken to reduce crime on a deeper structural level – what could social workers do in order to enable such a change?

I started working in a criminal justice social work setting with a good understanding regarding the context of the work carried out in this area, and the challenges service users encounter when attempting to achieve change in their lives. The majority of my work is based around working with service users who have had a community-based penalty, such as probation. I felt quite optimistic going into work in this environment as my own values are in keeping with offering support to assist service users to achieve positive change in their lives.

It was evident, when I first started, that not all offenders come from disadvantaged backgrounds, however, in my experience, most of the service users faced social and economic disadvantage, such as coming from either working-class or other minority backgrounds. What propelled most of them into criminal activity was not that they themselves were naturally bad people, it was the circumstances in which they had grown up or in which they lived. I often thought that if life had dealt them another hand and they had grown up in a different environment then they would not have come into contact with criminal justice and they could have led happy lives as normal members of society. Many had faced multiple adversities throughout their lives, encountering problems such as poverty, relative deprivation, poor housing conditions, poor education, relationship and family difficulties, and employment difficulties. Quite often, these difficulties will have affected the development of their social skills, too, which disadvantages them further. Many service users will also have substance-misuse issues and face all manner of difficulties in accessing support services. Without adequate support services people with substance issues can further endanger their health, on the one hand, but, more importantly, substance use can lead to criminal activity in order to finance that use. It was these factors that I saw as being important in shaping who they are as people and why they ended up engaging in criminal activity.

It is also evident that many service users encounter being stigmatized and rejected by society. This creates an obvious barrier towards promoting social inclusion and integration. I found that many find it difficult disengaging from their present lifestyles, as often low self-esteem is a barrier towards being confident enough to maintain change in their lives. Hence, service users often seem to be stuck in an 'environmental bubble' or subculture, and criminal justice social work faces the challenge of providing assistance and access to services in order to facilitate change. Moving people into a new way of life where they can develop themselves and leave their old ways of being behind is, unsurprisingly, very difficult and fraught with many problems!

I often got a sense that some of the service users would come across with confidence and bravado, however this often appeared to be more of a performance. This is understandable, as service users will use mechanisms to ensure that they do not 'lose face', and thereby this seems to be a technique for protecting their sense of self and identity. This was especially evident when working with offenders in different environments. For example, I worked with one service user both in a group environment and on a one-to-one basis. In the group environment he would come across as quite bold and appeared to boast about his offending behaviour, however his manner was quite different when I met him individually. It was evident that he had low self-esteem and talked openly about the adversities he had faced throughout his life. Both the group work sessions and the individual sessions are mainly based around a cognitive-behavioural approach to intervention, encouraging the offenders to examine their own behaviour and also the impact this has on others. I feel as if this type of intervention is really worthwhile, however this should be used alongside a more ecological and social approach, assisting service users with problems relating to housing, education, employment, substance misuse issues and finance.

As mentioned before, the social inclusion of offenders is high on the government policy agenda. Therefore, I found it surprising that some homeless charities have faced cutbacks to their services. Some charities have had to close down projects, which were valuable for service users working towards stability and hence reducing re-offending. Service users with substance misuse issues will also have a lengthy wait before accessing methadone programmes and addiction counselling. Indeed, most services have strict criteria, with some service users not always 'fitting in the box', thereby not being eligible for support. Often service users will have a wide range of social difficulties; however, there are scarce resources to enable them to achieve more stability in their lives. This was especially evident in relation to service users who have experienced custodial sentences. They often leave custody without any stable accommodation to go to, often staying in temporary bed and breakfast accommodation. Consequently, this has a problematic effect towards promoting social inclusion and assisting them to integrate back into the community. Hence, some service users are actually leaving custody faced with more instability than before they went to prison.

Working in criminal justice social work is challenging yet rewarding. However, it is clear that the vast majority of time is spent supporting service users in crisis and attempting to access services that are scarce and not always available. As a result, it is sometimes difficult to find the time to focus on the actual offending, including any meaningful programmatic or cognitive-behavioural work, which assists service users with addressing their individual behaviour. Ideally, it would be appropriate to balance addressing individual behaviour alongside addressing the wider social issues. However this is not always possible, with some service users facing issues such as homelessness, substance misuse and the lack of services available.

Further Reading

For further depth and detail on sociological aspects of crime, the following can provide useful coverage:

Croall, H. (2010) *Crime and Society in Britain,* 2nd edn. London: Longman.

Downes, D. and Rock, P. (2007) *Understanding Deviance: A Guide to the Sociology of Crime and Rule Breaking,* 5th edn. Oxford: Oxford University Press.

10

Intimacies and Relationships

Megan Todd, Steve Hothershall and Janet Owen

> ## Key themes
>
> - Ideas of family and intimate relationships vary across cultures and over time.
> - Modern sociology tends to study wider intimacies as opposed to the 'traditional' family unit.
> - Various demographic changes have occurred that pose questions of how people construct and maintain intimate relationships in the twenty-first century.

> ## Keywords
>
> family, intimacies, relationships, domestic violence, divorce, patriarchy, heteronormativity

Introduction

Being in some form of relationship with others is an integral part of human life. We all expect, or wish for, to be part of an arrangement with another person or other people that provides us with not just financial security but also emotional fulfilment and a sense of completion in our personal life narratives. For many people, however, relationships can be complex and challenging. Problems or social censure can be encountered, or the relationships can lead not to emotional fulfilment but to emotional upset or trauma. One of the main (but by no means exclusive, as we shall see) forms of relationship in contemporary society remains 'the family'. What a family is, however, can differ greatly from the common perception of a man and woman with their children. Nor is heterosexuality the only expression of human affection.

In this chapter we shall consider what it means to talk of 'the family'; does this remain a meaningful concept in the twenty-first century? In doing so, we examine ideological conceptualizations of the family, the role state intervention plays in shaping received notions of what the family is, and the potentially oppressive nature of the bonds of kinship. From this, we encounter different forms of family and different expressions of sexuality.

Sociology Focus

The family, for many, may seem like a 'haven in a heartless world', a source of comfort and security. Such a commonsense and, perhaps, romantic view of the family is an easy image to succumb to when it is an institution that most of us feel we know. This conventional perception, stereotype even, of the family is questioned and explored from different perspectives by sociologists:

> The family is an essential component of almost everyone's taken-for-granted world. It is all the more necessary to gain some distance from this taken-for-granted perspective if one is to understand what the institution is all about ... Familiarity breeds not so much contempt as blindness ... Sociology tries to introduce a sufficient element of artificial strangeness into what is most familiar to us in order that we may be able to describe the familiar in clearer ways. (Berger and Berger, 1976, pp. 93–4)

Most families are based on kinship – a social bond of blood ties, marriage or adoption – but who is included under the umbrella term 'family' changes over time and across different cultures. Rather than being a 'natural' unit, therefore, the family could be said to be another example of a social construction. Many sociologists have suggested that the family is interesting to study because of the way it is shaped by society, and the way in turn it helps to shape society. The family is interesting and important in other ways as an object of sociological enquiry, as the family is:

- a legally sanctioned institution and central to many governments' policies and party political rhetoric;
- also at the centre of one of the fundamental paradoxes in our lives: the fact that we are individuals but we are also social beings;
- often seen as playing a central role in reproducing and producing links between the individual and society.

Sociological understandings of the family and relationships have shifted over time, as is reflected in the title of this chapter. What traditionally has been known as the sociology of the family (with a focus on the structure of the idealized, white, nuclear family) is increasingly being conceptualized as the sociology of intimacies and relationships. This shift in emphasis allows for a more flexible focus on the emotional content of relationships (Smart, 2008). As such, it then becomes possible to include a variety of relationships between friends, sexual partners, family and kin instead of perceiving the traditional family as the only possible model of personal relationships.

ACTIVITY

What advantages do you perceive in exploring intimacy, in its fullest sense, as opposed to 'the family', in regard to relationships between people?

DEFINITION

The **family** is a social unit traditionally understood as those affiliated by legal or blood ties, or by co-residence. **Intimacies** or **intimate relationships** refer to those relationships whereby people may not necessarily be linked by blood or legal ties but nevertheless see themselves as constituting a meaningful unit. Jamieson (1998) suggests there are four key types of intimacies: couple relationships; parent–child relationships; sexual relationships; and those between friends and kin.

Theories of the Family

The broad theories of family life have been developed alongside trends in mainstream sociology and are summarized as follows.

More information on gender issues can be found in Chapter 3.

Marxist Interpretations of Family Life

Marxist theories regard the family as an exploitative institution, which serves to reproduce social inequalities and uphold capitalism (Zaretsky, 1976). Engels (1884/1972), in *The Origin of the Family: Private Property and the State*, analysed the emergence of the nuclear family and male dominance in Western societies, suggesting that the growth of private property and patriarchy evolved together. Within the nuclear family, it is argued, women are relegated to the private sphere, enabling men to work in the public sphere and accumulate wealth, the suggestion being that if women were able to participate in the public sphere their lot would be improved. Delmar (1977, p. 287) has argued that Engels's major contribution was to suggest that 'women's oppression was a problem of history, rather than biology'. Identifying that women were oppressed because of social convention as opposed to biological fate entails that changes in society could improve the situation of women. Many feminists have been sceptical, though, of the suggestion that if women had more involvement with the economy their status would be improved. There is evidence that women who go out to work are also left with the majority of housework, the so-called 'double burden' of domestic and paid labour. Women also often take on 'service' work which can be seen as an extension of their housework, for example, nursing, and such work has a relatively low status, and low pay, in our society (Stewart et al., 1980).

Functionalist Theory

Functionalist approaches have viewed the family as an important 'organ' in the 'body' of society (for example, Parsons and Bales, 1955). For functionalist sociologist George Murdock (1949), the 'traditional' nuclear family, with its rigid gender roles of the father as breadwinner and mother as carer and housewife, provides the best opportunity for the socially controlled expression of the sex drive. More importantly, they argue that the family serves an important role in society in terms of maintaining social stability and order by socializing children and stabilizing adults. Such expectations of the family are reflected in many governmental initiatives outlined below. Although the work of Parsons and Murdock is important in that it acknowledges the importance of the family unit in society, there have been various criticisms of functionalist perspectives on the family. A key problem is that functionalist theory places the nuclear family as the 'norm' and renders other forms of kinship as dysfunctional or deviant – problematic when in fact very few families conform to the nuclear family ideal. Functionalist theory also does not pay enough attention to the gendered economic and power inequalities within many intimate relationships, and the harms that these can lead to, an omission that feminists have criticized.

Feminist Approaches to 'The Family'

A third approach emerged with the early second wave feminist theories of the 1970s, providing some of the most comprehensive challenges to understandings of the family. Early arguments were that family structures were in no way natural or inevitable, and that the family was a major site of the subordination of women (Mitchell, 1971; Oakley, 1972). Feminists revealed that the gendered divisions of the family were socially constructed and served to perpetuate patriarchy. Sylvia Walby describes patriarchy as 'a system of social structures and practices in which men dominate, oppress, and exploit women' (1989, p. 214). Feminists also drew attention to the false separation of the public sphere from the private. First, feminists argued that women were excluded from participating in the public sphere because of their reproductive duties in the private realm of the family. Feminists then called into question the understanding of the family as private due to the fact that the household and women's roles within it were heavily scrutinized and policed by state policies, hence the famous feminist slogan 'the personal is political'.

ACTIVITY

Which of the above perspectives do you think most accurately understands 'family life'?

Breakdown, Democratization or Continuities?

In addition to the perspectives presented above, there have been more recent debates concerning intimacies and relationships. Gillies (2003) has identified that contemporary understandings of intimacies and relationships broadly follow one of three directions, which are outlined in greater detail below.

New Right Thinking

DEFINITION

In the 1980s the the Conservative Party in the UK and the Republican Party in the United States introduced what became known as the **'New Right'**. This ideology emphasized self-reliance, individualism, traditional family values, free-market capitalism, and minimal state intervention.

A study of the annual government census reveals a striking feature of contemporary society: changing household and marriage patterns in the UK. In a thirty-year period, from 1971 to 2001, there were more childless couples, increasing numbers of single-person households, and lone-parent households doubled. There has been a decline in first marriages (40 per cent fewer first marriages in 1994 than in 2001), a rise in the age of marriage (on average men and women are getting married six years later than they were thirty years ago) and a rise in divorce (the figure has doubled in thirty years). Certain groups in society regard such statistics as signaling a worrying social breakdown. New Right thinkers in countering feminist perspectives of the family have argued that such trends are linked with the political goals of feminism, which are, in turn, threatening the very foundations of society. Women, they warned, were increasingly placing their own needs before those of their children and their husbands, and undermining men's incentive to work (Davies, 1993). The result, they predicted, would be a decline in moral responsibilities and an unstable social order. Charles Murray (1990), for example, claimed that a rise in undesirable social phenomena such as illegitimacy and single parenthood would produce an 'underclass' of individuals dependent on the welfare state. Only a return to government policies that promoted the traditional family unit for the New Right would prevent an economic and moral decline.

Democratization

> **DEFINITION**
>
> **High modernity** and **reflexive modernity**, though different in emphasis, refer to modernity from the late twentieth century onwards. An increasing loss of tradition and a rapid loosening of rigid social structures mark this phase of modernity. As such, individuals are required to invest more time in reflecting on their sense of self and identity in this changing and fluid social landscape.

More recently, it has been argued, a new form of society emerged at the end of the twentieth century, a period of 'high modernity' (Giddens, 1992) or 'reflexive modernity' (Beck, 1994). A positive consequence of high modernity, for Giddens, was a loosening and blurring of the structural frameworks that underpin heterosexual relationships and the separation of sex and reproduction. Increasingly, he argues, men and women are compelled to reflexively create their identity through day-to-day decisions. This enables individuals to choose partnerships on a basis of mutual understanding, leading to 'pure relationships'. By a 'pure relationship' he refers to:

> a social relationship [which] is entered into for its own sake, for what can be derived by each person from a sustained association with another; and which is continued only in so far as it is thought by both parties to deliver enough satisfactions for each individual to stay within it. (Giddens, 1992, p. 58)

Partnerships entered into for their own sake, it is suggested, give rise to greater democracy and equality in relationships. Giddens focuses on same-sex relationships as leading the way in creating more democratic relationships. There have been many criticisms of Giddens' work, for example, he has been accused of failing to address continuing inequalities such as those based on social class and gender (Crow, 2002b; Smart and Neale, 1999).

Despite such criticisms, many sociologists have found Giddens's work of use, particularly in relation to same-sex partnerships (Weeks et al., 2001). Stacey (1996) argues that same-sex relationships represent an ideal postmodern kinship because their conscious efforts to form relationships are freed from the traditional patterns of family. Lacking any traditional role models or guidelines, such couples have had to be creative when forming intimate relationships. Giddens' work in many ways prefigured some of the work on the friendship/family continuum (Pahl and Prevalin, 2005).

Much has been written about friendship within sociology, frequently drawing on the work of Aristotle who defined three types of friendship – friends of virtue, friends of pleasure, and friends of utility (Pahl, 2000). A recent aspect of work on intimacies is a consideration of friendships as constituting 'families of choice'. 'Elective families' (Beck-Gernsheim, 1998) are often seen as being pioneered by gay men and lesbians, though they are by no means confined to them (Giddens, 1992). Several studies have shown that friends become a chosen family when they engage in similar practices, providing support in times of crisis, coming together for the major rituals of life surrounding birth, death and the other occasions that mark our progress through the life course (Charles et al., 2008; Pahl and Spencer, 2004). Giddens (1992) argues that the pursuit of personal happiness and stability through such relationships is of increasing importance in late modernity with the decline of a cohesive moral and social world, an argument that was in fact put forward as early as the eighteenth century by Scottish Enlightenment philosophers who saw intimate friendship as a 'modern' pattern emerging in their time (Silver, 1997). An increasing number of researchers have suggested that in fact friendships are so important in personal lives that we are witnessing a shift from the centrality of the couple to a more fluid network of intimates (Roseneil and Budgeon, 2004; Spencer and Pahl, 2006). So it would seem that the term 'family' can be used to describe a variety of selected relationships, friends as well as blood relatives.

Continuities

Those researchers who have argued either that the changes we are witnessing are detrimental to the social order or promote positive changes in the ways in which we conduct our intimate relationships have been very dominant. A quieter voice in the debate is the one that argues that in fact we are overemphasizing social change. Crow (2002b), for example, suggests that family relationships have always shown plurality and diversity; there have throughout history been lone parents, same-sex couples and co-habitees, what has changed is our labels for them. Others point to the continued importance that individuals place on intimate relationships (Ribbens McCarthy et al., 2003).

ACTIVITY

Changes to families and other intimate relationships are, in many ways, undeniable. Which of the above perspectives do you agree with? What evidence can you identify to support your answer?

Intimate Relationships and the State

A neo-liberal focus on family, community and responsibility has pushed 'the family' onto the centre stage of the social policy agenda. Although in itself this is not a new concept, the deliberate positioning of family life as a public rather than a private concern heralds a new direction in government policy. In many ways, the government's view of the family follows that of functionalist approaches, in that it sees the family as the foundation for an ordered and moral society (Gillies, 2008). Much has been written about the ways in which the state shapes and perhaps even controls our intimate relationships. Media attention tends to portray the UK as a 'nanny state' in which the government scrutinizes every aspect of family life, from how many fruit and vegetable portions children are given, to keep-fit classes for over-weight parents, to the use of compulsory parenting classes for those parents with 'problem' children. Many sociologists have noted that such intrusions into family life are highly classed, that those families who do not fit with the ideal middle-class model of family life are demonized. Walkerdine and Lucey's (1989) UK study, for example, showed how middle-class childrearing practices are articulated as normal and desirable. Rather than using the New Right discourse of the 'underclass', however, the government has softened the language and instead talks of 'social exclusion' (Levitas, 2005; MacDonald and Marsh, 2005). The drive to 'social inclusion' has arguably led to an increasingly authoritarian raft of family policies. What we are witnessing, it is argued, is the scapegoating of working-class families (mothers in particular), enabling governments to place the blame for the cause of society's ills onto 'poor parents' rather than focus on the social and structural inequalities (Gillies, 2008). Former Cabinet Minister Hilary Armstrong illustrated this approach in her Foreword to *Reaching Out*:

> People who want to turn their lives around can ... Government can't do it all. For too many people the problems have appeared insurmountable and the system too inaccessible, preventing them from taking responsibility for their lives ... This Action Plan will help individuals and the services that support them unlock their aspiration and help lift them out of poverty and exclusion. (Armstrong, 2006, p. 6)

The state has also played a significant part in determining what is (and what is not) regarded as a legitimate relationship. One clear example is the ways in which same-sex couples have been treated in government policies. Section 28 of the Local Government Act 1988, an Act that has been described as the most successful piece of homophobic legislation since the 1800s (Smith, 1994), was passed under Margaret Thatcher's government. It stated that a local authority 'shall not intentionally promote homosexuality or publish material with the intention of promoting homosexuality' or 'promote the teaching in any maintained school of the acceptability of homosexuality as a pretended family relationship'. The Act caused many individuals to feel they had to hide their sexual identity in certain situations because of a perceived rise in anti-gay feeling. Certainly, the Act does seem to have had an influence on the ways in which society responded to same-sex relationships, as during the Thatcher administration homophobic attitudes in society increased markedly. The British Social Attitudes Survey recorded 62% of respondents disapproving of gay relationships in 1983. By 1985 this had risen to 69% and rose again to 74% in 1987. That figure had reduced by 1992 to 58%. Section 28 was not repealed until 21 June 2000 in Scotland and 18 November 2003 in the rest of the UK. There have also been differing ages of consent for heterosexuals and gay men (lesbians have not historically been included in age of consent laws, not because their relationships have been socially accepted but more because when the first age of consent laws were passed there was a fear that talking about lesbians would 'spread the contagion'; see Weeks, 1989). In 1967 the age of consent for gay men was twenty-one, compared to sixteen for heterosexuals; in 1979 it was reduced to eighteen. In January 2001, under the Sexual Offences (Amendment) Act, the age of consent for gay men was reduced from eighteen to sixteen in line with heterosexuals, but there was, however, much objection from the moral right and religious groups at the time. Further lesbian, gay, bisexual and transgender (LGBT) issues are raised in the lived experience.

The state also decides who can and cannot be married. For example, until very recently same-sex couples could not register their relationships. On 5 December 2005 the Civil Partnership Act 2004 came into operation, meaning that same-sex couples could legally register if they live together, as civil partners of each other; however civil partnerships are not (at the time of writing) open to heterosexual couples. Neither are they legally considered to be a 'marriage', though in many respects civil partnerships afford same-sex couples the same rights as a married couple in areas like tax, social security, inheritance and the workplace (see www.womenand equalityunit.gov.uk/civil partnership.htm for more details). Some have welcomed civil partnerships as heralding a new acceptance of same-sex couples, others have suggested that they represent a 'two-tiered' system that reinforces heteronormativity (Hull, 2006).

DEFINITION

Seeing heterosexuality as the only acceptable form of sexuality, intimacy and relationship, while lowering the status of other forms of relationships, especially homosexual relationships, is termed **heteronormativity**.

ACTIVITY

How much control should the state (that is, the government and agencies such as social work) have over family life and intimacies? Are there any contemporary examples that you can think of that support your answer?

Violence and Intimate Relationships

DEFINITION

Patriarchy as a concept refers to the male domination of society. This domination is maintained through cultural, linguistic, and political and legal means and is evident in many aspects of everyday life such as the media and representations of gender and gender roles. **Domestic violence** is a highly contested, though widely used term. Broadly, it refers to a range of abuses including physical, sexual, emotional and financial abuse, as well as the threat of abuse. Some prefer the term **domestic abuse** because domestic violence may encourage a focus on purely physical abuse. Others prefer **intimate violence** or **intimate abuse** because it allows for an understanding of violence between those who do not necessarily live together, and violence that may occur in a public place.

The family may be commonly regarded as a 'haven in a heartless world'; the reality is that, for many, the family constitutes a dangerous place. Since large numbers of women experience domestic violence perpetrated by men (21%, roughly 1 in every 5 women, according to Home Office statistics for 2004), the assumption is that it is, therefore, performed by a substantial percentage of men and is not the act of a pathological 'few' (Price, 2005). As Bourke (1999) argues, when domestic violence happens so frequently it can begin to look 'normal' and, for this reason, many feminist sociologists have argued for the necessity of thinking beyond the psychiatric approach that men who are violent in relationships must be sick and beyond the theological approach that such men are evil. This different perspective requires examining the social structures that allow and permit male violence against women. A critical explanatory concept for many feminist theories of men's violence is patriarchy. In other words, patriarchy can be explained as a consistent pattern of ideological and structural practices that serve to justify and perpetuate men's oppression of women. Walby (1989) identified six mechanisms of patriarchy: the mode of production; the realm of paid work; the state; the realm of sexuality; cultural institutions; and, crucially for this chapter, male violence against women. All these mechanisms serve to subjugate women, which, in turn, permits a range of violent acts.

The family, as an institution, has frequently been cited by feminists as one that has traditionally legitimated the commission of violence against women and children (Kelly, 1988). Historically, the dichotomy between the public and the private with regard to domestic violence has often been reflected in the ambivalence of most agencies, including the police, towards getting involved in situations which occurred 'behind closed doors' and away from public view (Yllo and Bograd, 1988). Violence in the home between inti-mates was frequently, and perhaps still is, perceived as different from vio-lence against a stranger in a public place (Stanko, 1985). The parameters of the 'family' were traditionally set aside as paradigmatically 'private' (Oakley, 1981). This public/private binary has resulted in attitudes that rendered domestic violence as not 'real' police work and therefore as not associated with criminal investigation, as police work was about maintaining public order whereas domestic violence was about marriage counselling and social work and not appropriate to their role (Yllo and Bograd, 1988). Many would argue much domestic violence has been regarded as trivial, and to a certain extent even considered as normal, inevitable and excusable, because it is also 'domestic' (Fineman, 1994; Stanko, 1985). Edwards (1986) con-cluded from interviews with police officers that domestic violence was seen by many as a 'normal' part of family life and, thus, not a matter for their concern except in severe cases. There was, and perhaps still is, a covert tol-eration of domestic violence. While domestic violence continued to be seen as a 'private matter', it was virtually impossible to redefine it as criminal. For example, until as recently as 1991 men could not be charged with raping their wives. The issue of privileging a 'private' domestic situation, where men are abusing women within a household, took much political cam-paigning on the part of feminists, in order to expose the hypocrisy and use of power against women's interests (Corrin, 1996). The family has also been recognized as an institution that places the very young and the elderly at risk (see below). For instance, it is estimated that at least half of the children living in abusive households will themselves become the victims of abuse. Although statistically men are overwhelmingly more likely to be the per-petrators of, and women and children the victims of, domestic violence, this does not mean that men cannot be victims and women are incapable of violence. Recently, for example, there have been studies on violence in same-sex relationships (see below and Ristock, 2002).

The End of 'Families'?

There would seem to be no doubt that our intimate relationships have undergone a transformation in recent years and there is no reason to think that this will not continue into the twenty-first century. Post-industrialization has led to the de-traditionalization and individualization of social life. Does this mean, then, the end of family life as we know it? Although society has seen a rise in the divorce statistics, we are still, it would seem, heavily invested in marriage and 'coupledom'. For example, although almost half of marriages will end in divorce, more than 40 per cent of marriages are remarriages. Remarriage often creates blended families, or re-configured families, consisting of a combination of biological and step-parents/siblings. There has been a rise in the numbers of couples co-habiting. December 2005 saw the first official civil partnerships (the legal union of same-sex couples), and in the ensuring 12 months 18,059 ceremonies took place. Many gay and lesbian couples will raise children from previous heterosexual relationships, or they will have adopted children. Increasingly, lesbian and gay couples are choosing to have their own biological children, using a variety of reproductive technologies (Gabb, 2008).

The work of David Morgan (1996) and others has shifted the field conceptually, through the development of the idea of family practices – families are what they do rather than being defined exclusively by kinship and marriage. The field has shifted so much that academics such as Jamieson (1998) and Smart (2008) refer to 'intimacies' and 'personal life' rather than 'the family'. Such terminological changes mean that when we talk of family it is less rigidly identified with the idealized nuclear family of the 1950s, but nevertheless, research reveals the fact that we remain heavily invested in intimate personal relationships, a fact reflected by the continued importance of families and intimate relationships for social work.

Social Work Focus

Social work practice is intricately and intimately tied to working both with and within families, however constituted or conceived. This is true irrespective of the field of social work or social care you work within, for example fieldwork with children and their families which may involve 'substitute' families (foster care), criminal justice, or community care or residential work with older people, children or people with a learning disability. What is clear is that at some level the 'family' will have relevance and a resonance that will impact on your practice. This chapter offers a valuable opportunity to look at social work and social care practice through a sociological 'lens' focusing on work with children and their families (Hothersall, 2008; Munro, 2008) and adult support and protection (Hothersall et al., 2008; Mantell and Scragg, 2008; Pritchard, 2007) in order to illustrate some of the themes and issues you will encounter in relation to the family in the course of your practice.

As Healy points out:

> Sociological discourse asserts that humans are profoundly social beings. It
> challenges individualistic explanations of social and personal problems by drawing
> attention to the social practices and social structures that sustain these problems.
> (2005, p. 59)

The 'comfort of strangers'

Historically, social work and social care provision has its roots in Victorian
philanthropy (see Payne, 2006; Reamer, 1993) whilst some forms of residential provision emerged from the vestiges of the Poor Laws and the
workhouses (Fraser, 2009; Hothersall and Bolger, 2010), with particular
types of residential provision for some client groupings, notably 'the mad,
the sad and the bad', evolving with particular views on how to *care for* and
control people very evident in their design and function (Foucault, 1991b,
2001; Wolfensberger, 1975). Parton (1985) citing Donzelot (1980) refers to
the emergence of the 'social' sphere (and hence *social* work) as that space
between the private space of the family and the public space of the state.
The *social* sphere acts as the intermediate and mediating forum between
these other spaces and here philanthropy and ultimately social work
emerged and flourished.

As a social worker you will act, in some form or another, as an agent of
the state; anyone employed by a local authority social services department
or by a voluntary organization will have some obligation to the state, either
by virtue of the statutory obligations they have towards certain vulnerable
people or groups (Hothersall and Maas-Lowit, 2010) or by reference to the
requirements of the agency's funding which invariably will have a governmental component to it, or (more likely) both. These aspects echo
Foucault's notions of *governmentality* (Foucault 1991a) and this can help us
to understand from a broader sociological perspective the ways in which
the state can be seen to 'shape' human relations by use of the law, policy,
regulation and practices designed to promulgate and, some might suggest,
enforce *normalcy* upon those deemed to be acting outside the broad expectations and prescriptions of the state (Rose, 1999). Social work can be
interpreted as doing this to some extent, although such an analysis at this
level is clearly inadequate to do justice to the many facets of this position
and fails to acknowledge the benefits social work can bring to many, many
individuals. Furthermore, within social work practice there is an inherent

tension between *professional* social work usually taking place within an *organizational* context (Payne, 2006). Sometimes the professional elements of social work may collide with the organizational and operational requirements of the particular organization.

The development of social work generally, and especially in relation to direct work with children and their families and 'vulnerable' adults, has a long, chequered and interesting history, practically and philosophically (Buckley, 2007; Hendricks, 2005; Hothersall, 2008; Reamer, 1993; Wolfensberger, 1972) and such a history is useful to us in that it helps us to see how social work practice often 'mirrors' the particular issues deemed by society and the government of the day to be 'worthy' of attention and intervention. It can often be the case that 'moral panics' (Cohen, 2002; Critcher, 2006; Goode and Ben-Yehuda, 2009) are at the root of particular policy and practice initiatives; currently, youth crime would be seen by some as falling within that category, as would the support and protection of *adults* at risk of harm and abuse, whereas other areas of social work like safeguarding children (a relatively new turn of phrase for child care and protection) have been on the political agenda for many years, although particular variants of and issues within it seem to take precedence at different times (Frost and Parton, 2009; Parton, 2006). For example, it was not until the 1960s that society in general awoke to the 'fact' that some parents deliberately harm their children and the phrase 'Battered Baby Syndrome' (Kempe et al., 1962) was coined. As Garland (1990, p.1) notes, 'Giving a proper name to an entity can often make it seem more substantial or more unified than it actually is'. In a similar way, the whole issue of suspected child sexual abuse within the family and how this ought to be responded to was not widely nor publicly acknowledged as a cause for concern until the events of Cleveland and Orkney brought the matter to wide public attention (Butler-Sloss, 1988; Clyde, 1992). Child neglect and physical abuse have similarly been highlighted by a number of high-profile cases over the years (Hammond, 2001; Laming, 2003, 2009; O'Brien et al., 2003) emphasizing in many ways the tensions that exist between the 'private' arena of the family and the 'public' arena within which social work practice takes place and the tensions this generates (Blom-Cooper, 1985). Ashenden articulates some of the complexities of managing this phenomenon when she says that:

> Child protection is one set of practices through which relations between families and the state are constituted and regulated. This set of practices enables us to examine the negotiation of the relationship between public and private life.

Modern management of the legal, social and cultural boundaries between families and the state is effected by the mobilization of a range of professional forms of knowledge and practice such as law, medicine, psychology and social work, specializing in determining where and when intervention is reasonable and legitimate, all of which are premised on the idea of the 'best interests of the child'. (2004, p. 10)

In the area of work with adults, there are individuals who, because of age, infirmity or other conditions (for example, a mental illness or learning disability), are *more* vulnerable to exploitation and abuse from others and are less able to protect themselves or alert others to their plight (Hothersall and Maas-Lowit, 2010). Across Scotland (Hothersall et al., 2008) and England and Wales (Brown et al., 2008), new legislation has (recently) been enacted (Mandelstam, 2008; Mantell and Scragg, 2008) which enhances the potential for the state and its agents to intervene in situations where adults are at risk, although the efficacy of such measures has yet to be determined, in particular because of the issue of the determination of *capacity* or otherwise of any adult to consent or otherwise to interventions of any sort, irrespective of the actions of others (Gearty, 2007; Johns, 2007). This area, because of the issue of capacity (see *HL* v *United Kingdom*: the *Bournewood* Judgment[1] and Dickenson, 2001), demonstrates well the difficulties of state intervention in private life and is an area not well tested at this time, although *Bournewood* does offer guidance in certain areas (Robinson and Scott-Moncrieff, 2005).

From an ideological perspective, the role of the state as a provider of welfare is historically predicated on the collectivist/socialist approach (George and Wilding, 1985; Hothersall, 2010a, 2010b), which would maintain that the state has a level of responsibility to ensure that its citizens are protected and in receipt of sufficient 'primary goods' (Rawls, 1971). This view of the world saw the light of day in the aftermath of the Second World War when the government of the day implemented plans that brought about the 'welfare state' (Fraser, 2009). However, the New Right/ neo-liberal policies of the Thatcher (and in the United States, the Reagan)

---

1 The *Bournewood* Judgment: the *Bournewood* case concerned an autistic man with severe learning disabilities who was informally admitted to Bournewood Hospital under common law (i.e. voluntarily), although he did not actively agree (or disagree) to this because of his disability. The European Court of Human Rights found that he had been deprived of his liberty unlawfully without a legal procedure with safeguards and rapid access to a court of appeal. The court made it clear that the question of whether someone has, in fact, been deprived of liberty depends on the particular circumstances of the case. *HL* v *United Kingdom* [2004] ECHR.

era heralded a shift away from a focus on state involvement *per se* to a view of the world that emphasized the importance of *individualism* (Vinen, 2009). More recently, the 'Third Way' of New Labour (Garrett, 2004) appeared to represent itself as a somewhat relativistic and pragmatic ideology, which, whilst espousing its commitment to underlying socialist values, appeared to do so within a broad neo-liberal framework that it continued to develop and operate within. As a result, social policies in Scotland (Hothersall and Bolger, 2010) and the rest of the UK have tended to adopt an orientation predicated upon 'what works', although this may beg the question of what works for whom?

The family and social work

Within this context, the family is still regarded as one of the main loci for primary socialization (Maccoby, 2000). From a sociological perspective, we need to consider which *model* of the family is dominant by reference to the assumptions that governments, welfare organizations and practitioners make about it. Reference was made earlier to Marxist, functionalist and feminist accounts of the family as well as perceived changes to the form and function of the family within the context of modernity. It could be argued that elements of most if not all of these perspectives and the effects of these changes in the way we think about the family can be seen on a day-to-day basis within the context of law, policy and practice. For example, it is now the case that some children who are 'looked after' by the local authority will be placed with single people and same-sex couples who are approved as foster carers, and statute and concomitant regulation now acknowledges their right to apply to be prospective adopters. However, as we saw above, some writers and thinkers would argue that the family is an easy target as a scapegoat for the broader ills of society, with poorer families bearing the brunt of this criticism with claims that poor parenting, anti-social behaviour and criminal behaviour are loosening the 'fabric' or 'moral cement' of society because of the effects of these things upon the (idealized, functionalist) family.

In relation to child care practice within social work, Lorraine Fox Harding (1997) has summarized four value perspectives that have, to a greater or lesser extent, permeated child care policy and practice at different periods of time and reflect the shifting view of the locus of the *governmental* functions of the family, between the family unit itself and the agents and agencies of the state. There are elements of these different positions evident most of the time, although some aspects are more dominant than others (Fox Harding, 1997, p. 9):

1. *Laissez-faire and patriarchy.* A perspective with deep historical roots, often associated with the nineteenth century and industrialization. This view would hold that the power of and within the family should not be disturbed or encroached upon except in extreme circumstances. The role of the state is seen as being minimal, with the *male* being credited as the head of the household, thus supporting and perpetuating *patriarchy*.

2. *State paternalism and child protection.* This perspective can be seen to have emerged with the growth of welfare provision *per se* in the late nineteenth/early twentieth centuries. State intervention in order to care for and protect children is legitimated, although the actions of the state may at times be seen as authoritarian (as in the Cleveland and Orkney cases) and the issue of the importance of biological bonds and the rights of parents minimized. The *child's* welfare is seen as being paramount, although what constitutes 'the child's best interests' is defined and controlled by the state.

3. *The modern defence of the birth family and parent's rights.* This (current?) view is associated with the expansion of welfare provision generally in the form of state-sponsored 'family' policies. State intervention is legitimate, but its form aims to avoid paternalism, offering structured interventions at all levels to support the maintenance of the family unit. Wider structural influences are acknowledged as important variables to be considered taken in relation to the reasons for and the nature of interventions.

4. *Children's rights and child liberation.* This advocates for the child to be seen as the subject, as an independent person, with rights of their own, and has gained momentum with the emergence of the ECHR, the UNCRC and the Human Rights Act 1998. Within social work practice we can see the emphasis upon involving children and young people in decision-making, although how meaningful some of this might be in terms of outcomes has yet to be clearly established.

In reality, there are elements of each of these broad perspectives to be seen in everyday practice, and each one could have a 'weak' or a 'strong' form in any particular epoch. In fact, if we think about the recent case of Baby Peter (Laming, 2009), we could say that public opinion has voiced its 'surprise' at the apparent lack of *state paternalism* in this situation, whereas in the case of the children removed from the Orkney Islands in the 1990s, *defence of the birth family* was clearly the perspective seen to be the one in favour, even though in both cases *differing perspectives* appear to have been applied by the state and the professionals involved simultaneously. These are good examples of how the perceived management of difficult and painful events can lead to relatively sudden, and sometimes polarized, responses; the *zeitgeist* can change very quickly when we are talking about vulnerable children who are seen as having *not* been protected when they clearly should have been (Baby Peter) or when families are perceived to have been split up unnecessarily by social workers when many feel they should not have been (Orkney). In their respective wakes, changes in the law, policy, practice and *perceptions* are inevitable (see Dale, 2004; Dingwall et al., 1983; Parton, 1985, 2006). Similarly, cases involving serious harm to adults have highlighted failings in the systems as well as differing and conflicting perspectives operating simultaneously (MWC, 2006; SWSI, 2004).

It appears that both the form and to a large extent the *function* of the family have changed in recent years, particularly since the beginning of the 1970s when a number of global factors occurred that would subsequently compound and herald the rise of globalization (George and Wilding, 2002): electronic and other forms of mass media, individualization, ontological (personal) insecurity (Bauman, 2005; Kramer and Roberts, 1996), social anxiety and a shift in the *governmental* function of the family. The family has always been seen as having a governance function, usually in the form of *patriarchy*, although this is increasingly being replaced by 'social parenting' whereby growing numbers of children are often cared for by adults who are not their biological parent. The expectations around these governmental functions of the family have to some extent been increased because of the cult of individualism whereby families are assumed to be able to 'get on with it', but when difficulties do emerge these are similarly couched in *individualistic* terms and *pathologized* with the parent(s) being seen as in some ways inadequate. These changes, compounded within the context of the neo-liberal policies of the New Right and Margaret Thatcher, have subsequently had an effect on the relationships between the family and the state and, as we saw above, those families which appear not to conform to the ideal of 'benign functionalism' are invariably labelled as *dysfunctional* and become the subject of increased surveillance and intervention. In those situations where there are legitimate concerns for the well-being of children, these are conceptualized as arising from within the family itself rather than being seen as (in part at least) a response to the broader socio-economic and cultural forces impacting on society in these times of late modernity (Beck, 1992; Rodger, 2000).

The intricacies of intimacy

As we saw above, the neo-liberal focus on the family over recent years and its somewhat nascent position as one of the perceived moral anchor-points of late modernity has been paralleled by a raft of governmental and other initiatives designed to support it in its claim as the foundation-stone of, amongst other things, social order, morality and primary socialization (often couched in terms of 'effective parenting'). Inevitably, these essentially stereotypical generalizations bring with them increased and perhaps unrealistic expectations that tend to reflect the norms of the ruling class, in this instance the middle classes and their behaviours, which are 'normalized' and then extrapolated for others to emulate.

Walkerdine and Lucey's (1989) study illustrates one example of this in the area of parenting whilst Gillies's (2003) position could support the claim that working-class parents effectively become the target of (stigmatizing?) *selective* welfare policies masquerading as 'universal beneficence'. Similarly, earlier comments regarding the governance of the family by the state should afford us a clear sense that available interpretations of child and family law, policy and practice *are* open to interpretation and, in that respect, should be available for negotiation. In the current climate (2010) surrounding the safeguarding of children, there is a clear tendency towards prescription, regulation and monitoring on the part of government agencies, which appears to compromise the capacity of professionals to use their professional knowledge and judgement in the way it was designed to be used, with the result that defensible decisions are now seen as being those that are largely made on *economic* rather than *professional* and *welfare* grounds.

An obvious example of the interface between the family and the state is that of social work with children and their families. Children are variously regarded as 'innocent', a manifestation of our futures and simultaneously demonized; witness the current demonization of 'hoodies' and other young people who engage in what is described as 'anti-social behaviour'. This is not a new phenomenon; on the contrary, such divergent, confused, yet often-parallel views have existed for millennia and represent the constructivist and relativistic nature of 'childhood' as a phenomenon (Berger and Luckman, 1979; Cunningham, 2006; James and Prout, 2003; Postman, 1995; Searle, 1995; Smith, 2010).

The family is seen as having a pivotal role to play in relation not only to the *care* of children but also in relation to their *control*. These differing dimensions are usually seen as two sides of the same coin, relative to the age and perceived level of ability and, ergo, of the *responsibility* of the child or young person concerned. However, much social work practice is focused on the *protection* of children and young people, usually from harm occasioned upon them by others, sometimes from the harm they may do to themselves, unwittingly or otherwise, and the (re-?)education of parents in relation to, amongst other things, 'effective' parenting (Ghate, 2002; Harnet, 2007; Howe, 2005).

Where a child is seen as being in need of protection, it is usually the case that such harm is likely to befall them at the hands of parents or other significant persons who have care or control of them on a regular basis. In most situations, the family is usually the core unit from within which the harm arises. The notion that the abuse of children is something generally perpetrated by strangers is something of an 'urban legend' and whilst an awareness of 'stranger danger' is a useful, culturally sanctioned, self-protective strategy for children and young people, the real dangers tend to lie much closer to home (Crittenden, 2008).

Child abuse and neglect in its many forms and facets (Corby, 2006; Ferguson, 2004) is a culturally relative phenomenon and one that 'rarely presents with unambiguous evidence' (Munro, 2005, p. 381). The same can be said in relation to the abuse and neglect of vulnerable adults (Hothersall and Maas-Lowit, 2010). The protection of adults at risk of harm (Mantell and Scragg, 2008; Pritchard 2001, 2007), especially harm occasioned upon them by family members, is another area where our expectations and perceptions regarding the family, often built up on the basis of *functionalist* interpretations, are being challenged. That is not to say that the abuse of vulnerable adults within and by their family or by those entrusted with their care (usually those with some sort of 'professional' status) is something new; clearly it isn't. What *is* new however is the formal sanctioning by the state of activity to (hopefully) prevent and minimize such incidents.

As you can see, these comments are made in relation to the broadly functionalist perspective of the family adopted by the state. The issue of domestic or intimate partner violence and the state response to this can similarly be seen to be a reaction to what is labelled as *individual* pathology within an otherwise (functionally speaking) *benign* institution. This issue has latterly been given high priority by successive UK governments, and social work services in conjunction with the police and other agencies (including the courts) have developed fairly sophisticated response mechanisms. The social work literature is replete with practice-based and other forms of research into this issue (see Geffner et al., 2003; Letourneau et al., 2007; Mullender et al., 2002; Wolfe et al., 2003) and the findings and recommendations are important. However, dependent upon the ideological view of the family in operation, differing interpretations might be offered to explain such phenomena and to inform the development and implementation of particular interventions (Abrahams, 2007; Cleaver et al., 2007).

Clearly, the family offers itself to our scrutiny in many guises and presents anachronisms at every turn. It is, however, the main unit and agent of socialization, certainly *primary* socialization, and the role of the state in relation to oversight and monitoring is one that is largely determined by reference to constructivist theories of the family as an institution. Certainly social work and its tasks are largely defined by reference to these *ideologies of the family* and, whilst powerful, these are open to contestation in much the same way that social work as an activity is very much contested, although its rationale tends to be one that mirrors the prevailing ideology, rather than perhaps developing its *own ideology of well-being.*

Lived Experience

Janet Owen is Regional Community Development Worker with MESMAC North East, a gay and bisexual men's community support service. Within her work Janet offers direct support provision to MESMAC's service user remit group of men who have sex with men (MSM) and also joins community development workers from other agencies to improve access to services around specific topics within lesbian, gay, bisexual and transgender sectors.

As you read the lived experience it would be useful to consider the issues that have been discussed in both the sociology and the social work focus. Doing so should help you relate what can seem quite abstract theories and concepts to real life examples.

The following prompts should prove helpful:

- Relate the points concerning working with LGBT people that Janet raises below to the sociological theories outlined in the sociology focus.
- Reflect on why people who not subscribe to a heterosexual identity are discriminated against in society.

- Consider the issue of domestic violence in relation to the theories and research advanced in both the sociology and social work focus.

When working with LGBT people it's important to remember that an individual's status as an LGBT person may, *or may not*, have something to do with why they need support from you, however its also possible to say that the majority of LGBT people will have a history which may have included discrimination because of their LGBT status and this may have had an impact on the way they access any type services at all.

In our society LGBT people of all ages are bombarded with messages (hidden or overt) that can lead many of them to decide to keep their sexual orientation or gender identity a secret for fear of discrimination, especially bullying or harassment. Keeping this secret, or sometimes witnessing/experiencing the consequences of not keeping this secret, means living a lie and can cause huge pressures that can affect all areas of life, even when accessing support/care services.

Our heterocentric society assumes day to day that everyone either is or should be straight/heterosexual and this assumption can make it easy for people who aren't straight, or who don't fit stereotypical views of gender identities, to feel isolated, set apart, vulnerable. Often negative experiences around these issues begin in the education system and have lasting implications into adulthood.

Reflecting on formative education years it is possible to recognize that for the majority of LGBT people they will not have had access to positive role models, they will certainly not have had positive reinforcement that it's okay if they or any one else is LGBT, they will not have had an opportunity to have their questions answered or their myths and stereotypes about LGBT people challenged, and to varying extents the subject of LGBT status remains taboo or is treated as a dirty little secret.

With all of that to take into account it's a wonder that any LGBT person ever feels able to present the issue they need your support around and this can, of course, cause barriers to your work.

You may find, for example, that someone who is in a same-sex domestic abuse relationship doesn't recognize that what is happening to them is domestic abuse because, in our society, for the last thirty or so years domestic abuse has been recognized as 'men hitting women'. Even if they do recognize what's happening to them they may fear seeking help from anyone in an authority position – for instance, approaching the local authority for any services and having to 'out' themselves as LGBT is sometimes intimidating because they may fear a homophobic or transphobic response ... many LGBT people would struggle with the idea of contacting the police, even if their life was in danger, for exactly the same reasons. Even where a same-sex relationship is acknowledged to be violent/controlling there is a real lack of appropriate support to signpost people to. The majority of domestic abuse (DA) support agencies across the country (at the time of writing) are for women who suffer abuse from men and who don't have a remit around supporting same-sex domestic abuse victims/survivors, and there are no perpetrator programmes around LGBT relationships. When people do try to access support its often through generic LGBT support agencies where most workers don't feel well enough informed about DA to be effective. If DA support agencies are approached, most workers don't feel well enough informed about LGBT issues to be effective. Sometimes lesbians are given places in women's refuges, which can have a positive outcome, but can also carry a significant risk that other residents and workers may not be understanding or receptive to the situation and may respond in a homophobic manner.

When dealing with service users/clients for whom LGBT status is a factor it's crucial to take your lead from that person, and to know your limits. If you are not familiar with LGBT issues and that is an integral part of the situation you're trying to deal with, then seek professional support from experts in the field of LGBT support. While the majority of LGBT support agencies will exist within the voluntary/community sector, it's important to recognize that they are still professional organizations run in a professional manner (if you're in any doubt you can check this out with the individual organizations you contact), and that it is possible to create working relationships across statutory and voluntary/community (or even private) sectors. If, in order to achieve the best possible outcome for the client/service user, you need to set up multi-agency/multi-sector case conferences, then do that. Even if you don't feel that you can share information then perhaps it's worth exploring whether there are some aspects of support that your client can get from a specialist LGBT support organization and some that they can get from you. Get to know what LGBT support there is in your geographic area, make your contacts and keep in touch with them so that you have an immediate link should you need it, and do it before you have a client/service user in crisis, as that's the wrong time to be trying to network!

Further Reading

Excellent coverage of sociological aspects of relationships and intimacies can be found in the following two texts:

Jamieson, L. (2002) *Intimacy: Personal Relationships in Modern Societies*. Cambridge: Polity Press.

Smart, C. (2008) *Personal Life*. Cambridge: Polity Press.

11

Community and Social Capital

Steven MacLennan, Keith Muir
and Susan Thoms

Key themes

- Community is conceptually highly problematic.
- Community can refer not only to a geographic area, but also to people who share a collective identity, common interests and common situations.
- The continuing existence of community is highly contentious, with research indicating a mixed, fluid and highly varied state of affairs.
- Areas of groups of people with high social capital arguably can experience better health, lower crime and a variety of other positive social goods.
- For social workers community work can help to tackle the deeper causes of social problems, inequalities and injustice.

Keywords

community, identity, urban, rural, social capital, empowerment, crisis intervention

Introduction

Working with people not just as individual service users but also as part of a wider community is an important part of social work practice. For example, social workers may provide services for people who are unwell or disabled and who have contacts with a community of interest comprising medical, nursing, home care, welfare rights, welfare benefits and job centre staff, or they may work with children and families in city or rural communities where problems will relate to local services, schools or employment opportunities. They may also work in teams that are geographically situated within particular areas, in health centres with a defined catchment area or in residential units that are part of a particular community within a town or part of a city.

This chapter explores the concept of community, teasing out issues of definition and the capacity of community to be a positive resource in people's lives, allowing them to experience a better, healthier and safer life. To do so, the work of the Chicago School and David Putnam will be drawn on in order to describe, explain and define the concepts of community and social capital. The Chicago School were a group of academics, working and studying in Chicago from around 1910 to 1930, and their work was important in the establishment of a group of cognate studies now referred to as 'urban sociology'. Their studies generated many influential, if not classic, post-Second World War urban and community studies in Britain and elsewhere. Attention then turns to the equally influential and contemporary work of David Putnam, and the theory of 'social capital', for which he is best known. Social capital is a current social theory of community, which sees community as embedded in social networks and civic engagement, and is generally, though not always, regarded as an advantageous asset for individuals and society as a whole. The social capital thesis has captured a large audience outside of academia, and has been used to inform policy research designed to facilitate social capital.

Both of the above are applied examples of how sociological research is important in explaining social problems and, by association, point to how such problems could be alleviated. Such research is therefore crucially relevant to issues outside of academia and can influence social policies. In turn this work modifies institutional discourses (especially at a social policy level), and affects local social work practices.

Sociology Focus

Community

Community has long been a subject of sociological study. The reason for this interest relates to the massive transformations and upheavals that occurred in European societies during the Industrial Revolution, a period of transition from predominantly rural to increasingly urban societies (starting around the mid-1800s). Industrialization and the rise of capitalism in Western societies made people more geographically and socially mobile, changed the physical structures they inhabited, facilitated a distinction between places of work and home, restructured economies and centralized the provision of public services (Crow and Allan, 1994; Savage et al., 2002). These changes also impacted upon the social roles and identities of individuals and how they interacted with one another (Simmel, 1950 [1905]; Tönnies, 1963 [1887]).

This move to city and urban life, as indicated above, radically altered people's lives. Urban life, its cultures and ways of relating to people were in stark contrast with the rural life that most people had previously experienced. Ferdinand Tönnies (1887) characterized the differences between the rural and urban as two different types of social relations: *Gemeinschaft* (community) and *Gesellschaft* (association). *Gemeinschaft* refers to the strong emotional bonds, sustained by kinship, customs and an emotional attachment and loyalty to place, found in communities. *Gesellschaft* refers to rational and impersonal relationships, regulated by contracts and the law, found in business organizations and large populations. George Simmel's (1950) *The Metropolis and Mental Life* contrasted modern city living with rural and urban dwellers from an earlier epoch and argued that cities were in a state of constant change. As a result, the individual's senses were constantly stimulated, resulting in an intensification of emotional life. Savage et al. (2002, p. 123) point to four interrelated urban forms evident in Simmel's works:

1. Intellectuality means urban dwellers react with their head instead of their heart.
2. Urban dwellers instrumentally weigh up the advantages and disadvantages of each action, i.e. they are calculative.
3. Urban dwellers distance themselves from each other emotionally.
4. Individuality, reserve and an aversion to other people create a blasé attitude.

The sociological interest in 'community' has often focused on the concept as being a state of affairs that is desirable, wholesome and connoting warm images of friendly neighbours, people to call on in times of trouble, and a source of identity. This brief outline probably accords with most people's intuitive understanding of what community is and what it means. After all, in the United Kingdom, at least, popular culture is replete with images of some form of 'community'. Television soap operas such as *EastEnders, Coronation Street, Hollyoaks,* and the now classic *Brookside,* all, in their own way, deal and have dealt with issues of community. The community life depicted in those series might not always be rosy, might be often beset by problems, with the occasional punch-up in the pub, but underlying them all is the ideal that people should be able to live harmoniously with their neighbours.

The sociological research into community has revealed that community may, however, be much more diffuse than the above brief treatment would suggest. Community is actually a notoriously difficult concept to define succinctly and in fact has many meanings (Crow and Allan, 1994). One can witness how community refers to a variety of quite different relationships, interactions and spatial arrangements (where people live). So, for example, in the British soaps mentioned above, community is the 'classic' image of a group of people living in a distinct place, while the 'business community' refers to people who do not necessarily live (or even work in the same place) but yet have some attribute in common. These difficulties do not mean we should abandon any attempt to define community. The following interrelated themes frequently emerge in the literature:

- *Common situation.* Communities often share a common feature that binds them, such as class, ethnicity or religion, which may be, but is not essentially, territorial. For example, it is not enough simply to live in an area to be part of the community (Crow and Allan, 1994), and conversely online community members need not be in physical contact with each other.
- *Common interests.* Communities involve interpersonal relationships and emotional bonds that are not centred just on work, or politics, etc., but also encompass most areas of everyday life (Tönnies, 1963 [1887]; Wilmott, 1986).
- *Collective identity.* There is a group identity that individuals recognize and to which they are emotionally attached and feel loyalty (Lee and Newby, 1983). Regardless of place, communities are contained within socially constructed 'symbolic boundaries' (Cohen, 1985). That is, people use the idea of community to generate and sustain their sense of belonging. The notion of community provides some basis for their identity, especially in terms of insiders and outsiders, i.e. those who are similar, and those who are different (Cohen, 1985).

The continuing existence of community also needs to be considered. Much sociological research and theorizing has strongly suggested that society today is marked not so much by being a member of a community but by being an individual. Theoreticians such as Beck (2001) and Giddens (1981), for a variety of reasons, maintain that 'individualization' is a strong dynamic in contemporary society. People either do not have the time for, nor do they attach the same importance to, the building of bonds with their neighbours. Empirical research is also suggestive of this trend. Young and Willmott's classic (1957) study of life in the East End of London identified what for many people would be an archetypical location-based community. People engaged in regular acts of mutual-aid with strong matriarchial figures guiding and maintaining community cohesion. A follow-up study in the 1970s on the same people, after they had been moved to a new

estate, found that the community bonds had broken and given way to
more privatized and individual pattern of relationships. Recent research
commissioned by the BBC (Sillito, 2008) also suggested a weakening of
community among the British public, with just over a fifth of Britons thinking that British neighbourhoods are not as friendly as they used to be.

These pessimistic accounts though have to be balanced by other research
that indicates that community, even though hard to maintain, is still important for many people. Mumford and Power (2003), for example, found that,
for poor women, lone-parents bonds' and connections with other women
on their estates were an important and valued resource on which to call in
times of need. Overall, it is difficult accurately to assess the community
balance sheet and make definitive claims as to the existence or otherwise
of community. What is sure, however, is that with many different social
processes and impulses operating simultaneously, community is becoming
a much more complex phenomenon to study and to understand. Cattell
(2004), in her work on community in declining neighbourhoods, found
examples of both high individualization and of strong community bonds,
the existence of either being contingent on factors such as poverty, existing
community interaction, and the will of people to initiate and maintain
interactions with others.

The next theory we examine indicates the potential of community and
association to create positive change and circumstances for people.

Social Capital: A Contemporary Theory of Community

Social capital is not a new idea. As a concept it has been around in various
guises and formats and has been recognized and reincarnated by many scholars
and writers over the past century (Farr, 2004). However, Robert Putnam's
(1993, 1995, 1996, 2000) thesis has captured the popular and political imagination. Putnam's concern centred on the analysis that social capital had been in
decline in the United States, especially since the 1940s. However, what is
social capital? Field's (2003: 1) definition is comprehensive and clear:

> By making connections with one another, and keeping them going over time,
> people are able to work together to achieve things they could not achieve by
> themselves, or could only achieve with great difficulty. People connect through
> a series of *networks* and they tend to *share some common values* with other mem-
> bers of these networks; to the extent that these networks constitute a resource,
> they can be seen as a form of capital. As well as being useful in its immediate
> context, this stock of capital can often be drawn on in other settings. In general

then, it follows, the more people you know, and the more you share a common outlook with them, the richer you are in social capital. [emphases added; note the emphasized elements of Field's definition that resonate with the thematic outline of community offered above]

In addition, Halpern (2005) adds that there are three irreducible features of social capital that should be recognizable in any associational form (for example a community): a *network*; shared *norms, values* and *expectancies*; and *sanctions* (i.e. punishments and rewards) that maintain the norms and network. Putnam (1995) also identified the features of *trust* and *reciprocity*, which should also be added to this list. Furthermore, there are sub-types of social capital, *bonding* and *bridging*. 'Bonding social capital brings together people who are alike in important respects (ethnicity, age, gender, social class etc.) whereas bridging social capital refers to social networks that bring together people who are unlike one another' (Putnam and Goss, 2002, p. 11). Bridging is generally viewed as a positive type of social capital, whereas bonding can have negative consequences if groups are homogeneous and exclude others, whilst promoting solely their own interests, such as criminal gang activity, or underpinning institutional discrimination (Field, 2003; Halpern, 2005; Putnam and Goss, 2002).

Putnam's (1995, 2000) 'bowling alone' metaphor neatly summarizes his concern that people are less likely to engage in social activities, such as playing in teams in organized bowling leagues against regular sets of opponents, or being involved in civil engagements such as trade unions, Parent Teacher Associations and voting. The metaphor of someone bowling alone is derived from the popular American pastime of ten-pin bowling. In the 1950s, being part of a bowling league was commonplace for most Americans. It was by associating with individuals on a regular basis that common bonds could be forged and maintained, the argument being that this style of activity helps to build and sustain 'a wider set of networks and values that foster general reciprocity and trust, and in turn facilitate mutual collaboration' (Field, 2003, p. 32). As time has moved on, bowling still remains popular in the United States, but the leagues have declined, and thus people are much less likely to have the associations they once did in the 1950s and are now 'bowling alone'.

Putnam (1993), in his original social capital study, compared different regions in Italy to explain what made some regional governments more effective than others. He found that effectiveness was not due to budgets or policy, instead, the differences were based on the vibrancy of associational life and the level of trust between strangers. Furthermore, these differences were embedded in cultural and political practices (Putnam, 1993).

The North/South Italian divide was argued, by Putnam (1993), to be marked by higher levels of distrust, lower levels of voluntary association involvement (civil engagement) and a power-based (rather than participation-based) social organization in the South, which accounted for at least some of the North's higher economic performance. In this way it can be seen how social capital can affect not only the individual and local level, but also the regional and national.

Essentially, what makes social capital work is that the networks provide 'instrumental' and 'affective' support. Instrumental support refers to practical advice, creating useful contacts or assisting in distinct tasks ('lending a hand'), while affective resources include emotional support and helping someone cope with a crisis ('a shoulder to cry on'). These resources allow a whole host of positive outcomes and developments to occur for both individuals and communities if social capital is high. A range of research has associated good health, low crime rates and high educational attainment, for example, with high social capital (Halpern, 2005). There are many reasons why these outcomes arise, but essentially, it all returns to the basic premise of social capital that the more social capital one possesses, then the more affective and instrumental resources and supports there are, upon which one can call.

In the UK, Coulthard, Walker and Morgan (2002) used British General Household Survey data pertaining to the indicators of civic engagement, neighbourliness, social networks and social support, to operationalize the concept of social capital and correlate these findings with socio-demographic indicators (age, sex, ethnicity, etc.). Their study was comprehensive, but in brief, people who scored positively in one area were likely to score positively in the other areas, and less likely to score negatively in all the other areas (i.e. social capital encompasses most areas of social life). Those with low social capital tended to be young, female, belong to an ethnic minority, be more poorly educated, have dependent children, be renters (as opposed to owner occupiers), and have recently moved house. These findings point to the idea that community life facilitates social capital, and those that are socially, not just economically, deprived are more likely to have low social capital. If people do not have access to social networks that support social capital, and this is coupled with other factors such as low wages or unemployment, then they are unlikely to have equal access to social capital resources (Field, 2003).

In rounding up this introduction to the concepts of community and social capital, community, as a certain type of social relation, can be regarded as being of benefit to individuals because it involves cohesiveness, solidarity and trustworthiness and is also important for the well-being of individuals. Furthermore, when those types of social relations are in place they promote social networks and facilitate individual and community action through the solution of collective problems (Halpern, 2005). If community is taken as a certain form of social relation between people, then social capital can be regarded as a beneficial outcome of it. The two concepts are mutual and interlinked: communities foster and facilitate social capital. As Putnam and Goss (2002) argue, isolation and community stagnation are a result of civic disengagement, and civic disengagement leads to a decline in social capital. The social capital thesis points to the ways in which communities may be constituted contemporaneously, that is, it is not so much the place that is important, it is networks involving people who trust each other and can collaborate with each other to obtain collective social goods, although it is also recognized that these can be used for selfish and disruptive ends too.

Social Work Focus

Social work has long concerned itself with the social environment and context of people's lives, as much as with individual difficulties or personal traits. The problems that an individual or perhaps a family will have in coping with life's difficulties can be relatively easy to understand (if not necessarily so straightforward to fix!). Responding to an issue involving large numbers of individuals can seem rather more daunting, however. In such a scenario we may understandably be tempted to view those large numbers of people as so many individual cases, often with the result of pathologizing each of those individuals, that is, seeing the problems of the larger group as just being a collection of individual problems. In this section, building on the insights provided by sociology, we shall explore how community-based social work can effect positive change at a deeper social level. By attempting change at this wider social level, social work can prove, in many respects, to be more effective in challenging and addressing the problems of individual clients.

Social work approaches – the individual or the community?

First of all, it may be useful briefly to consider different models of social work before considering how and why working on a community-wide basis could be of use to social work. This reflection is important to undertake, as how one conceptualizes social work (thinking about what social

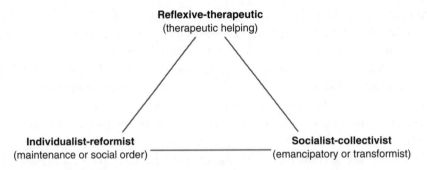

Figure 11.1 *Discourses of the social work task (Payne, 2005, p. 10)*

work is meant to do) determines the form of social work practice (how social work is carried out in the 'real world'). In considering what exactly social work is, Payne (2005) suggests a triangle (Figure 11.1), which identifies the three competing and complementary discourses of the social work task as follows:

- **Reflexive-therapeutic** – this approach forms the basis of most social work. It is centred on bringing about the best possible approach to improving the situation for individuals or communities so that they can avoid and transcend problems by being encouraged to increase their personal power.
- **Socialist-collectivist** – this is a more radical approach to social work. It operates on the principle that those who are discriminated against, or who are disadvantaged, may be able to take more control over their lives by banding or working together. The role of the social worker is to encourage and facilitate this process.
- **Individualist-reformist** – this approach could be seen as a compromise between the above approaches. While seeking to meet the needs of the individual, the social worker is also trying to make relevant welfare services, including social work, more efficient, effective or responsive. In this respect, the individualist-reformist approach may be seen as less ambitious, and, some may say, more realistic than the socialist-collectivist approach.

If we accept the above as a useful identification of the main aspects of social work we could argue that much of current practice is concerned with the therapeutic and reformist approaches to needs within society. These approaches may seem a helpful way forward with their concern for, and focus on, helping individuals and maintaining social order. Unease has been mooted by some social workers in relation to social work operating in this manner. As Culpitt (1999), prompted by the theories of Foucault, claimed, the primary function of the welfare state may not be about poverty or social exclusion, but be about identifying, classifying and regulating deviant individuals and groups. What Culpitt is arguing here is that social work, following an individualist and therapeutic approach, is only dealing with the surface problems of society and the individual and not tackling the deeper underlying causes of problems such as poverty or inequality. What sociology tells us is that problems may appear to be the property of the individual, but this is only a partial, if not misleading, understanding of the causes of the issues that social work clients face in their daily lives. Problems have, instead, a deeper social origin. Unless they are tackled or reduced at that level then they will continually be reproduced.

Accepting deeper causes of social problems creates interesting challenges for social work and social workers. Social workers are, after all, *required* by the various regulatory bodies in the United Kingdom not only to be *non*-discriminatory but also, more actively, to be *anti*-discriminatory and to *challenge oppression* wherever they come across it. In order to adopt this more progressive deeper approach, it is not enough to help someone in an often unjust, unequal and oppressive society; we have instead to be concerned with the very factors that create these unacceptable conditions.

An instructive example can be drawn from C. Wright–Mills. Addressing unemployment, he states that 'when, in a city of 100,000, only one man is unemployed, that is his personal trouble, and for its relief we look to the character of the man, his skills and his immediate opportunities. But when in a nation of 50 million employees, 15 million men are unemployed, that is an issue and we may not hope to find its solution within the range of opportunities open to any one individual' (Wright–Mills, 1959, p. 9).

Of course some of those people who are unemployed may have needed help with a variety of aspects in their personal lives before becoming unemployed, some may now need help as a consequence of becoming unemployed and some may manage to get by without any outside intervention, perhaps through relying on their own resources or with support from family or other contacts. The point, however, is that the problem is not 15 million individual problems but rather one societal problem.

It is in response to this kind of dilemma where individual people and families are undoubtedly suffering, but the scale of the problem is such that it is about much more than individuals, that we need to consider the place of communities in tackling social problems.

Continuing the analogy for a little further, we might want to consider the nature of large-scale unemployment as forming a community of interest as well as a geographical community and that there is a great deal of common lived experiences between a family living on state benefit in

Swansea or in, say, Manchester. Indeed, the same argument could be made about an individual with a serious drug problem living in Strabane compared to one living in Kidderminster. In other words, there is a locality element to community, but there can also be a shared experience element that can transcend place, linking people who live in quite separate places in a common cause.

Working with communities

Community, as we have seen throughout this chapter, is not then a static concept, but rather one that has many different applications across time and space, as was discussed in the sociology section. Into this equation we can add the concept of alienation. This particular concept can be understood as a situation where an individual or a wider group of people feel that they have little or no commitment to the ideals, aspirations or indeed the benefits of being part of wider society. Often this alienation is connected to beliefs and feelings that somehow the individual or group do not have the means to access resources that people in wider society would tend to take for granted. Again, thinking about unemployment, if a school leaver's parents, neighbours and siblings are persistently unemployed, then it is not likely to be a surprise if that young person does not see the relevance of seeking employment for him/herself. Indeed, it is even more likely to reinforce negative aspects about society should that person attempt to find meaningful employment and fail, than if they never attempt it in the first place. Either course of action is unlikely to lead to a more cohesive society.

More recently the term social 'inclusion' has become a more accepted one, although once again the concept has a range of differing meanings depending on the point one wishes to make. For New Labour in the early twenty-first century, the term tended to equate with individuals being in employment whilst social exclusion was, from this perspective, primarily about unemployment.

Interestingly, the concept derives from a European perspective that focuses on geographical communities where there is a wide level of deprivation experienced by the inhabitants of that area. The key issue here is that, in the European discourse, it is communities that are excluded rather than the individuals that make up those communities. This is an important distinction, as it would tend to imply that it is the communities that require support rather than merely the individuals who make up the community.

Such a position might, incidentally be seen to be very much in line with the European traditions of social solidarity which stands in contrast with recent British social policy that tends to emphasise the individual at the expense of structural or wider societal factors.

In order to challenge social inequalities it is therefore necessary to seek to help people to become empowered. Ledwith describes this as the process through which 'people have their dignity and self respect restored' and 'which is the consequence of critical consciousness: the understanding that life chances are prescribes by structural discrimination' (Ledwith, 2009, p. xii). The crucial aspect of this approach is that it is emancipatory (creates freedom) and transformative (makes changes). It does not merely try to tidy up problems, as is implied in the individual and therapeutic models above, but seeks rather to use the power of the community to eradicate those problems. One rather obvious criticism of this approach can be made right away: such wide-scale change is too ambitious, and indeed it is. We are never going to create Utopia. That does not mean, however, to say that such a goal is not worthy of pursuit, and, even if only some change is made, then that is still of benefit to many people.

One of the difficulties facing the practice of social work arises from the profession's large representation in local government service. Community work, in terms of trying to help communities of interests, often within geographically located communities, flourished in the 1960s and 1970s. It could be argued that the activities and projects, while successful in some areas, were inadequately embedded to have lasting success, were inadequately funded in order to become embedded or, significantly, were overwhelmed by political will. In this last respect, the legacy of the Conservative governments of Prime Minister Margaret Thatcher in the 1970s and 1980s was the dismantling of community work as a mainstream social work activity. Social work became distinct from community work, which became a separate strand, often linked with youth work, and delivered from a less powerful position in the hierarchy of local government. The task for social workers now is to re-establish the awareness of community, perhaps more as a reflection of a continuum of service provision.

Probably the first task is to identify the community, remembering that it does not have to be geographical, although it may well be. As we discussed earlier, communities can either be based on a locality or can be based on shared interests or a common experience of exclusion and oppression. The point here is to find the commonality, whether in relation to where they live, common experiences or some aspect of their self-identity that binds a particular group of people together.

Next it is necessary to identify the needs and issues within the particular community. The approach to this task, which is commonly used by bureaucratic organizations or agencies, is for that organization, for example, the local authority, to undertake an assessment and work out what needs to be done to improve the community. Again, such an approach may sound beneficial for a community, as bureaucracies and organizations can exercise great power and potentially will have access to a variety of resources. Trying to effect positive change via this approach does have two notable drawbacks. First, what the bureaucracy identifies as a problem may not be what the community itself regards as being a problem. It may suit an organization to define something as a problem based on the specific resources they may have at their disposal to deal with it. They may, therefore, ignore what they cannot solve. Second, actions by an organization can be seen to be a 'top-down' approach. People in the community become passive actors as opposed to active agents, as control and power over what happens in their community are taken away from them.

ACTIVITY

Can you see a problem here? Does this 'top down' approach seem to equate with the concept of 'empowerment'?

In order to prevent this top-down approach imposing outside solutions on communities, one solution is to undertake a community profile in partnership with the community. We might liken this to an assessment based on an exchange model in which the worker is the expert in the theory and knowing how to navigate the external systems and bureaucracies, but the residents of the community are the experts in what life is like in that community. Again this applies to communities of interest as well as geographical communities. Travellers may be a very dispersed community, but their experiences can only be unique to their own community. As a static person, I may know how to advise on the best approaches to the various authorities, but I cannot know what it feels like to be a traveller in either the positive or the negative aspects.

As a social work intervention, community work may be said to have suffered from a lack of clarity in defining what both the concept and practice actually are. However, it could be argued that in the twenty-first century, with the variety of welfare provision and economic factors, community work may have a particular part to play in working alongside groups of people in order to promote change in 'issues of poverty, exclusion, racism and disadvantage and how these feed into local problems of inadequate facilities, crime, ill-health, isolation, breakdown in relationships and so on' (Stepney, 2006, p. 1300).

To review the role of social work then:

- We need to be involved in identifying some area of common purpose in a group of people, or at least the potential for a sense of purpose.
- There will be some shortfall in either the physical means to advance that purpose, in the knowledge of how to advance the purpose, or in both.
- There is likely to be a sense of injustice and equally likely to be a sense of hopelessness or impotency ('nothing can be done so why bother trying').
- The worker can assist in identifying the goal but *must not* seek to impose his/her own agendas. In this the method is very similar to Task Centred work (Coulshed and Orme, 2006) with individuals in that the nature of the problem to be addressed must first be negotiated by the service user in relationship with the social worker and then specific achievable tasks or goals are agreed in the same way. Albeit as a community approach, this is undertaken with a very different type of service user.

Similarities can also be drawn from the Crisis Intervention model (Coulshed and Orme, 2006). In this model, individuals experiencing a state of crisis, in which their normal balance or comfort is upset, may be motivated to address change in order to remove the crisis. The aim is to achieve a crossover into a wider field of functioning, and this may be the further goal of a community approach. So, if a community or elements within it are able to accept that they can have some influence on what happens in their lives in one situation, they are likely to refuse meekly to accept unreasonable imposed conditions in any other area of their lives. Notice that as with Crisis Intervention, a sense of crisis that incorporates hopelessness is part of the problem, and changing that hopelessness is part of the solution.

It is not always necessary to succeed totally in altering the target of change as long as people in the community feel that they have been able to make some impact on the situation which they have identified as problematic. To this end the old song 'It ain't what you do it's the way that you do it' seems very appropriate as a theme tune for community work.

However, the challenge facing social work is large. In the managerial culture within which social work operates, it is difficult to deliver effectively at a wider community level. Alan Twelvetrees (2002) has noted how much of community work is based on projects, 'task centred', in other words. These projects take time to set up, and perhaps by the time they are in operation, funding may be cut, staff will have been dispersed and little achieved in the way of any consistent improvement.

ACTIVITY

Compare the discussion of social capital in Chapter 9 on Crime with some of the underlying themes in this chapter.

Social workers in the twenty-first century will be faced with the need to communicate with policy-makers how the themes of community, addressed within this chapter, can have an implication for the problems faced by individuals. The whole premise is based on the importance of relationships, of networks, of continuity: in a system that relies on the policies of politicians, these features, particularly continuity, are hard to maintain.

Lived Experience

For the lived experience, community worker Susan Thoms reflects on her experiences working with people in deprived communities. As you read the lived experience it would be useful to consider the issues that have been discussed in both the sociology and the social work focus. Doing so should help you relate what can seem quite abstract theories and concepts to real life examples.

The following prompts should prove helpful:

- Consider how the sociological perspectives outlined in the sociology focus relate to how Susan defines and describes the communities with which she works.
- Reflect on how other examples of disadvantage and inequality we have explored elsewhere in this book are relevant to this account of contemporary communities.
- Identify how the initiatives with which Susan is involved could potentially build social capital in that community.

The concept of 'community' is hard to define, and being a member of a community does not necessarily lead to a collective view, or a harmonious, united population. The communities I work in are defined geographically, where the sense of community comes from where you live. They are also defined by poverty and disadvantage, being amongst the most deprived in the country.

The statistics relating to poor health, low educational attainment, high unemployment, low income, inadequate housing and a lack of access to facilities and services, are stark and revealing. The reality has a major impact on people's quality of life and well-being. For individuals this can result in isolation, alienation, a feeling of powerlessness and a lack of capacity to participate in society. For a community it can result in social conflict, a lack of community cohesion and a poor reputation.

In turn, communities can become areas with a high turnover of residents, and are seen as a 'last resort' rather than somewhere to live through choice. When people have an attachment to a place it can help stabilize the neighbourhood, foster the development of social networks and community ties, and encourage a positive engagement. Strong social networks can act as a defence against some of the worst problems in a deprived area, and increase trust and feelings of security. Having neighbours to turn to, groups and activities to be involved in and support and advice available, can help make life easier. And where the community comes together to tackle common issues, such as community safety, or to organize community events, this can increase the feeling that the area is a good place to live, and help to build stronger, more resilient communities.

The role of community workers within such neighbourhoods is to support the community to increase social inclusion, and develop community capacity and engagement. The social aspects of disadvantage, such as crime, drugs, disaffected young people and anti-social behaviour, can be tackled by building aspirations and expectations amongst those who may be poorly educated, low-skilled and demotivated. Education offers a potential route to empowerment and equality. People who are more confident, skilled and knowledgeable have the ability not only to change their own individual circumstances, but also to get involved in their local communities, to make changes, take action, feel in control and to be engaged.

I am involved in a wide number of initiatives that support communities in this way, providing opportunities for personal development and community involvement. Usually the two are linked, for example, involvement in an informal art and craft group, or literacy class, may lead to people becoming involved in a media project, making films about community issues, producing community newsletters, presenting topical, locally based community radio shows. And through the process people are learning, accessing training, becoming more confident, talking to decision-makers and politicians, putting their views across and getting their voices heard.

The formal education system all too often fails people, particularly those from disadvantaged backgrounds. Lack of support from parents, who may have had a negative educational experience themselves, combined with an attitude from teachers and peers that 'they will never amount to anything' can result in young people leaving school with few qualifications and poor job prospects. We want our young people to be 'effective contributors' and 'active citizens' yet their life chances are often more or less defined from the day they are born. Youth work involves engaging with young people, often non-participants, in a way that is sympathetic to their interests. Using methods such as residential trips, combining outdoor activities with discussion time, using interactive media such as video or drama are ways of enabling young people to put their views across in ways more appropriate to them; engaging with young people on the streets and conducting meetings in an informal style can also encourage young people to get involved.

One aim might be to get young people involved in consultative forums or Community Councils, where they can get involved in neighbourhood planning and decision-making, and represent the views of other young people in their area. For some more vulnerable groups of young people, the aims may be less ambitious, but just as vital. Support to deal with chaotic lifestyles that may include drug misuse and homelessness should be available in a non-judgemental way. Empathy is vital in understanding the needs and issues facing young people, and it is important to recognize the potential they have. Peer education is one way for young people to learn from each other and share experiences. A young mothers' group may be set up principally for pregnant teenage girls and mothers, to teach them life skills, build their confidence, and give support that may not be available elsewhere. To have the same girls visiting classes at the local school, passing on their experience and knowledge to their peers, can potentially reduce incidents of teenage pregnancy in a way that is more relevant and effective than teachers, parents, books, or leaflets may be.

Further Reading

A good all-round introduction on sociology and communities is provided by:
Savage, M., Warde, A. and Ward, K. (2002) *Urban Sociology, Capitalism and Modernity*, 2nd edn. Basingstoke: Palgrave Macmillan.

While the following provides a useful social work perspective:
Twelvetrees, A. (2002) *Community Work*. Basingstoke: Palgrave Macmillan.

References

Abrahams, H. (2007) *Supporting Women After Domestic Violence: Loss, Trauma and Recovery*. London: Jessica Kingsley.

Abrams, L. (1998) *The Orphan Country*. Edinburgh: John Donald.

Acheson, D. (1998) *Independent Inquiry into Inequalities in Health*. London: The Stationery Office.

Adams, R. (1996) *The Personal Social Services*. Harlow: Longman.

Adams, R. (2008) *Empowerment, Participation and Social Work*. Basingstoke: Palgrave Macmillan.

Adams, R., Dominelli, L. and Payne, M. (2002) *Social Work: Themes, Issues and Critical Debate*. Basingstoke: Palgrave.

Adams, R., Dominelli, L. and Payne, M. (eds) (2009) *Critical Practice in Social Work*. Basingstoke: Palgrave Macmillan.

Aggleton, P. (1987) *Deviance*. London: Tavistock.

Aldridge, J. and Sharpe, D. (2007) *Pictures of Young Caring*. Loughborough: ESRC and Loughborough University.

Allen, K. (2004) *Max Weber: A Critical Introduction*. London: Pluto Press.

Andrews, M. (1999) 'The seductiveness of agelessness', *Ageing and Society*, 19: 301–18.

Arber, S. and Ginn, J. (1993) 'Gender and inequalities in health in later life', *Social Science and Medicine*, 36(1): 33–46.

Arber, S. and Ginn, J. (1995) 'Women and ageing', *Reviews in Clinical Gerontology* 4(4): 93–102.

Armstrong, H. (2006) *Foreword to Reaching Out: An Action Plan on Social Exclusion*. www. cabinetoffice.gov.uk/social exclusion task force/publications/reaching out/pdf

Ashenden, S. (2004) *Governing Child Sexual Abuse: Negotiating the Boundaries of Public and Private, Law and Science*. London: Routledge.

Association of Directors of Social Work (ADSW) (2003) ADSW Policy Statement on Criminal Justice Social Work. www.adsw.org.uk/documents/ADSWCJPOLICY. 1103.doc (accessed 12 November 2003).

Atkin, K., Waqar, I.U. and Jones, L. (2002) 'Young South Asian deaf people and their families: negotiating relationships and identities', *Sociology of Health and Illness*, 24(1): 21–45.

Atkinson, R. (1998) 'The life story interview', *Qualitative Research Methods*. Series 44, A SAGE University Paper.

Bagguley, P. and Mann, K. (1992) 'Idle thieving bastards? Scholarly representations of the "underclass"'. *Work, Employment and Society* 6(1): 113–26.

Bailey, R. and Brake, M. (1975) *Radical Social Work*. London: Edward Arnold.

Baker, S. and MacPherson, J. (2000) *Counting the Cost: Mental Health in the Media*. London: MIND.

Balibar, E. (1991) 'Is there a neo-racism?', in E. Balibar and I. Wallerstein (eds), *Race, Nation, Class: Ambiguous Identities*. London: Verso, pp. 17–28.

Banks S. (2001) *Ethics and Values in Social Work*. Basingstoke: Palgrave.

Barclay Report (1982) *Social Workers: Their Role and Tasks. Report of a Working Party*. London: Bedford Square Press.

Barnardo's (2006) *Hidden Lives – Unidentified Young Carers in the UK*. Ilford: Barnardo's.

Bauman, Z. (1989) *Modernity and the Holocaust*. Ithaca, NY: Cornell University Press.

Bauman, Z. (1998) *Work, Consumerism and the New Poor*. Buckingham: Open University Press.

Bauman, Z. (2005) *Liquid Life*. Cambridge: Polity Press.

Beck, U. (1992) *Risk Society: Towards a New Modernity*. London: SAGE.

Beck, U. (1994) 'The reinvention of politics: towards a theory of reflexive modernization', in U. Beck, A. Giddens and S. Lash (eds), *Reflexive Modernization: Politics, Tradition and Aesthetics in the Modern Social Order*. Cambridge: Polity Press, pp. 1–55.

Beck, U. (2001) *Individualization: Institutionalized Individualism and its Social and Political Consequences*. London: SAGE.

Beck-Gernsheim, E. (1998) 'On the way to a post-familial family: from a community of needs to elective affinities', *Theory, Culture and Society*, 15(3–4): 53–70.

Becker, H.S. (1953) 'Becoming a Manhuana User', *The American Journal of Sociology*, 59(3): 235–242.

Becker, H. (1963) *Outsiders: Studies in the Sociology of Deviance*. New York: Free Press.

Becker, H. (1964) *The Other Side: Perspectives on Deviance*. New York: Free Press.

Beckett, C. and Maynard, A. (2005) *Values and Ethics in Social Work – An Introduction*. London: SAGE.

Berger, P. and Berger, B. (1976) *Sociology: A Biographical Approach*. Harmondsworth: Penguin.

Berridge, D. and Brodie, I. (1996) 'Residential child care in England and Wales: the enquiries and after', in M. Hill and J. Aldgate (eds), *Child Welfare Services: Developments in Law, Policy, Practice and Research*. London: Jessica Kingsley.

Beveridge, W. (1942) *Social Insurance and Allied Services*. London: HMSO.

Black, D., Morris, J., Smith, C. and Townsend, P. (1980) *Inequalities in Health: Report of a Research Working Group*. London: Department of Health and Social Security.

Blackburn, R. (1998) *The Making of New World Slavery: From the Baroque to the Modern, 1492–1800*. London: Verso.

Blom-Cooper, L. (1985) *A Child in Trust: The Report of the Panel of Inquiry into the Death of Jasmine Beckford*. London: London Borough of Brent.

Blumer (1969) *Symbolic Interaction: Perspective and Method*. Berkley, CA: University of California Press.

Bochel, H., Bochel, C., Page, R. and Sykes, R. (2009) *Social Policy: Themes, Issues and Debates*, 2nd edn. London: Pearson–Prentice Hall.

Bond, J., Peace, S., Dittmann-Kohli, F. and Westerhof, G. (eds) (2007) *Ageing in Society*, 3rd edn. London: SAGE.

Bottero, W. (2005) *Stratification: Social Division and Inequality*. London: Routledge.

Bourdieu, P. (1984) *Distinction: A Social Critique of the Judgement of Taste*. London: Routledge and Kegan Paul.

Bourke, J. (1999) *An Intimate History of Killing: Face-to-Face Killing in Twentieth Century Warfare*. London: Granta.

Bradley, H. (1996) *Fractured Identities: Changing Patterns of Inequality*. Cambridge: Polity Press.

Braithwiate, J. (1989) *Crime, Shame and Reintegration*. Cambridge: Cambridge University Press.

Brandon, D., Brandon, A. and Brandon, T. (1995) *Advocacy: Power to People with Disabilities*. Birmingham: Venture.

British Association of Social Workers (2002) The Code of Ethics. www.basw.co.uk/Default.aspx?tabid=64

Brogden, M. (2001) *Geronticide: Killing the Elderly*. London: Jessica Kingsley.

Brown, R., Barber, P. and Martin, D. (2008) *Mental Health Law in England and Wales: A Guide for Approved Mental Health Professionals*. Exeter: Learning Matters.

Buckley, R. (2007) 'Social work with children and families: a case study of the integration of law, social policy and research in the development of assessment and intervention with children and families', in J. Lishman (ed.), *Handbook for Practice Learning in Social Work and Social Care*. London: Jessica Kingsley.

Burke, B., Cropper. A. and Harrison, P. (2000) 'Real or imagined - Black women's experiences in the Academy', *Community, Work & Family*, 3(3): 297–310.

Butler, J. (1999) *Gender Trouble: Feminism and the Subversion of Identity*. New York: Routledge.

Butler, R.N. (1969) 'Age-ism: another form of bigotry', *The Gerontologist*, 9: 243–6.

Butler-Sloss, E. (1988) *Report of the Inquiry into Child Abuse in Cleveland*. London: The Stationery Office.

Byrne, D. (2005) *Social Exclusion*, 2nd edn. Buckingham: Open University Press.

Callinicos, A. (1995) *Race and Class*. London: Bookmarks.

Carter, B. and Virdee, S. (2009) 'Racism and the sociological imagination', *British Journal of Sociology* 59(4): 661–79.

Carter, R. and Fenton, S. (2010) 'From re-thinking ethnicity to not thinking ethnicity', *Journal for the Theory of Social Behaviour* 40(1): 1–18.

Case Con Manifesto. Available at www.radical.org.uk/barefoot (accessed 31 August 2009).

Cattel, V. (2004) ' "Having a laugh and mucking in together": using social capital to explore dynamics between structure and agency in the context of declining and regenerated neighbourhoods', *Sociology* 38(5): 939–57.

Central Council for Education and Training in Social Work (1989) Paper 30: *Rules and Requirements for the Diploma in Social Work*. London: CCETSW.

Charcot, J.M. (2009 [1881]) *Clinical Lectures on the Diseases of Old Age*. Cornell: Cornell University Library.

Charles, N., Aull Davies, C. and Harris, C. (2008) *Families in Transition: Social Change, Family Formation and Kin Relationships*. Bristol: Policy Press.

Christie, A. (1998) 'Is social work a "non-traditional" occupation for men?' *British Journal of Social Work,* 28(4): 491-510.

Christie, A. (2006) 'Negotiating the uncomfortable intersections between gender and professional identity in social work', *Critical Social Policy*, 26(2): 390-411.

Clark, T.N. and Lipset, S.M. (1991) 'Are social classes dying?', *International Sociology* 6(4): 397–410.

Cleaver, H., Nicholson, D., Tarr, S. and Cleaver, D. (2007) *Child Protection, Domestic Violence, and Parental Substance Misuse: Family Experiences and Effective Practice.* Philadelphia: Jessica Kingsley.

Clyde, Lord (1992) *Report of the Inquiry into the Removal of Children from Orkney, February 1991.* London: The Stationery Office.

Coello, M.H., Casanas, J.A. and Rocco, S.R. (2004) 'Understanding critical race theory: an analysis of cultural differences in healthcare education', *Image*, 17(49): 1–10.

Cohen, A. (1985). *The Symbolic Construction of Community.* London: Routledge.

Cohen, S. (2002) *Folk Devils and Moral Panics.* Abingdon: Routledge.

Cohen, S. (2002 [1973]) *Folk Devils and Moral Panics.* London: Paladin.

Coleman, C. and Moynihan, J. (1996) *Understanding Crime Data: Haunted by the Dark Figure.* Buckingham: Open University Press.

Collins, P.H. (2007) *Critical Race Theory.* College Park, MD: University of Maryland.

Connell, R.W. (1995) *Masculinities*, 2nd edn. Cambridge: Polity Press.

Connell, R.W. (2002) *Gender.* Cambridge: Polity Press.

Cooley, C.H. (1909) *Social Organisation: A Study of the Larger Mind.* New York: Charles Scribner's Sons.

Corby, B. (2006) *Child Abuse: Towards a Knowledge Base*, 2nd edn. Maidenhead: Open University Press.

Corrin, C. (ed.) (1996) *Women in a Violent World: Feminist Analyses and Resistance Across 'Europe'.* Edinburgh: Edinburgh University Press.

Coulshed, V. and Orme, J. (2006) *Social Work Practice*, 4th edn. Basingstoke: Palgrave Macmillan.

Coulthard, M., Walker, A. and Morgan, A. (2002) *People's Perceptions of their Neighbourhood and Community Involvement. Results form the Social Capital Module of the General Household Survey 2000.* London: Office for National Statistics.

Crawford, K. and Walker, J. (2004) *Social Work with Older People.* Exeter: Learning Matters.

Critcher, C. (ed.) (2006) *Critical Readings: Moral Panics and the Media.* Buckingham: Open University Press.

Crittenden, P. (2008) *Raising Parents: Attachment, Parenting and Child Safety.* Cullompton: Willan.

Croall, H. (1998) *Crime and Society in Britain.* London: Longman.

Crompton, R. (2008) *Class and Stratification: An Introduction to Current Debates*, 3rd edn. Cambridge: Polity Press.

Cross, S. and Bagilhole, B. (2002) 'Girls' jobs for the boys? Men, masculinity and non-traditional occupations', *Gender, Work and Organization*, 9(2): 204–226.

Crow, G. (2002a) 'Families, moralities, rationalities and social change', in Carling, A., Duncan, S. and Edwards, R. (eds), *Analysing Families: Morality and Rationality in Policy and Practice.* London: Routledge, pp. 285-296.

Crow, G. (2002b) 'Fifty years of community studies', *Sociological Research Online*, 7(3). Available from www.socresonline.org.uk/7/3/crow.html (accessed 27 February 2009).

Crow, G. and Allan, G. (1994) *Community Life: An Introduction to Local Social Relations*. Hemel Hempstead: Harvester Wheatsheaf.

Crow, I. (2007) *The Treatment and Rehabilitation of Offenders*. London: SAGE.

CSDH (Commission on Social Determinants of Health) (2008) *Closing the Gap in a Generation: Health Equity through Action on the Social Determinants of Health. Final Report of the Commission on Social Determinants of Health*. Geneva: World Health Organization.

Culpitt, I. (1999) *Social Policy and Risk*. London: SAGE.

Cunningham, J. and Cunningham, S. (2008) *Sociology and Social Work*. Exeter: Learning Matters.

Dale, P. (2004) 'Like a fish in a bowl: parents' perceptions of child protection services', *Child Abuse Review*, 13: 137–157.

Dalrymple, J. and Burke, J. (2006) *Anti-Oppressive Practice: Social Care and the Law*, 2nd edn. Maidenhead: Open University Press.

Daniel, C. (2007) 'Outsiders-within: critical race theory, graduate education and barriers to professionalization', *Journal of Sociology and Social Welfare*, 34(1): 1–13.

David, M. (1996) 'Fundamentally Flawed', in *Charles Murray and the Underclass: The Developing Debate*. London: IEA Health and Welfare Unit, 150–55.

Davidson, N. (1999) 'The Trouble with "Ethnicity', *International Socialism, Second Series*, 84 (3): 3-30.

Davies, J. (1993) *The Family: Is It Just Another Lifestyle Choice?* London: Institute for Economic Affairs.

Davis, A. (2007) 'Structural approaches to social work', in J. Lishman (ed.), *Handbook for Practice Learning in Social Work and Social Care*. London: Jessica Kingsley, pp. 27–38.

Davis, K. (1942) 'A conceptual analysis of stratification', *American Sociological Review* 7(3): 309–21.

Davis, K. and Moore, W.E. (1945) 'Some principles of stratification', *American Sociological Review*, 10(2): 242–49.

Dean, R.G. (2001) 'The myth of cross-cultural competence', *Families in Society: The Journal of Contemporary Human Services*, 82(6): 623–30.

Delgado, R. and Stefancic, J. (2007) *Critical Race Theory: An Introduction*. New York: New York University Press.

Delmar, R. (1977) 'What is feminism?', in J. Mitchell and A. Oakley (eds), *What Is Feminism?* Oxford: Blackwell.

Dickenson, D. (2001) 'Decision-making competence in adults: a philosopher's viewpoint', *Advances in Psychiatric Treatment*, 7: 381–7.

Dingwall, R., Eekelaar, J.M. and Murray, T. (1983) *The Protection of Children: State Intervention and Family Life*. Oxford: Blackwell.

Dominelli, L. (2008) *Anti-Racist Social Work*, 3rd edn. Hampshire: Palgrave Macmillan.

Dominelli, L. (2009) 'Women's reproductive rights: issues and dilemmas for practice', in R. Adams, L. Dominelli and M. Payne (eds), *Critical Practice in Social Work*. Basingstoke: Palgrave Macmillan.

Downes, D. and Rock, P. (2003) *Understanding Deviance: A Guide to the Sociology of Crime and Rule Breaking*, 5th edn. Oxford: Oxford University Press.

Doyal, L. (2001) 'Sex, gender and health: the need for a new approach', *British Medical Journal* 323: 1061–3.

DWP (Department for Work and Pension) (2009) The Pensioners' Incomes Series 2007–08, www.dwp.gov.uk/asd/asd6/Press_Release_0708.pdf (accessed 29 May 2009).

Edwards, A. (1986) 'Male violence in feminist theory: an analysis of the changing conceptions of sex/gender violence and male dominance', in J. Hanmer and M. Maynard (eds), *Women, Violence and Social Control*. London: Macmillan, pp. 13–29.

Elias, N. (1985) *The Loneliness of the Dying*. Oxford: Blackwell.

Emslie, C., Ridge, D., Zieband, S. and Hunt, K. (2006) 'Men's account of depression: reconstructing or resisting hegemonic masculinity?', *Social Science and Medicine*, 62: 2246–57.

Engels, F. (1884/1972) *The Origin of the Family, Private Property and the State*. London: Lawrence and Wishart.

Esping-Anderson, G. (1990) *The Three Worlds of Welfare Capitalism*. Cambridge: Polity Press.

Estes, C. (1979) *The Aging Enterprise*. San Francisco, CA: Jossey–Bass.

Ewald, F. (1991) 'Insurance and risk', in C. Gordon and P. Miller (eds), *The Foucault Effect: Studies in Governmentality*. Chicago, IL: University of Chicago Press. pp. 197–210.

Farr, J. (2004) 'Social capital: a conceptual history', *Political Theory*, 32(1): 6–33.

Featherstone, M. and Hepworth, M. (1991) 'The mask of ageing and the postmodern lifecourse', in M. Featherstone, M. Hepworth, and B.S. Turner (eds), *The Body: Social Process and Cultural Theory*. London: SAGE.

Featherstone, M. Hepworth, M. (1995) 'Images of positive ageing: a case study of Retirement Choice Magazine', in M. Featherstone and A. Wernick (eds), *Images of Ageing: Cultural Representations of Later Life*. London: Routledge.

Ferguson, H. (2004) *Protecting Children in Time: Child Abuse, Child Protection and the Consequences of Modernity*. Basingstoke: Palgrave Macmillan.

Ferguson, I. (2003) 'Challenging a "spoiled identity": mental health service users, recognition and redistribution', in S. Riddell and N. Watson (eds), *Disability, Culture and Identity*. Harlow: Pearson.

Ferraro, K.F. and Farmer, M.M. (1996) 'Double jeopardy to health hypothesis for African Americans: analysis and critique', *Journal of Health and Social Behavior*, 37: 27–43.

Field, J. (2003) *Social Capital*. London: Routledge.

Fineman, M. (1994) 'Preface', in M. Fineman and R. Myktiuk (eds), *The Public Nature of Private Violence: The Discovery of Domestic Abuse*. London: Routledge.

Finkelhor, D. (1994) 'Current information on the scope and nature of child sexual abuse', *The Future of Children*, 4(2): 3-53.

Flouri, E. (2005) *Fathers and Child Outcomes*. New York: Wiley.

Foucault, M. (1991a) 'Governmentality', in G. Burchell, C. Gordon and P. Miller (eds), *The Foucault Effect: Studies in Governmentality*. Hemel Hempstead: Harvester Wheatsheaf, pp. 87–104.

Foucault, M. (1991b) *Discipline and Punish: The Birth of the Prison*. Harmondsworth: Penguin.

Foucault, M. (2001) *Madness and Civilisation*. Abingdon: Routledge Classics.

Fox Harding, L. (1997) *Perspectives in Child Care Policy*, 2nd edn. London: Longman.

Fraser, D. (2009) *The Evolution of the British Welfare State*, 4th edn. Basingstoke: Palgrave Macmillan.

Fraser, S. and Matthews, S. (2008) *The Critical Practitioner in Social Work and Health Care*. London: SAGE/Open University.

Freeark, K., Rosenberg, E., Bornstein, J., Jozefowicz-Simben, D., Linkevich, M. and Lohnes , K. (2005) 'Gender differences and dynamics shaping the Adoption Life Cycle', *American Journal of Orthopsychiatry*, 75(1): 86–101.

Frost, N. and Parton, N. (2009) *Understanding Children's Social Care: Politics, Policy and Practice*. London: SAGE.

Gabb, J. (2008) *Researching Intimacy in Families*. Basingstoke: Palgrave Macmillan.

Gallie, D. (1994) 'Are the unemployed an underclass? Some evidence from the social change and economic life initiative', *Sociology*, 28(3): 737–757.

Gans, H.J. (1995) *The War against the Poor: The Underclass and Antipoverty Policy*. New York: Basic Books.

Garland, D. (1990) 'Frameworks of inquiry in the sociology of punishment', *British Journal of Sociology*, 41(1): 1–15.

Garrett, P.M. (2004) 'How to be modern: New Labour's neo-liberal modernity and the *Change for Children* Programme', *British Journal of Social Work*, 38: 270–289.

Gearty, Y. (2007) 'The mental capacity to act: the Office of the Public Guardian and the New Court of Protection', *Journal of Adult Protection*, 9(3): 39–46.

Geffner, R., Igelman, R. and Zellner, J. (2003) *The Effects of Intimate Partner Violence on Children*. New York: Haworth Press.

George, V. and Wilding, P. (1985) *Ideology and Social Welfare*. London: Routledge & Kegan Paul.

George, V. and Wilding, P. (2002) *Globalization and Human Welfare*. Basingstoke: Palgrave Macmillan.

Ghate, D. (2002) *Parenting in Poor Environments*. London: Jessica Kingsley.

Giddens, A. (1973) *The Class Structure of Advanced Societies*. London: Hutchinson.

Giddens, A. (1981) *A Contemporary Critique of Historical Materialism*. Vol. 1: *Power, Property and the State*. London: Macmillan.

Giddens, A. (1991) *Modernity and Self-Identity: Self and Society in Late Modern Age*. Cambridge: Polity Press.

Giddens, A. (1992) *The Transformation of Intimacy: Sexuality, Love and Eroticism in Modern Societies*. Cambridge: Polity Press.

Giddens, A. (2006) *Sociology*, 5th edn. Cambridge: Polity Press.

Gillies, V. (2003) 'Family and intimate relationships: a review of the sociological research', Families & Social Capital Research Group Paper 2. London: South Bank University.

Gillies, V. (2008) 'Childrearing, class and the new politics of parenting', *Sociology Compass*, 2(3): 1079–95.

Gilroy, P. (1982) 'Steppin' out of Babylon – race, class and autonomy', in Centre for Contemporary Cultural Studies, *The Empire Strikes Back: Race and Racism in 70's Britain*. London: Routledge.

Goffman, E. (1968) *Stigma: Notes on the Management of a Spoiled Identity*. Harmondsworth: Penguin.

Goldthorpe, G.H. (1987) *Social Mobility and Class Structure in Modern Britain*, 2nd edn. Oxford: Clarendon.

Goode, E. and Ben-Yehuda, N. (1994) *Moral Panics: The Social Construction of Deviance.* Oxford: Blackwell.

Goode, E. and Ben-Yehuda, N. (2009) *Moral Panics: The Social Construction of Deviance,* 2nd edn. London: Wiley–Blackwell.

Green, F. (2001) 'It's been a hard day's night: the concentration and intensification of work in late twentieth-century britain', *British Journal of Industrial Relations*, 39(1): 53–80.

Halpern, D. (2005) *Social Capital.* Cambridge: Polity Press.

Hammond, H. (2001) *Child Protection Inquiry into the Circumstances Surrounding the Death of Kennedy McFarlane (17/4/97).* Dumfries and Galloway Child Protection Committee.

Harnet, P.H. (2007) 'A procedure for assessing parents' capacity for change in child protection cases', *Children and Youth Services Review,* 29(9): 1179-1188.

Harris, J.B. (2006) *The Social Work Business.* London: Routledge.

Harris, R., Tobias, M., Jeffreys, M., Waldegrave, K., Karlsen, S. and Nazroo, J. (2006) 'Racism and health: The relationship between the experience of racial discrimination and health in New Zealand', *Social Science and Medicine*, 63(6): 1428-1441.

Hattersley, L. (2005). 'Trends in Life Expectancy by Social Class: an update': *Health Statistics Quarterly* 2: 16-24.

Healy, K. (2005) *Social Work Theories in Context: Creating Frameworks for Practice.* Basingstoke: Palgrave Macmillan.

Hicks, S. (2000) '"Good Lesbian, Bad Lesbian…": regulating heterosexuality in fostering and adoption assessments', *Child and Family Social Work*, 5(2): 157-168.

Hendricks, H. (ed.) (2005) *Child Welfare and Social Policy: An Essential Reader.* Bristol: Policy Press.

Hobdell, E.F., Grant, M.L., Valencia, I., Mare, J., Kothare, S.V., Legido, A. and Khurana, D.S. (2007) 'Chronic sorrow and coping in families of children with epilepsy', *Journal of Neuroscience Nursing*, 39(2): 76–82.

Holmes, M. (2007) *What Is Gender? Sociological Approaches.* London: SAGE.

Holmes, M. (2009) *Gender and Everyday Life.* London: Routledge.

Home Office (2009) British Crime Survey. www.homeoffice.gov.uk/rds/bcs1.html; www.scotland.gov.uk/Publications/2008/06/02124526/8 (accessed 25 April 2010).

Hothersall, S.J. (2008) *Social Work with Children, Young People and Their Families in Scotland,* 2nd edn. Exeter: Learning Matters.

Hothersall, S.J. (2010a) 'What *is* Social Policy?', in S.J. Hothersall and J.L. Bolger (eds), *Social Policy for Social Work, Social Care and the Caring Professions: Scottish Perspectives.* Kent: Ashgate.

Hothersall, S.J. (2010b) 'Ideology: how ideas influence policy and welfare', in S.J. Hothersall and J.I. Bolger (eds), *Social Policy for Social Work, Social Care and the Caring Professions: Scottish Perspectives.* Kent: Ashgate.

Hothersall, S.J. and Bolger, J.I. (eds) (2010) *Social Policy for Social Work, Social Care and the Caring Professions: Scottish Perspectives.* Kent: Ashgate Publishing.

Hothersall, S.J. and Maas-Lowit, M. (eds) (2010) *Need, Risk and Protection in Social Work Practice.* Exeter: Learning Matters.

Hothersall, S.J., Mass-Lowit, M. and Golightley, M. (2008) *Social Work and Mental Health in Scotland.* Exeter: Learning Matters.

Houchin, R., (2005) *Social Exclusion and Imprisonment in Scotland*. Glasgow: Scottish Prison Service.

Howe, D. (2005) *Child Abuse and Neglect: Attachment, Development and Intervention*. Basingstoke: Palgrave Macmillan.

Hull, K. (2006) *Same-Sex Marriage: The Cultural Politics of Love and Law*. Cambridge: Cambridge University Press.

Imrie, R. (1996) *Disability and the City: International Perspectives*. London: Paul Chapman.

Imrie, R. (2006) *Accessible Housing: Quality, Disability and Design*. London: Routledge.

Jamieson, L. (1998) *Intimacy: Personal Relationships in Modern Societies*. Cambridge: Polity Press.

Jenkins, R. (2008) *Social Identity*, 3rd edn. London: Routledge.

Johns, R. (2007) 'Critical commentary: who decides now? Protecting and empowering vulnerable adults who lose the capacity to make decisions for themselves', *British Journal of Social Work* 37(3): 557–64.

Johnston R.J., Gregory, D., Pratt, G. and Watts, M. (eds) (2000) *The Dictionary of Human Geography*. Oxford: Wiley-Blackwell.

Jones, C. (1998) 'Social work and society', in R. Adams, L. Dominelli and M. Payne (eds), *Social Work: Themes Issues and Critical Debate*. Basingstoke: Macmillan.

Jones, I.R., Hyde, M., Victor, C.R., Wiggins, R.D., Gilleard, C. and Higgs, P. (2008) *Ageing in a Consumer Society: From Passive to Active Consumption in Britain*. Bristol: Policy Press.

Karlsen, S. and Nazroo, J.Y. (2002) 'The relationship between racial discrimination, social class and health among ethnic minority groups', *American Journal of Public Health*, 95: 312–23.

Karlsen, S. and Nazroo, J.Y. (2004) 'Fear of racism and health', *Journal of Epidemiology and Community Health*, 58: 1017–18.

Katz, M. (1990) *The Undeserving Poor: From the War on Poverty to the War on Welfare*. New York: Pantheon.

Katz, M. (1996) *In the Shadow of the Poorhouse: A Social History of Welfare in America*, 10th Anniversary Edition. New York: Basic Books.

Kelly, L. (1988) *Surviving Sexual Violence*: Cambridge: Polity Press.

Kelley, N. (2005) *The MIND Guide to Advocacy*. London: MIND.

Kelly, G. and Gilligan, R. (eds) (2000) *Issues in Foster Care: Policy, Practice and Research*. Phildadelphia/Taylor and Francis.

Kempe, H., Silverman, F., Steele, B., Droegemueller, W. and Silver, H. (1962) 'The battered child syndrome', *Journal of the American Medical Association*, 181(1): 17–24.

King, T.E., Parkin, E.J., Swinfield, G., Cruciani, F., Scozzari, R., Rosa, A., Lim, S-K., Xue, Y., Tyler-Smith, C. and Jobling, M.A. (2007) 'Africans in Yorkshire? The deepest-rooting clade of the Y phylogeny within an English genealogy', *European Journal of Human Genetics*, 15: 288–93.

Kramer, S. and Roberts, J. (eds) (1996) *The Politics of Attachment: Towards a Secure Society*. London: Free Association Books.

Krieger, N., Chen, J.T., Waterman, P.D., Rehkopf, D.H. and Subramanian, S.V. (2005) 'Painting a truer picture of US socioeconomic and racial/ethnic health inequalities: the Public Health Disparities Geocoding Project', *American Journal of Public Health*, 95: 312–23.

Laming, Lord Justice H. (2003) *The Victoria Climbié Inquiry Report* (Cmnd 5730). London: The Stationery Office.

Laming, Lord Justice H. (2009) *The Protection of Children in England: A Progress Report*. (HC330). London: The Stationery Office.

Laslett, P. (1996) *A Fresh Map of Life: Emergence of the Third Age*. London: Palgrave Macmillan.

Lawson, T. and Heaton, T. (1999) *Crime and Deviance*. Basingstoke: Macmillan.

Lea, J. (2002) *Crime and Modernity: Continuities and Left Realist Criminology*. London: SAGE.

Ledwith, M. (2007) 'Reclaiming the radical agenda: a critical approach to community development', *Concept* 17(2): 8–12. Reproduced in the encyclopaedia of informal education. www.infed.org/community/critical_community_development.htm (accessed 3 September 2010).

Lee, D. and Newby, H. (1983) *The Problem of Sociology*. London: Hutchison.

Lemert, E. (1952) *Social Pathology*. New York: McGraw–Hill.

Lemert, E. (1972) *Human Deviance, Social Problems and Social Control*, 2nd edn. Englewood Cliffs, NJ: Prentice–Hall.

Letourneau, N.L., Fedick, C.B. and Willms, J.D. (2007) 'Mothering and domestic violence: a longitudinal analysis', *Journal of Family Violence*, 22: 649–59.

Levitas, R. (2005) *The Inclusive Society? Social Exclusion and New Labour*, 2nd edn. Basingstoke: Palgrave.

Lewis, O. (1961) *The Children of Sanchez*. New York: Random House.

Llewellyn, A., Agu, L. and Mercer, D. (2008) *Sociology for Social Workers*. Cambridge: Polity Press.

London Child Poverty Commission (2008) *Capital Gains*. London: London Councils.

Lymbery, M. (2007) *Social Work with Older People, Context, Policy and Practice*. London: SAGE.

Lynch, J.W., Davey-Smith, G., Kaplan, G.A. and House, J.S. (2000) 'Income inequality and mortality: importance to health of individual income, psychosocial environment, or material conditions', *British Medical Journal*, 320: 1200–4.

Maccoby, E.E. (2000) 'Parenting and its effects on children: on reading and misreading behaviour genetics', *Annual Review of Psychology*, 51: 1–27.

MacDonald, R. and Marsh, J. (2005) *Disconnected Youth? Growing Up in Britain's Poor Neighbourhoods*. Basingstoke: Palgrave Macmillan.

MacDonald, R., Shildrick, T., Webster, C. and Simpson, D. (2005) 'Growing up in poor neighbourhoods: the significance of class and place in the extended transitions of "socially excluded" young adults', *Sociology*, 39(5): 873–89.

Mackay, R. (2007) 'Empowerment and advocacy', in J. Lishman (ed.), *Handbook for Practice Learning in Social Work & Social Care*. London: Jessica Kingsley, 269–84.

MacPherson, W. (1999) *The Stephen Lawrence Inquiry: Report of an Inquiry by Sir William MacPherson of Cluny*. London: The Stationery Office.

Mcguire, I. (ed.) (1995) *What Works: Reducing Offending*. Chichester: John Wiley.

McNeill, F. and Whyte, B. (2007) *Reducing Reoffending: Social Work and Community Justice in Scotland*. Cullompton: Willan.

McRobbie, A. and Garber, J. (1976) 'Girls and subcultures: an exploration', in S. Hall and T. Jefferson (eds), *Resistance through Rituals: Youth Sub-cultures in Post-War Britain*. London: Hutchinson, pp. 209–223.

Malik, K. (1996) *The Meaning of Race*. Basingstoke: Palgrave.

Mandelstam, M. (2008) *Safeguarding Vulnerable Adults and the Law*. London: Jessica Kingsley.

Mantell, A. and Scragg, T. (2008) *Safeguarding Adults in Social Work*. Exeter: Learning Matters.

Marchbank, J. and Letherby, G. (2007) *Introduction to Gender: Social Science Perspectives*. Harlow: Pearson Education.

Marx, K. (1975 [1844]) 'The economic and philosophical manuscripts', in *Karl Marx: Selected Writings*. Harmondsworth: Penguin.

Marx, K. and Engels, F. (2005 [1848]) *The Communist Manifesto*. Harmondsworth: Penguin.

Maynard, M. (1994) '"Race", gender and the concept of "difference" in feminist thought', in H. Afshar and M. Maynard (eds), *The Dynamics of 'Race' and Gender: Some Feminist Interventions*. London: Taylor and Francis, pp. 9–25.

Milner, H.R. (2008) 'Critical race theory and interest convergence as analytic tools in teacher education policies and practices' (Report), *Journal of Teacher Education*, 59(4): 332–46.

Ministry of Justice (2009) *Jack Straw: new virtual courts launched and intensive Community Payback extended*. http://www.justice.gov.uk/news/newsrelease120509a.htm (accessed 25/04/10)

Ministry of Justice/HMSO (2009) 'Statistics on Women and the Criminal Justice System', Institute for Criminal Policy Research, Kings College, London.

Minois, G. (1989) *History of Old Age: From Antiquity to the Renaissance*, trans. Sarah Hanbury-Terison. Oxford: Oxford University Press.

Mitchell, J. (1971) *Women's Estate*. Harmondsworth: Penguin.

Mooney, G. and Scott, G. (2005) *Exploring Social Policy in the 'New' Scotland*. Bristol: Policy Press.

Moore, G. and Whyte, B. (1998) *Social Work and Criminal Law in Scotland*. Edinburgh: Mercat Press.

Morgan, D. (1996) *Family Connections: An Introduction to Family Studies*. Cambridge: Polity Press.

Morris, L. (1994) *Dangerous Classes: The Underclass and Social Citizenship*. London: Routledge.

Mullender, A., Hague, G., Imam, U., Kelly, L., Malos, E. and Regan, L. (2002) *Children's Perspectives on Domestic Violence*. London: SAGE.

Mumford, K. and Power, A. (2003) *East Enders: Family and Community in East London*. Bristol: The Policy Press.

Munro, E. (2005) 'What tools do we need to improve identification of child abuse?', *Child Abuse Review*, 14: 374–88.

Munro, E. (2008) *Effective Child Protection*, 2nd edn. London: SAGE.

Murdock, G. (1949) *Social Structure*. Basingstoke: Macmillan.

Murray, C. (1984) *Losing Ground: American Social Policy 1950–1980*. New York: Basic Books.

Murray, C. (1990) *The Emerging British Underclass*. London: IEA Health and Welfare Unit.

Murray, C. (1996) *Charles Murray and the Underclass: The Developing Debate*. London: IEA Health and Welfare Unit.

Murray, C. (2001) *Underclass +10*. London: Civitas.

MWC (Mental Welfare Commission for Scotland) (2006) *Report of the Inquiry into the Care and Treatment of Mr L and Mr M*. Edinburgh: Mental Welfare Commission for Scotland.

National Association of Social Workers (2008) *Code of Ethics of the National Association of Social Workers*. Washington: NASW.

Nazroo, J.Y. (1997) *The Health of Britain's Ethnic Minorities: Findings from a National Survey*. London: Policy Studies Institute.

Nazroo, J. (1998) 'Genetic, cultural or socio-economic vulnerability? Explaining ethnic health inequalities in health', *Sociology of Health and Illness*, 20: 710–30.

Nettleton, S. (1995) *The Sociology of Health and Illness*. Cambridge: Polity Press.

Newstone, S. (1999) 'Men Who Foster', in A. Wheal (ed.), *The RHP Companion to Foster Care*, 2nd edn. Lyme Regis: Russell House Publishing.

O'Brien, R., Hunt, K. and Hart, G. (2005) '"It's caveman stuff, but that is to a certain extent how guys still operate": men's accounts of masculinity and help seeking', *Social Science and Medicine*, 61(3): 503–16.

O'Brien, S., Hammond, H. and McKinnon, M. (2003) *Report of the Caleb Ness Inquiry*. Edinburgh and Lothian Child Protection Committee.

Oakley, A. (1972) *Sex, Gender and Society*. London: Maurice Temple Smith.

Oakley, A. (1981) *Subject Women*. Oxford: Martin Robertson.

Office for National Statistics (2008) *Social Trends 38*. Basingstoke: Palgrave MacMillan.

Olney, M.F. and Brockelman, K.F. (2003) 'Out of the disability closet: strategic use of perception management by select university students', *Disability in Society* 18(1): 35–50.

Oliver, M. (1990) *The Politics of Disablement*. Basingstoke: Macmillan.

ONS (The Office for National Statistics) (2005) *Focus on Older People*. London: HMSO.

ONS (Office for National Statistics) (2006) *Focus on Health*. Newport: The Office for National Statistics.

ONS (The Office for National Statistics) (2009a) *Statistical Bulletin: 2009 Annual Survey of Hours and Earnings*. Newport: The Office for National Statistics.

ONS (The Office for National Statistics) (2009b) *Social Trends 2009*. Newport: The Office for National Statistics.

Oppenheim, C. and Harker, L. (1996) *Poverty: The Facts,* 3rd edn. London: Child Poverty Action Group.

Orme, J. (2009) 'Feminist social work', in R. Adams et al (eds), *Critical Practice in Social Work*. Basingstoke: Palgrave Macmillan.

Pahl, R. (1989) 'Is the Emperor naked?', *International Journal of Urban and Regional Research*, 13(4): 711–20.

Pahl, R. (2000) *On Friendship*. Cambridge: Polity Press.

Pahl, R. and Spencer, E. (2004) 'Personal communities: not simply families of "Fate" or "Choice"', *Current Sociology*, 52(2): 199–221.

Pahl, R. and Prevalin, D. (2005) 'Between family and friends: a longitudinal study of friendship choice', *British Journal of Sociology*, 56(3): 433–50.

Pakulski, J. and Waters, M. (1995) *The Death of Class*. London: SAGE.

Parsons, T. and Bales, R. (1955) *Family, Socialization and Interaction Process*. New York: Free Press.

Parton, N. (1985) *The Politics of Child Abuse*. Basingstoke: Macmillan.

Parton, N. (2006) *Safeguarding Childhood: Early Intervention and Surveillance in a Late Modern Society*. Basingstoke: Palgrave Macmillan.

Patel, B. and Kelley, N. (2006) *The Social Care Needs of Refugees and Asylum Seekers*. Bristol: Social Care Institute for Excellence.

Payne, M. (2005) *Modern Social Work Theory*, 3rd edn. London: Macmillan.

Payne, M. (2006) *What Is Professional Social Work?*, revised 2nd edn. Bristol: Policy Press.

Payne, S., Horn, S. and Relf, M. (2000) *Loss and Bereavement*. Buckingham: Open University Press.

Penketh, L. (2000) *Tackling Institutional Racism: Anti-Racist Policies and Social Work Education and Training*. Bristol: Policy Press.

Phillipson, C. (1998) *Reconstructing Old Age: New Agendas in Social Theory and Practice*. London: SAGE.

Piliavin, I. & Scott Briar, S. (1964) 'Police encounters with juveniles', *American Journal of Sociology*, 70(Sept): 206-214.

Pierson, J. (2002) *Tackling Social Exclusion*. London: Routledge.

Pollack, O. (1961) *The Criminality of Women*. New York: A.S. Barnes.

Price, L. (2005) *Feminist Frameworks: Building Theory on Violence Against Women*. Black Point, NS: Fernwood Publishing.

Pritchard, J. (2001) *Male Victims of Elder Abuse: Their Experiences and Needs*. London: Jessica Kingsley.

Pritchard, J. (2007) *Working with Adult Abuse: A Training Manual for People Working with Vulnerable Adults*. London: JKP.

Procacci, G. (1991) 'Social economy and the government of poverty', in C. Gordon and P. Miller (eds), *The Foucault Effect: Studies in Governmentality*. Chicago: University of Chicago Press. pp. 151–68.

Putnam, R. (1993) *Making Democracy Work: Civic Traditions in Modern Italy*. Princeton, NJ: Princeton University Press.

Putnam, R. (1995) 'Bowling alone: America's declining social capital', *Journal of Democracy*, 6(1): 65–78.

Putnam, R. (1996) 'Who killed civic america?', *Prospect*, 7(24): 66–72.

Putnam, R. (2000) *Bowling Alone: The Collapse and Revival of American Community*. New York: Simon & Schuster.

Putnam, R. and Goss, K. (2002) 'Introduction', in R. Putnam (ed.), *Democracies in Flux: The Evolution of Social Capital in Contemporary Society*. Oxford: Oxford University Press.

Ramchandani, P., Stein, A. Evans, J. and O'Connor, T. (2005) 'Paternal depression in the postnatal period and child development: a prospective population study, *The Lancet*, 365(9478): 2201-2205.

Rawls, J. (1971) *A Theory of Justice*. Cambridge, MA: Harvard Press.

Ray, M., Bernard, M. and Phillips, J. (2009) *Critical Issues in Social Work with Older People*. London: Palgrave Macmillan.

Reamer, F.G. (1993) *The Philosophical Foundations of Social Work*. New York: Columbia University Press.

Redley, M. and Weinberg, D. (2007) 'Learning disability and the limits of liberal citizenship: interactional impediments to political empowerment', *Sociology of Health and Illness*, 29(5): 1–20.

Reiman, J.H. (1979) *The Rich Get Richer and the Poor Get Poorer – Ideology, Class and Justice*. Hoboken, NJ: John Wiley & Sons.

Ribbens McCarthy, J., Edwards, R. and Gillies, V. (2003) *Making Families: Moral Tales of Parenting and Step-Parenting*. York: Sociology Press.

Ristock, J. (2002) *No More Secrets: Violence in Lesbian Relationships*. London: Routledge.

Ritchie, B. (2008) 'An anti-racist strategy for individual and organisational change', in A. Barnard, N. Horner and J. Wild (eds), *The Values Base of Social Work and Social Care*. Maidenhead: Open University.

Ritzer, G. (1996) *The McDonaldization of Society*, 2nd edn. Thousand Oaks, CA: Pine Forge Press.

Roberts, K. (2001) *Class in Modern Britain*. Basingstoke: Palgrave Macmillan.

Robinson, R. and Scott-Moncrieff, L. (2005) 'Making sense of Bournewood', *Journal of Mental Health Law* May: 17–25.

Rodger, J.J. (2000) *From a Welfare State to a Welfare Society: The Changing Context of Social Policy in a Post-Modern Era*. Basingstoke: Palgrave Macmillan.

Rogers, A. and Pilgrim, D. (2005) *A Sociology of Mental Health and Illness*. Maidenhead: McGraw-Hill.

Rose, N. (1999) *Governing the Soul: The Shaping of the Private Self*, 2nd edn. London: Free Association Books.

Rose, S. (2005) *Lifelines: Life Beyond the Gene*. London: Vintage.

Roseneil, S. and Budgeon, S. (2004) 'Cultures of intimacy and care beyond the family: personal life and social change in the early twenty-first century', *Current Sociology* 52: 135–59.

Ross, H. (2008) 'Justice reinvestment: what is it and why it may be an idea to consider it in Scotland', CJ Scotland. www.cjscotland.org.uk/index.php/cjscotland/dynamic page/?id=66 (accessed 8 July 2008).

Ross, R.R. and Fabiano, E. (1985) *Time to Think: A Cognitive Model of Delinquency Prevention and Offender Rehabilitation*. Johnson City, TN: Institute of Social Sciences and Arts.

Sahlins, M. (1974) *Stone Age Economics*. London: Routledge.

Saunders, P. (1989) *Social Class and Stratification*. London: Routledge.

Saunders, P. (1996) 'Might Britain be a meritocracy?', *Sociology*, 29 (1): 23–41.

Savage, M. (2000) *Class Analysis and Social Transformation*. Buckingham: Open University Press.

Savage, M. (2002) 'Social exclusion and class analysis', in P. Braham and L. Janes (eds), *Social Differences and Divisions*. Oxford: Blackwell, pp. 59–100.

Savage, M., Bagnall, G. and Longhurst, B. (2001) 'Ordinary, ambivalent and defensive: class identities in the Northwest of England', *Sociology* 35(4): 875–92.

Savage, M., Warde, A. and Ward, K. (2002) *Urban Sociology, Capitalism and Modernity*, 2nd edn. Basingstoke: Palgrave Macmillan.

Sayer, T. (2008) *Critical Practice in Working with Children*. Basingstoke: Palgrave.

Schön, D. (1983) *The Reflective Practitioner: How Professionals Think in Action*. London: Temple Smith.

Scottish Government (2003) *The Framework for Social Work Education in Scotland*. Edinburgh: Scottish Government.

Scottish Government (2006) *High Level Summary of Equality Statistics: Key Trends for Scotland*. Edinburgh: Scottish Government.

Scottish Government (2008) *Protecting Scotland's Communities, Fast Fair and Flexible Justice*. Edinburgh: Scottish Government.

Scottish Government (2010) *Child Protection Statistics 2009/09*. Edinburgh: Scottish Government. Available at www.scotland.gov.uk/Resource/Doc/286274/0087182.pdf.

Scottish Poverty Unit (2002) *Poverty in Scotland*. Glasgow: Glasgow Caledonian University.

Scottish Social Services Council (2005) *Code of Practice for Social Service Workers and Employers*. Dundee: SSSC.

Shakespeare, T. (2006) *Disability Rights and Wrongs*. London: Routledge.

Silver, A. (1997) '"Two Different Sorts of Commerce", or, Friendship and Strangership in Civil Society', in J. Weintraub and K. Kumar (eds), *Public and Private Thought in Practice: Perspectives on and Dichotomy*. Chicago: The University of Chicago Press, pp. 43–74.

Sillito, D. (2008) *The Neighbours who Never Speak*. http://news.bbc.co.uk/1/hi/uk/7385655.stm (accessed 4 March 2010).

Simmel, G. (1905) 'The Metropolis and Mental Life', in K. Wolff (1950) *The Sociology of Georg Simmel*. New York: Free Press.

Singh, G. (2000) 'Developing black perspectives in practice teaching'. Report of an Action Research Project, Coventry University.

Singh Koli, H. (2008) 'Gone out for a curry. I may be some time …', *Observer*, 16 November.

Sklair, L. (2000) *The Transnational Capitalist Class*. Chichester: Wiley-Blackwell.

Smale, G., Tuson, G. and Stratham, D. (2000) *Social Work and Social Problems*. Basingstoke: Palgrave.

Smart, C. (2008) *Personal Life*. Cambridge: Polity Press.

Smart, C. and Neale, B. (1999) *Family Fragments?* Cambridge: Polity Press.

Smith, A. (1994) *New Right Discourse on Race and Sexuality*. Cambridge: Cambridge University Press.

Smith, M.K. (2002) 'Casework and the Charity Organization Society', *The Encyclopedia of Informal Education*, www.infed.org/socialwork/charity_organization_society.htm (accessed 31 August 2009).

Smith, P. and Natalier, K. (2005) *Understanding Criminal Justice, Sociological Perspectives*. London: Sage.

Smith, R. (2010) *A Universal Child?* Basingstoke: Palgrave Macmillan.

Social Work Services Inspectorate (SWSI) (2004) *Investigations into Scottish Borders Council and NHS Borders Services for People with Learning Disabilities: Joint Statement from the Mental Welfare Commission and the Social Work Services Inspectorate.* Edinburgh: Scottish Executive.

Spencer, L. and Pahl, R. (2006) *Rethinking Friendship: Hidden Solidarities Today.* Princeton, NJ: Princeton University Press.

Stacey, J. (1996) *In the Name of the Family: Rethinking Family Values in the Postmodern Age.* Boston, MA: Beacon Press.

Stanko, E. (1985) *Intimate Intrusions: Women's Experience of Male Violence.* London: Routledge.

Stanley, N.M. and Bradley, J.G. (2000) *Responding Effectively to Students' Mental Health Needs: Project Report.* University of Hull.

Steadman Jones, G. (1984) *Outcast London: A Study in the Relationship Between Classes in Victorian Society.* London: Penguin.

Stepney, P. (2006) 'Mission Impossible? Critical practice in social work', *British Journal of Social Work*, 36(8): 1289–1307.

Stewart, A., Prandy, K. and Blackburn, R. (1980) *Social Stratification and Occupations.* Teaneck, NJ: Holmes and Meier.

Stuart-Hamilton, I. (2006) *The Psychology of Ageing – An Introduction*, 4th edn. London: Jessica Kingsley.

Swain, French, S., Barnes, C. and Thomas, C. (2005) *Disabling Barriers – Enabling Environments.* London: SAGE.

Tawney, R. (1938) *Religion and the Rise of Capitalism.* Harmondsworth: Penguin.

Tew, J. (2005) *Social Perspectives in Mental Health London.* London: Jessica Kingsley.

Thane, P. (2000) *Old Age in English History: Past Experiences, Present Issues.* Oxford: Oxford University Press.

Thomas, N. (2005) *Social Work with Young People in Care: Looking After Children in Theory and Practice.* Basingstoke: Palgrave-Macmillan.

Thompson, N. (1993) *Anti-Discriminatory Practice* (3rd edn, 2001; 4th edn, 2006). Basingstoke: Macmillan/Palgrave.

Thompson, N. (2007) 'Anti-discriminatory practice', in M. Davies (ed.), *The Blackwell Companion to Social Work.* Oxford: Blackwell.

Tönnies, F. (1963[1887]) *Community and Society (Gemeinschaft und Gesselschaft).* New York: Harper and Row.

Tulle, E. (ed.) (2004) *Old Age and Agency.* Hauppauge, NY: Nova Science.

Tulle, E. and Mooney, E.A. (2002) 'Moving to "age-appropriate" housing: government and self in later life', *Sociology*, 36(3): 683–701.

Tumin, M.M. (1953) 'Some principles of stratification: a critical analysis', *American Sociological Review*, 18(4): 387–94.

Twelvetrees, A. (2002) *Community Work.* Basingstoke: Palgrave Macmillan.

Twigg, J. (2006) *The Body in Health and Social Care.* Basingstoke: Palgrave Macmillan.

Twigg, J. (2007) 'Clothing, age and the body: a critical review', *Ageing & Society*, 27: 285–305.

Union of the Physically Impaired Against Segregation (UPIAS) (1976) *Fundamental Principles of Disability.* London: UPIAS.

Urry, J. (2007) *Mobilities.* Cambridge: Polity Press.

Vennard, J., Sugg, D. and Hedderman, C. (1997) *The Use of Cognitive-Behavioural Approaches with Offenders: Messages from the Research. Home Office Research Study 171.* London: HMSO.

Victor, C. (2005) *The Social Context of Ageing: A Textbook of Gerontology.* London: Routledge.

Vincent, J.A. (1999) *Politics, Power and Old Age.* Buckingham: Open University Press.

Vinen, R. (2009) *Thatcher's Britain: The Politics and Social Upheaval of the 1980s.* London: Simon & Schuster.

Walby, S. (1989) 'Theorising patriarchy', *Sociology,* 23(2): 213–34.

Walby, S. (1990) *Theorizing Patriarchy.* Oxford: Blackwell.

Walker, A. (1980) 'The social creation of poverty and dependency in old age', *Journal of Social Policy,* (9):49–75.

Walker, C. and Walker, A. (2002) 'Social policy and social work', in R. Adams, L. Dominelli and M. Payne (eds), *Social Work: Themes, Issues and Critical Debates,* 2nd edn. Basingstoke: Palgrave.

Walkerdine, V. and Lucey, H. (1989) *Democracy in the Kitchen.* London: Virago Press.

Ward, T. and Maruna, S. (2007) *Rehabilitation.* Routledge: Abingdon.

Webb, S. (2006) *Social Work in a Risk Society.* Basingstoke: Palgrave Macmillan.

Weber, M. (1946) *From Max Weber: Essays in Sociology,* 2nd edn (H.H. Gerth and C. Wright-Mills, eds). Oxford: Oxford University Press.

Weber, M. (1992) *Economy and Society,* New Edn. Berkeley, CA: University of California Press.

Weeks, J. (1989) *Sex, Politics and Society: The Regulation of Sexuality Since 1800.* London: Longman.

Weeks, J., Heaphy, B. and Donovan, C. (2001) *Same Sex Intimacies: Families of Choice and Other Life Experiments.* London: Routledge.

Welshman, J. (2006) *Underclass: A History of the Excluded, 1880 – 2000.* London: Hambledon: Continuum.

Welshman, J. (2007) *Underclass: A History of the Excluded, 1880–2000.* London: Continuum.

West, C. and Zimmerman, D.H. (1987) 'Doing gender', *Gender and Society* 1(2): 125–51.

Wilkinson, R.G. (1996) *Unhealthy Societies: The Afflictions of Inequality.* London: Routledge.

Williams, S.J. (1999) 'Is anybody there: critical realism, chronic illness and the disability debate', *Sociology of Health and Illness,* 21(6): 797–819.

Wilmott, P. (1986) *Social Networks, Informal Care and Public Policy.* London: Policy Studies Institute.

Wilson, K., Ruch, G., Lymbery, M. and Cooper, A. (2008) *Social Work: An Introduction to Contemporary Practice.* London: Pearson Longman.

Wilson, W.J. (1987) *The Truly Disadvantaged: Inner City, the Underclass and Public Policy.* Chicago, IL: University of Chicago Press.

Wilson, W.J. (1996) *When Work Disappears.* New York: Knopf.

Wimberley, R.C., Fulkerson, M.G. and Morris, L.V. (2007) 'Predicting a moving target: postscript for *The Rural Sociologist* on global rural-to-urban transition dates', *The Rural Sociologist,* 27(3): 19–22.

Wineburgh A.L. (2000) 'Treatment of children with absent fathers'. *Child and Adolescent Social Work Journal*, 17(4): 255-277.

Wirth, L. (1938) 'Urbanism as a way of life', *American Journal of Sociology*, 44(1): 1–24.

Wolfe, D.A., Crooks, C.V., Lee, V., McIntyre-Smith, A. and Jaffe, P.G. (2003) 'The effects of children's exposure to domestic violence: a meta-analysis and critique', *Clinical Child & Family Psychology Review*, 6: 171–87.

Wolfensberger, W. (1972) *Normalisation*. New York: NIMH.

Wolfensberger, W. (1975) *The Origin and Nature of Our Institutional Models*. New York: Human Policy Press.

Woodcock, J. and Tregaskis, C. (2008) 'Understanding structural and communication barriers to ordinary family life for families with disabled children: a combined social work and social model of disability analysis', *British Journal of Social Work*, 38: 55–71.

Wright, E.O. (2000) *Class Counts* (Student Edition). Cambridge: Cambridge University Press.

Wright-Mills, C. (1959) *The Sociological Imagination*. Harmondsworth: Pengion.

Yllo, K. and Bograd, M. (eds) (1988) *Feminist Perspectives on Wife Abuse*. London: SAGE.

Young, I.M. (1980) 'Throwing like a girl: a phenomenology of feminine body comportment motility and spatiality', *Human Studies*, 3(1): 137–56.

Young, J. (1999) *The Exclusive Society: Social Exclusion, Crime and Difference in Late Modernity*. London: SAGE.

Young, J. (2007) *The Vertigo of Late Modernity*. London: SAGE.

Young, M. and Willmott, P. (1957) *Family and Kinship in East London*. London: Routledge.

Zaretsky, E. (1976) *Capitalism, the Family and Personal Life*. London: Pluto Press.

Index